Principles of Architectural History

THE FOUR PHASES OF ARCHITECTURAL STYLE, 1420–1900

THE MIT PRESS Massachusetts Institute of Technology, Cambridge, Massachusetts, and London, England

Principles of Architectural History

THE FOUR PHASES OF ARCHITECTURAL STYLE, 1420–1900

Paul Frankl

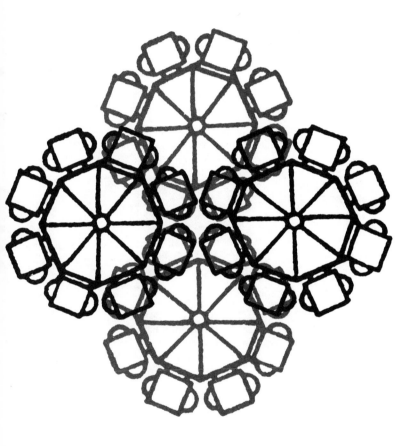

TRANSLATED AND EDITED BY JAMES F. O'GORMAN

WITH A FOREWORD BY JAMES S. ACKERMAN

Originally published in Germany in 1914 under the title
Die Entwicklungsphasen der neueren Baukunst.
Translated with permission of Verlag B. G. Teubner, Stuttgart.

Set in Linofilm Palatino and printed and
bound in the United States of America by Halliday Lithograph Corp.

ISBN 0 262 06024 8 (hardcover)
ISBN 0 262 56013 5 (paperback)
Second printing, first MIT Press paperback edition, June 1973
Third printing, November 1977

Library of Congress catalog card number: 68–18236

Respectfully dedicated to
Heinrich Wölfflin

Foreword

Paul Frankl, one of the last survivors of the golden age of German art history, died in Princeton, New Jersey, in 1962 at the age of eighty-three. He was born in Prague, and took his doctoral degree in Munich in 1910. After publishing his dissertation on fifteenth-century stained glass in southern Germany and a small handbook on early Renaissance architecture in Italy (1912), he began writing *Die Entwicklungsphasen der neueren Baukunst*, which appears here for the first time in translation. It was presented in 1914 as his *Habitationsschrift* (the work traditionally required in Germany of candidates for a university post) to the renowned professor of art history at Munich, Heinrich Wölfflin. It is characteristic of Frankl's intellectual independence that his book although in many ways inspired by Wölfflin's early architectural study, *Renaissance und Barock* (1888), was essentially an attack on, or at least a vigorous criticism of Wölfflin's thesis and method.

Appointed to a chair at Halle University in 1921, Frankl began to work on the subject that was to be his major interest during the next forty years—medieval architecture. Like Wölfflin, he believed that the specialist had a responsibility to inform the general reader, and his major books are historical surveys: *Die frühmittelalterliche und romanische Baukunst* (1926), *The Gothic: Literary Sources and Interpretations Through Eight Centuries* (1960), and *Gothic Architecture* (1962). In 1934 Frankl was dismissed from the University by the Nazis, and during the next four years he was occupied in preparing the manuscript for *Das System der Kunstwissenschaft* (1938), a monumental theoretical work of over a thousand pages. In 1938 he came to the United States. In 1940 he accepted a research position at the Institute for Advanced Study, at Princeton, which he held until his death.

Much of Frankl's influence as a teacher and scholar is due to his lifelong concern for historical and critical theory. He was convinced that history is a philosophical discipline and that the historian should present his data within a framework of explicitly stated principles. The ideas expressed first in *Die Entwicklungsphasen* became the core of *Das System der Kunstwissenschaft*, which Frankl felt to be his most important contribution to scholarship. It was the greatest disappointment of his career that his colleagues and the younger art historians were so put off by the length and impenetrable language of *Das System* that it had no impact on the field, and in his last years—until the day before his death—he was confidently engaged in writing a shorter and more accessible version. Another cause of the failure of *Das System* was an antagonism toward theory and abstraction that developed in the second generation of modern art historians and still survives today. On this account, the translation of *Die Entwicklungsphasen*, written over half a century ago, can be a timely proof of the effectiveness and necessity of analysis based on a theoretical position.

In *Principles of Architectural History*, Frankl proposes two interlocking systems, one critical, the other historical.

The critical system establishes four categories for the analysis of architectural monuments:

1. spatial composition
2. treatment of mass and surface
3. treatment of light, color, and other optical effects
4. relation of design to social functions

These subdivisions depart from those more commonly used in architectural criticism based on three categories established by the Roman architectural theorist Vitruvius: *Firmitas* (the use of materials and structural technique in design), *Commoditas* (the accommodation of the building's use to its design), and *Venustas* (the aesthetic and symbolic aspect of design). Perhaps because he is examining the evolution of an architectural epoch not radically affected by structural innovation, Frankl chooses to de-emphasize *Firmitas;* he retains the concept of *Commoditas* in his fourth category but interprets it more vividly than his predecessors. *Venustas* he expands into three categories. The first category, spatial composition, is an important innovation of the turn of the century in German architectural criticism. The historians Brinckmann, Riegl, and especially Schmarsow established the foundations on which Frankl's analysis is based. Critics of the nineteenth century, a period in which almost all architects concocted designs out of the vocabulary of past styles, experienced buildings not as spatial environments but as evocative forms and surfaces. Frankl recognizes this experience in the second category, which is the focus of Wölfflin's system in *Renaissance und Barock.* The new image of the architect as primarily a creator of spaces that elicit aesthetic responses parallels the principles of the radical modern designers working before the First World War, although there is no evidence that these principles directly influenced the historians. Frankl was probably more attuned to the architects of the Jugendstil than to the pioneers of the Modern Movement.

Frankl's third category is also indebted to innovations in contemporary European thought, primarily in the young science of psychology, to which he refers in the introduction to Chapter 3. While his observations on architectural space are based on an intellectual analysis of the abstract image of the ground plan, his "visible form" is based on the sensuous experience that emerges only as one moves round and through a building, that changes with every step, and is affected by the position and intensity of the light sources. In earlier criticism, buildings had been characterized from the point of view of an observer standing motionless and looking at a façade or an interior from the position a photographer might choose to obtain the most favorable single view. Frankl's innovation reconstructs the kinetic experience of the observer who arrives at a single image as the product of many partial images. This is the only way to analyze adequately later Baroque and Rococo buildings, and it is not surprising that the method of Frankl's predecessors was both the result and the cause of their preference for the more static design of Renaissance architecture. Frankl's "visible form" draws into the orbit of architectural criticism an analysis of the processes of perception that had revolutionized the approach to the figural arts at the close of the nineteenth century, through the theories of Hildebrandt, Fiedler, and Riegl (whose distinction between "haptic" and "optic" experiences must have influenced Frankl's separation of "corporeal" and "visible" form). Frankl's statement at the beginning of Chapter 3:

We interpret as three-dimensional every single image of an object that we receive from any one viewpoint, but what is essential in viewing architecture is that we accept these isolated images as merely preliminary arrangements, not as ends in themselves. To see architecture means to draw together into a single mental image the series of three-dimensionally interpreted images that are presented to us as we walk through interior spaces and round their exterior shell. When I speak of the *architectural image*, I mean this *one mental image*.

reminds us that the principles of Gestalt psychology were formulated in Germany during the years in which this book was written.

The final category, "purposive intention" (*Zweckgesinnung*), offers a critical tool that Wölfflin had excluded from his formalist system: the analysis of the relationship of buildings to the social institutions for which they are conceived. As Frankl says, the occasional earlier writers who recognized the significance of cultural history for architectural criticism had been content to introduce their discussion of a building or a style with a summary of the historical events of the preceding years— a device that seldom furthered an understanding of the actual relationship between social processes and architecture. Frankl focuses attention on one aspect of this relationship: the way in which the spatial conception of a building, its furnishings, and ornament are suited to the activities for which they are designed. His formulation of the problem raises the interpretation of Vitruvian "commodity" to a high intellectual level at which meaningful connections can be made between art and other aspects of a culture. This principle also was stimulated by changes in his environment: the emergence of "functionalism" as central to modern architectural theory and the impact of sociology and anthropology on the writing of history. An earlier but less effective attempt had been made by Henry Adams in *Mont-St.-Michel and Chartres* (1905). Frankl does not consider the symbolic function of architectural spaces, forms, and ornament—the "iconography" of architecture—which was to become an important feature of more recent criticism, partly through the influence of his most distinguished student, Richard Krautheimer.

The historical framework within which these criteria are tested subdivides post-medieval architecture into four "phases":

1. 1420–1550, with examples chosen primarily from the work of Italian architects from Brunelleschi to Antonio da San Gallo the Younger

2. 1550–1700, encompassing, like the remaining phases, the whole of European architecture

3. the eighteenth century

4. the nineteenth century

Frankl thus ignores the widely accepted differentiation between the styles of 1420–1500 ("early" Renaissance) and of 1500–1550 ("high" Renaissance), which later historians have represented as quite distinct. Following Wölfflin, he suggests that the architecture of the later 1500's already shows the characteristics typical of the following century and should be classed as "Baroque," although he is reluctant to use this term, which was then still so charged with negative overtones. The third phase encompasses primarily the Rococo style, and the last phase, the many architectural modes of the nineteenth century.

Frankl's summary treatment of the fourth phase is probably due to the difficulties he encountered in attempting to represent nineteenth-century architecture as a stage in the evolution of Renaissance style, a thesis he accepted from another influential predecessor, Heinrich von Geymüller. Today, from a distance of another half century and with the aid of voluminous scholarship on the architecture of the last two hundred years, we generally identify the twilight of the Renaissance tradition with the Rococo and Neo-Palladian styles of the later eighteenth century. If Frankl had revised this text in his later years, he probably would have eliminated his fourth phase.

Within each of the four critical categories, the four historical phases are examined in turn with a further subdivision, where required, between religious and secular architecture.

As in Wölfflin's essay, the historical evolution of forms follows a predetermined path, so that the individual architect can only adjust to rules somehow imposed upon him by the logic of preceding steps. Although the architect is mentioned by name, when known, he does not appear to be responsible for the dynamics of style: the true protagonists of Frankl's four phases are immanent style-forces (Riegl's *Kunstwollen*). "The *development* of style," he says, "is an intellectual process overriding national characteristics and individual artists." But the development is not simply linear: it proceeds by the action and counteraction of "polar opposites." An instance of this Hegelian scheme at work would be the transition from the organization of spaces by *addition* in the first phase to organization by *division* in the second.

As the architect is the servant of pervasive historical forces, so we, as observers, are servants of the aesthetic forces of architecture. In a Gothic cathedral, "If an ambulatory encircles the polygonal choir, the entire movement within the space catches the spectator in an endless whirl. He has no thought of return, and the path forward pulls him toward an unattainable goal in infinity." In the central-plan church of the Renaissance, on the other hand, "Just as the pure group [of spaces] permits no one to enter, it permits no one to leave; we must remain forever in this central point." Spatial organization creates personified forces capable of their own movement or stasis independent of and obviously superior to the action we may choose within the building.

This idealist criticism in the tradition of German nineteenth-century philosophy implies that the aesthetic values in a work of art exist even if we are not present to receive them; when we are present, they can be received properly only in the one correct way. Recent criticism, under the impact of modern perception psychology and of the major trends of twentieth-century philosophy, has repudiated this position and gives far greater attention to the contribution of the observer to an aesthetic experience, interpreted as a kind of dialogue between subject and object. But the philosophical presuppositions of Wölfflin and Frankl have had a powerful influence on architectural analysis that has not waned: the characterization of the Gothic cathedral just quoted remains the model for today's handbook writers and college lecturers, who rarely read philosophical and psychological treatises and are often unaware of the theoretical roots of their descriptions.

The personification of disembodied forces acting in space is paralleled by the reading of the masses of Renaissance architecture in terms of the human body: "The Gothic cathedral takes root in the earth like a plant and spreads its upward surging forces out through thin stalks to its ribs. . . . A building of the first phase of post-medieval architecture is rather like a man. It is not rooted to the earth but stands with its socle firmly upon the earth's surface. . . ." The metaphor allows us to think of structural members as bones and muscles and wall surfaces as skin; the excitement we derive from certain buildings comes from a bodily identification with the apparent play of their forces. This is precisely the explanation of the psychological roots of our experience of Renaissance architecture proposed in another, more celebrated, architectural criticism published in 1914, Geoffrey Scott's *The Architecture of Humanism*. Scott carries the argument a step further than Frankl, proposing that the humaneness of Renaissance and Baroque architecture makes it superior to that of other periods. Frankl avoids comparative judgments of styles, but his book, like Scott's, helped to induce his reluctant contemporaries to approach Baroque architecture sympathetically.

Since the time of Frankl and Scott there have been no encompassing historical-critical treatments of Renaissance and Baroque architecture,* although a large literature has accumulated that attempts to gain recognition of a Mannerist style of architecture in the period 1520–1600, between Frankl's first and second phases. The writings of the more positivist generation following Frankl attempted to arrive at definitions of style as the result of examining the evidence in individual buildings and drawings, and in writings on architecture, so that monographs on individual architects and essays on the style of a single generation have replaced the grander but more arbitrary systems represented by the *Principles*.

A number of the superficial obstacles to appreciation of Frankl's text that existed in the original edition have been removed in the translation. The arrangement of the material in the long first chapter has been clarified by new subheadings. Many of the references to buildings that are not to be found in the well-known handbooks are accompanied by additional illustrations. Above all, the imaginative translation of Frankl's difficult and often private language enables the reader to perceive the brilliance of the over-all conception and of the many individual analyses. In addition to the broad concepts, there are in these pages more valuable and more varied models of practical criticism for the professional critic or amateur of architecture than in any book of its kind I know. We may criticize it for one or another aspect, but in over fifty years we have not managed to produce a work that surpasses it in vitality and significance.

James S. Ackerman
Cambridge, Massachusetts
February 1968

* The Wölfflin-Frankl tradition was continued, however, in Sigfried Giedion's book on the architecture of the nineteenth and twentieth centuries, *Space, Time and Architecture* (1st ed. 1941).

Translator's Note

Paul Frankl's *Entwicklungsphasen der neueren Baukunst* was written more than half a century ago for a limited audience of scholars. The scholar must still read the original: this translation is intended for a more general public. For this reason I have tried to make Frankl's thesis more palatable by omitting anything (including most of his Introduction) that does not contribute directly to the development of his main argument; rearranging or rewriting his misplaced or badly stated passages where necessary; correcting his poorly edited text in the light of subsequent scholarship; eliminating all obsolete bibliographic references (without consistently adding newer references); and, finally, augmenting the sparse photographs. Most of these changes have been made silently; I believe none alters Frankl's intention. The notes within square brackets are mine.

A direct translation of the German title would have been both unwieldy and misleading. Frankl wrote this work in answer to *Renaissance und Barock,* by Heinrich Wölfflin, whose ideas are better known to English-speaking readers through one of his later works, *Kunstgeschichtliche Grundbegriffe,* translated as *Principles of Art History.* The title of the present book, *Principles of Architectural History,* was chosen to make clear the association between these two scholars.

Further information about the buildings mentioned here can be found in the volumes of the *Pelican History of Art,* edited by Nikolaus Pevsner, that discuss European architecture of the fifteenth to nineteenth centuries.

This translation would not exist without the encouragement of James S. Ackerman, who suggested it. I am grateful to Hermann G. Pundt for checking an early draft, and to Richard Betts for correcting many errors in what might have been the final draft.

J. F. O'G.

Preface

This book contains the tentative results of a study that began when I first picked up Heinrich Wölfflin's *Renaissance und Barock*[1] more than a dozen years ago. Although I did not consider myself capable of investigating the problem of stylistic development as fruitfully as Wölfflin had, and although, as a mere novice, I could do no more than try to see buildings through his eyes, I felt from the beginning that he had not completely solved the problem. Since then I have studied his book intensely at least once a year, acquainted myself with the material by traveling and by reading other works, and tried to clarify the problem myself. My most important tools were the analysis of buildings according to four basic elements: space, corporeality, light, and purpose, and the conception of the Renaissance and Baroque as polar opposites.

I subsequently found essential support for both these methods, first in the writings of August Schmarsow, which explore the basic elements of art, and then in Wölfflin's summer lectures at Munich in 1912, in which he developed his systematic quest for polarity. I benefited greatly from both, without losing my own independence or making my own reflections seem superfluous. Schmarsow not only assigned a specific element to each of the plastic arts (to architecture, space; to sculpture, corporeality; to painting, light) but also arbitrarily assigned one dimension to each (respectively, depth, height, and width).[2] There is some truth in what he says, but his reasoning led to one-sided conclusions. Wölfflin began by listing his five polarities for painting and then demonstrated their applicability to sculpture.[3] But he scarcely mentioned architecture. I had begun with architecture, however, and arrived at very different polarities, so that these lectures gave me the opportunity to defend my principles against his complete and awe-inspiring system, and so strengthen my convictions. I can no longer say how many of Wölfflin's ideas found their way into the present work. Many certainly did. But it is quite impossible to give the source for each sentence. I have never repeated anything verbatim. It is obvious that we absorb the best ideas we encounter in order to renew and develop them. In the end I am not concerned in whose head a specific idea is born. Knowledge moves from person to person in order to complete, or perhaps to cease, its development.

I have not relied solely upon Schmarsow and Wölfflin, however. I hardly need to say that Jakob Burckhardt and Alois Riegl also stood as godfathers. I have frequently used Heinrich von Geymüller's works and have hauled along as traveling companion Cornelius Gurlitt's three volumes on the Baroque.[4] I should also thank other authors for books that are bad as well as good, for the bad ones often prove more stimulating in the long run. They are not produced in vain. And I hope the same kind judgment will be conferred upon this work, if it should prove to be a bad one.

The discussion in this book demands not an extensive knowledge of the literature but a great knowledge of monuments. Anyone who has not seen most of the churches and palaces mentioned in the first chapter—and if possible he should have seen them often—will find the reading difficult. Anyone for whom geometric descriptions are tedious and irksome is fundamentally unsuited for research in the history of architecture: he should confine himself to the remaining chapters. If these still seem difficult morsels to swallow, then I hope that the fare I offer, if not easy to chew, might nonetheless prove nourishing.

Paul Frankl
Gauting, near Munich
June 1913

Contents

Illustrations

(Line drawings are from Paul Frankl,
Die Entwicklungsphasen der neueren Baukunst, unless otherwise noted.)

Principles of Architectural History

THE FOUR PHASES OF ARCHITECTURAL STYLE, 1420–1900

Introduction[1]

To study stylistic change in architecture, that is, to establish the polar opposites separating the successive phases of one epoch, which is our main aim here, we must focus upon the comparable elements in the art of building and determine categories of similar features that remain constant over a period of time.

When we compare church façades, we must be aware that this concept is subject to the higher concept of façade in general. As soon as we disregard the special features of a church façade, the common characteristics of all façades (palace, church, villa) will become apparent, and the differences between street and courtyard façades will disappear. Façade itself is only the exterior elevation; it must display characteristics of style that can be observed from inside as well as outside. These general characteristics are also present on the ceiling and on the floor, despite their own peculiarities. Internal and external walls, floors, and roofs can all be included under the general concept of the tectonic shell. Corporeality is their common element; it completely distinguishes them from color and light, the merely visible, which forms a second category, and from the space they enclose, which forms a third.

The visual impression, the *image* produced by differences of light and color, is primary in our perception of a building. We empirically reinterpret this image into a conception of *corporeality*, and this defines the form of the *space within*, whether we read it from outside or stand in the interior. But optical appearance, corporeality, and space do not alone make a building. Distinctions between church, palace, villa, and city hall are based upon specific, typical forms, which crystallize for specific purposes. The forms are not retained for specific purposes, but are necessarily the products of purpose. The molded space is the theater for certain human activities, and these are the focus of our perception. Once we have reinterpreted the optical image into a conception of space enclosed by mass, we read its *purpose* from the spatial form. We thus grasp its spiritual import, its content, its meaning. The designing architect works in the opposite direction, of course. He begins with the building program. As he lays out the pattern of activities it demands, he produces a framework of circulation around which the rooms are arranged. When he has found his spatial form for this program, he begins to model the enclosing mass. Light and color are his last considerations. But this sequence can be altered in various ways during the design process. Lighting and the perspective image interact, and this can have a decisive effect upon the ultimate spatial form. The sequence is unimportant. We are interested only in the fact that space, light, corporeality, and purpose are the most general concepts we can find. They best characterize the differences between buildings. They are so different that there is no danger of repetition when we discuss them.

We are looking for the polar opposites of spatial form that separate the successive phases of one epoch and for the polar opposites within the other categories as well. But we are concerned only with the architecture of the post-medieval epoch. I had better explain what I mean by this term.

Renaissance architecture has been defined in many ways, but Geymüller's definition is the broadest. In various works he has described it as a combination of antique and Gothic forms extending in time from Frederick II of Hohenstaufen, in the thirteenth century, up to his own day, say 1900. I must reject part of this description.

In the early fifteenth century Brunelleschi consciously broke with the Gothic tradition and erected whole buildings in imitation of antique forms. He was imitated in turn by contemporary architects, and a new development was born. This new development was possible because the same ideas that led Brunelleschi to a revival of antique architecture were shared by his educated contemporaries. If architecture is the molded theater of human activity, of the joys and sorrows of a society, an architectural style can begin only when a culture has reached a state of maturity. Philosophy, religion, politics, and science—the whole of Renaissance culture—had to be ready before the fine arts could give them expression. "Renaissance Man" preceded the Renaissance artist. Of course Renaissance *culture* did not appear overnight, but the *architectural* historian can leave the problem of its development to other disciplines. The Renaissance begins for him at that moment in the middle of the Gothic tradition when Brunelleschi erected buildings that corresponded to the new spirit.

I cannot accept Geymüller's inclusion of Gothic forms in his definition of Renaissance architecture. Michelangelo's St. Peter's in the Vatican is no synthesis of antique orders and Gothic vaulting, no rebirth of ancient or medieval architecture, but an entirely new creation. Although Leonardo and Bramante produced designs for Milan Cathedral, and although Gothic vestiges can be found in the works of Brunelleschi and Michelozzo, the entire development indicates as clearly as do the sources that the Gothic was considered vanquished and was detested.

I agree with Geymüller, however, that after Brunelleschi there is no break in the tradition. The Renaissance began in Florence and spread through Tuscany to Rome, and from there throughout the Christian world. It took on a new aspect each time it crossed a border, of course, but it followed a basically continuous development according to its own inner logic. In the course of time its newly conquered territories became equally important as centers of stylistic development, until finally the crises of change occurred no longer in Rome but in Paris, Antwerp, or the many princely courts in Germany. We can study this development as a whole or in its local variations.

The *development* of style is an intellectual process overriding national characteristics and individual artists. It is a great man who can cope with the problems of his time, but the greatest genius is no more than the servant of this intellectual process.

I think it unnecessary to deal with the peculiarities of geography or race in this book. I shall discuss the entire continuous development from Brunelleschi to the end of the nineteenth century as one unit. I shall include not only Italy and France but the whole of Christianity. Local variations in the development might be of importance in other studies, or in the ultimate narration of the development, but they are unimportant here.

I refuse to call this entire period the Renaissance. This term is now firmly established for the first phase. If I include the Baroque in the Renaissance, I cannot characterize the two as polar opposites. I have chosen to call the entire period of architectural history between 1420 and 1900 simply "post-medieval." This seems harmless enough. The terms for the individual phases (Renaissance, Baroque, Rococo, Neoclassicism) are easier to do without than is commonly believed. I shall avoid them until I have defined each phase by stylistic polarity.

The reader now knows what to expect, and what not to expect. I restrict myself to post-medieval architecture in this work because it is provisional. I am investigating older epochs using the same method[2] and hope eventually to achieve insight into the organism of stylistic development by comparing all epochs and their development. I have no doubt that my subsequent studies will be made easier because of this one and that this one will need correction once I have completed them.[3]

1. Leonardo da Vinci,
Sketches for Centralized Churches.

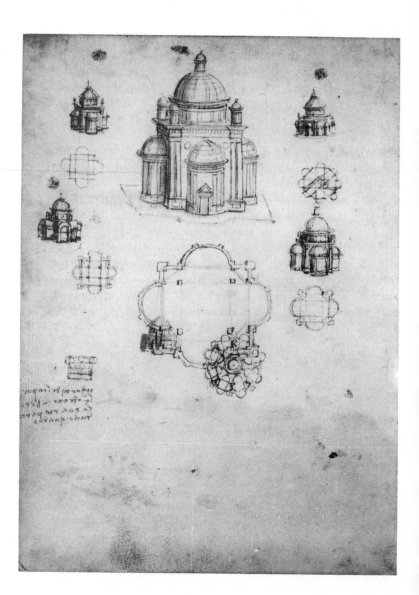

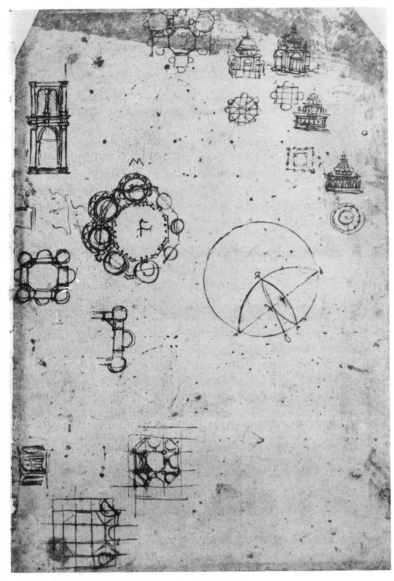

2. Leonardo da Vinci, Sketches for Centralized Churches.

ECCLESIASTICAL ARCHITECTURE

First Phase (1420–1550)

The notebooks of Leonardo da Vinci contain architectural sketches that are mostly designs for centralized churches (Figs. 1–2). They were not all drawn at one time, of course, since they are scattered throughout many codices, and even within the same codex are not all on one sheet, but we may be certain that they are not isolated doodles. They are, rather, the individual links of a logical chain. Leonardo wanted to know in a general way what forms he could give to the central-plan church, and set out systematically to find the answer. He realized that if he began with the simplest spatial forms

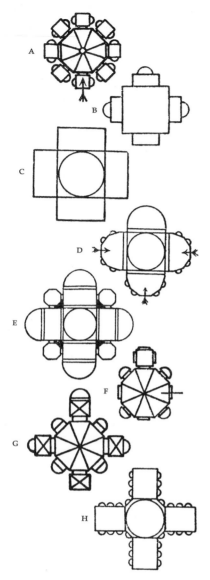

3. Centralized Churches of the First Phase. Diagrammatic Plans. (No common scale.)

A. Florence, Sta. Maria degli Angeli, 1434.
B. Mantua, S. Sebastiano, 1460.
C. Prato, Sta. Maria delle Carceri, 1485.
D. Todi, Sta. Maria della Consolazione, 1508.
E. Parma, Madonna della Steccata, 1521.
F. Florence, Sto. Spirito, Sacristy, 1489.
G. Milan, Sta. Maria della Passione (original plan), 1482.
H. Church shown in Raphael's "School of Athens," 1510.

(square, octagon, circle, or dodecagon), he would arrive at every conceivable central-plan church, without taxing his imagination, by the mechanical addition of circular, semicircular, square, rectangular, or octagonal ancillary spaces to the principal and cross axes of his basic figures. A complete series of related central-plan churches could be developed from a basic schema. For example, he could begin with a Greek cross (four square arms added to the sides of a central square), and then either replace the square space by an octagon, a circle, or a dodecagon, or replace the square arms with rectangles, octagons, circles, semicircles, or dodecagons. The imagination is limited in the formation of such basic schemas, which are found by geometric means, so that the creation of spatial forms becomes a matter of scientific combination.

1. SIMPLE GROUPS WITH COORDINATED ANCILLARY CENTERS

Sta. Maria degli Angeli in Florence, begun by Brunelleschi in 1434 and still unfinished, seems to have been the stimulus for this method of construction by combination. It attracted Leonardo's attention and he drew a plan of it with slight variations.[1] This first completely centralized church of postmedieval architecture is an octagon with rectangular ancillary spaces (chapels) on all eight sides (Fig. 3A). Each of these ancillary spaces is expanded by two semicircular niches so placed that those of adjacent chapels meet back to back. There are doors at this point of contact so that a circular movement is possible from one ancillary group (the chapel with its flanking niches) to the next round the octagon.[2] Leonardo radially expanded this arrangement in his sketch by adding a third niche to the outside of each chapel.

There are other executed variations of this schema. S. Sebastiano in Mantua, 1460, is a central square with a rectangular space added to each side (Fig. 3B). Each of these ancillary spaces is narrower than the side of the main square, and thus is clearly an independent space. Three of these have apses, which are in turn smaller in diameter than their sides. This produces a second set of re-entrant angles. A long rectangular cross space on the fourth side of the main square serves as a vestibule.

The Chapel of the Cardinal of Portugal, also of 1460, at S. Miniato al Monte above Florence, follows this schema except that it has rather shallow cross arms, is reduced to small dimensions, and lacks the ancillary spaces of the second zone (that is, the outer apses). The Cappella di Sta. Fina, 1468, at the Collegiata in S. Gimignano is similar. So is Sta. Maria delle Carceri in Prato, 1485, although there (Fig. 3C) the dimensions are greater and the cross arms are equal in width to the central square (forming a Greek cross). Sixteenth-century churches belonging to this same family are Sta. Maria della Consolazione at Todi (Fig. 3D), 1508; the Madonna di S. Biagio at Montepulciano, 1518; and the Steccata in Parma

(Fig. 3E), 1521.[3] The choir of the cathedral in Como, definitive design 1519, also follows this schema.

The sixteen-sided figure occurs only in the painted temple in Raphael's "Marriage of the Virgin," 1504. The hexagon in the small Cappella Emiliana, 1530, at S. Michele di Murano in Venice is also rare, as is the pentagon which appears in the spatially subordinate entrance to this same chapel.

2. SIMPLE GROUPS WITH RHYTHMICAL ANCILLARY CENTERS

This basic schema first becomes more complicated when the ancillary spaces are no longer identical but alternate in size and shape. This produces rhythm. The simplest examples of this are the Sacristy, 1489, of Sto. Spirito in Florence, which is an octagon with apses added to its diagonal sides and very shallow rectangular depressions added to its principal sides (Fig. 3F); the east end (the original church) of Sta. Maria della Passione in Milan, 1482, an octagon with square arms on the principal sides and semicircles on the diagonals (Fig. 3G); and the Tempietto, 1502, at S. Pietro in Montorio in Rome. The Tempietto (Fig. 62) is a circle with semicircular niches on its principal axes and small depressions on its diagonals. The latter are too small to be true spaces, but they do act as intervals to produce the cyclic rhythm *b a b a b* and so on.

The same rhythm also occurs when the central space is a square with truncated corners, rather than a regular octagon, as in the building shown in Raphael's "School of Athens," 1510, in the Vatican. The building has long rectangular cross arms and small niches in the corners of the central square (Fig. 3H). The Cappella Chigi, 1513, in Sta. Maria del Popolo in Rome is simpler; it has no cross arms. Rhythm also occurs if a regular octagon is supplemented by triangular corner spaces that enlarge it into a square, such as in Sta. Maria di Piazza in Busto Arsizio, 1518.

The regular dodecagon with alternating semicircular and rectangular chapels occurs in Leonardo's manuscripts,[4] and he also invented richer combinations within this same family. He added diagonal niches and square arms to an octagon, in a plan similar to that of Sta. Maria della Passione in Milan (Fig. 3G), but expanded each arm by adding an apse to each of its three free sides. (In addition, small domed circular spaces on the diagonals serve as vestibules.)[5] A variation of this design has octagonal rather than square arms.[6]

The Sacristy of S. Satiro in Milan was probably the inspiration for that of Sto. Spirito in Florence (Fig. 3F). The plan of the former, begun as early as 1478, is also an octagon with diagonal niches and very shallow rectangular depressions on its principal axes. I include it in this family although it is distinguished by an upper passage within the thickness of the wall. This is perhaps present merely for technical reasons, for it is so narrow and of so little use (notice the way the stair opening cuts into it, and the great distance between its floor and the top of its

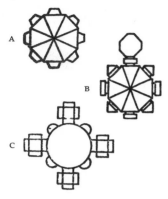

4. Centralized Churches of
the First Phase. Diagram-
matic Plans. (No common
scale.)
A. Lodi, Incoronata, 1488.
B. Pavia, Sta. Maria di
Canepanova, 1492.
C. Crema, Sta. Maria della
Croce, 1490.

railing) that we can hardly call it a gallery at all. This shallow
upper layer of space, which actually has more the effect of
relief than of space, recurs in several other centralized churches
of one and two zones, such as the Incoronata in Lodi, 1488 (with
coordinated ancillary spaces; Fig. 4A); Sta. Maria di Canepanova in Pavia, 1492; and S. Magno at Legnano, 1504 (both
with rhythmical ancillary spaces; Fig. 4B).

Rhythm between ancillary spaces seems to be nothing
other than a natural outgrowth of the rhythm that recurs between a central space and each of its ancillary spaces. Subordination of the ancillary centers to the main space seems also to
demand a change from a coordinated to an alternating relationship between the ancillary spaces themselves. Rhythmical
grouping is so characteristic of completely centralized churches
that even the simplest domed Greek cross, without any ancillary spaces or rhythmically distributed niches, gives the
impression of being grouped round a center. I call this a
"spatial group" in order to remind us of this impression. It
can also be said that coordinated ancillary spaces are *aligned,*
whereas rhythmically alternating ancillary spaces are *grouped.*

3. GROUPS OF THE SECOND ORDER
WITH COORDINATED ANCILLARY CENTERS

No matter how complicated they become through rhythmical alternation in one and two zones, spatial groups are
always still relatively simple if they have only one center.
If smaller spatial groups are added to the principal and diagonal
axes of a larger group, however, we have a group of groups,
that is, a centralized church of the second order.

Sta. Maria della Croce in Crema, 1490, is a domed space
with a fully developed Greek cross added to each end of its
principal axes (Fig. 4C).[7] I know of no other executed monuments of this type, but Leonardo's manuscripts contain similar
designs. One has a circular main space expanded by the addition of four small circular ancillary centers to both main axes,
and this is even combined with a rhythmical alternation of
the ancillary spaces of the main center.[8] In another an octagon
is surrounded by eight coordinated square ancillary centers
each of which is in turn expanded by a niche on each side
(Fig. 1).[9] The sketches, as well as their variants,[10] make us
aware that *these* spatial groups of the second order are based
upon the coordination of the ancillary centers.

4. GROUPS OF THE SECOND ORDER
WITH RHYTHMICAL ANCILLARY CENTERS

Using an octagonal main space in another drawing (Fig. 2,
top),[11] Leonardo experimented with the rhythmical alternation
of the ancillary centers themselves. At the ends of the main
axes he placed square spaces of one zone, but on the diagonals
he drew other niches which give access to octagonal ancillary
centers. Since the square spaces on the main axes have the
appearance of cross arms (that is, function as the first zone of

the main space), we need not count eight coordinated ancillary centers round the central octagon. Only those on the diagonals occupying the angles between the cross arms are true ancillary centers.[12] There is a corresponding system in groups of the second order. Leonardo started with a square center, added square or rectangular cross arms, and then placed ancillary centers on the diagonals between the cross arms.[13] The four ancillary centers are identical, and thus coordinated, but they are separated by cross arms of very different shape. The impression thus arises that the ancillary centers alternate rhythmically with the cross arms, that is, with the ancillary spaces of the main center. If there is already a rhythmical relationship between the main and ancillary spaces in much simpler compositions, then the rhythm here is more complex because the ancillary centers are rhythmically related not only to the cross arms but also to the total centralized formation. The four small spatial groups in the corners are subordinate to the large cross in the center, and if the ancillary centers themselves have rhythmically alternating spaces, then we have a rhythmical group of rhythmical groups.

If the ancillary centers are to be large enough to have any kind of monumental effect, the radius of the principal center must be very large. Thus spatial groups of the second order are effective only when their over-all dimensions are very great. The design of St. Peter's in the Vatican in Rome of about 1504 (foundation 1506) offered the perfect opportunity to explore the possibilities of a spatial group of the second order.

The central spatial group in Bramante's first design is a simple Greek cross the arms of which are two bays long and end in large apses (Fig. 5). Only the second bay in each of these arms is flanked by rectangular chapels. The first bay opens into ancillary centers that have arms analogous to the chapels. Only the outer arms of the ancillary centers could be closed with apses, and since the size of these apses makes them very prominent, the ancillary centers do not seem equally developed on all sides. Each of the smaller apses is opened by an entrance, just as are the great apses of the principal system. Beyond the smaller apses are porticoes, three bays wide and deep enough to permit the alignment of their façades with the ends of the main towers. This alignment also determines the dimensions of the corner sacristies (octagons with one zone of niches), which, as in some of Leonardo's sketches, were thought of as the ground floors of great corner towers. These towers define a large square beyond which project only the rectangular exteriors of the great apses placed in the centers of the sides.

The size of the piers sustaining the main dome is crucial for the axial relationships in this design. The piers correspond to the depth of the cross arms of the ancillary centers. For this

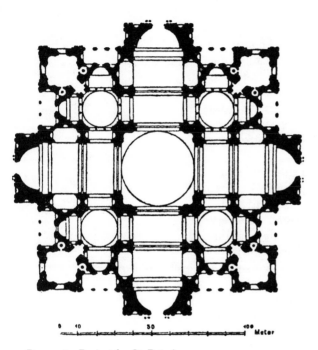

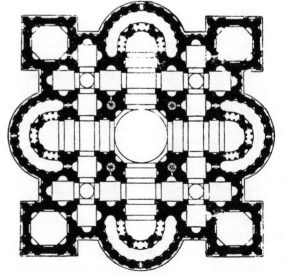

5. Bramante, Project for St. Peter's
in the Vatican, 1506. Plan.
6. Bramante (?), Project for St.
Peter's in the Vatican. Plan.

reason the axis of the first bay of each of the main cross arms runs through the centers of the ancillary groups, through the apses that close their arms, and into the porticoes beyond. The porticoes are thus placed on axis between the towers and the great apses; this axial alignment explains why a *second bay* was added to each of the main cross arms.

Bramante made essential corrections in the course of further revisions. In a later design (Fig. 6), he strengthened the dome piers in such a way that the main cross arms needed only *one bay*. The piers now correspond to the four arches sustaining the main dome; these are no longer paired arches but real *barrel vaults* reinforced by framing arches. Since the length of the cross arms of the ancillary groups is determined by the width of the piers sustaining the main dome, the axis of each of these smaller cross arms once again establishes the axis of the bay of each of the great arms. All that was required to complete these larger arms was the addition of a barrel vault, equal to those sustaining the main dome, at the end of each bay. The fact that the main arms are no longer *two bays* long is an improvement over the first design, because such duplication contradicts the threefold rhythm that is the vital element of any true spatial group. The cross arms are now actually one bay long. The bay is defined by two barrel vaults of almost equal length. They are reinforced by framing arches[14] and correspond to the width of the dome piers. But the central space of each of the ancillary groups is significantly smaller, and its arms significantly larger, than in the first design. These arms are now square; they overwhelm the apses added to their free sides in a second zone. The entrances into the ancillary groups are gone, as are the porticoes, so that the dimensions of the sacristies are now independent of the interior axial relationships. Each sacristy can be reached from one of the niches of an ancillary group. The niches, ten in each group, or forty in all, can now be used for altars. This too is an improvement over the first design, in which the doors into the ancillary groups made these spaces the crossing points of circulation, thereby demoting them to mere vestibules. In addition, the sacristies in the first design were to be entered diagonally, so that one corner of each of the secondary focal spaces was accented and the balance of the space was disturbed. In the second design there is no access to the ancillary centers from outside; the remaining entrances lead directly into the principal system. In order to facilitate transition from outside into the gigantic central system, Bramante placed a passage round each of the great apses. These are semicircular corridors *closed* by apses at each end. There is no access from two of these corridors to the cross arms of the ancillary centers, and access from the other two is through insignificant doors. Each of these four passages is completely isolated, so that they

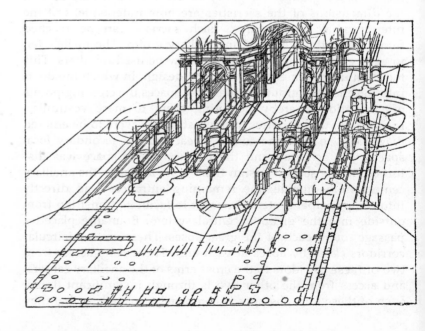

7. Peruzzi (?), St. Peter's in the
Vatican. Perspective-Section.

do not form a complete circulatory system round the building. In this sense they do not form a proper "ambulatory."[15] Geymüller conjectured that a gallery was to have been placed above them, and Burckhardt suscribed to this theory when he said that they were "undoubtedly of two stories."[16] But the extant interior perspective (Fig. 7), which corresponds exactly to this plan, does not show galleries, and, because of the pronounced spatial effect of such features, I doubt that they were forgotten or left out in order to enhance the clarity of the drawing.[17]

The large well-preserved model of St. Peter's by Antonio da San Gallo the Younger, 1539, which retains the essentials of Bramante's plan, also argues against this hypothesis (Figs. 8–10). The differences between Bramante's and San Gallo's plans concern spaces that do not belong to the interior space itself. They include a reduction in the size of the sacristies and the addition of an eastern façade and monumental vestibule. In addition to the desire for a transitional space, a compelling reason for the addition of the passages in the second design was the requirement of the cardinals that the new building should extend as far as the entrance to the old Constantinian basilica. Since the passages themselves did not quite accomplish this, however, Bramante added the entrance hall shown in plan in the perspective drawing (Fig. 7).[18] San Gallo tried to bind this eastern extension to the interior more organically but succeeded only in replacing the passage on this side by a domed vestibule-like space that gives access directly into the apse of the eastern arm of the main cross. The entrances through the ancillary centers have a greater impact upon the interior space.

Despite these differences, San Gallo's model is fundamental to any reconstruction of Bramante's partially preserved plan, and it can be assumed from the model that no galleries were planned. Yet Burckhardt's "two stories" is correct in a sense other than that he had intended, if we can interpret Bramante's intention accurately from San Gallo's model. An upper story is actually present above each passage in the model. It serves as a continuous buttress for the apsidal vaults, and was supposed to contribute basically to the static equilibrium of the entire building. That is to say, it forms a brace against the lateral thrust of the main dome, which is itself surrounded by tiers of similar arcades. These upper stories have no effect upon the interior; they do not belong to it. They are connected with it by very steep, slanting shafts through which the cross arms receive a minimum of indirect light (Fig. 9). A glance at the section shows the awkwardness of this arrangement, and the model itself demonstrates that to carry out such a project is unthinkable. If such a building had been executed, the upper stories would not have been seen from within, but

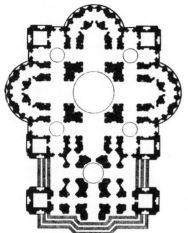

8. Antonio da San Gallo the
Younger, Project for St. Peter's
in the Vatican, 1539. Plan.

9. Antonio da San Gallo the
Younger, Project for St. Peter's in
the Vatican. Section.

10. Antonio da San Gallo, Project
for St. Peter's in the Vatican. Model.

unfortunately would have been apparent, for they would have made the space totally dark. We cannot assume that the interior of the executed building would have been as dark as the interior of the model, which stands in a closed room and receives no direct sunlight. Even if the model were placed in the open, it would provide no true conception of the illumination in the actual building, in which the amount of light as well as the dimensions would have increased. Nonetheless, the model makes it clear that the colossal space would have been as good as dark. Large windows were planned in the apses of the main cross arms; they are below the entablature of the great order, and receive light through an inclined shaft leading only to the floor above the passages. There are lunette windows above the entablature, but these too receive light only from the upper galleries and not from the outside.[19] In the model there are no windows in the cross arms.[20] Bramante intended to cut through the barrel vault above each cross arm with lunette windows, as is clearly visible in the perspective drawing (Fig. 7),[21] but they would not have helped much because the domes and drums of the ancillary centers were to tower up outside them. Since the windows of the great drum beneath the main dome do not open directly to the outside but into an arcade, the cross arms of the executed building would not have received adequate light through them either. In the model only the outer passages are brightly illuminated, although they have no windows in their ground stories, and they too receive light through inclined shafts leading down from upper windows. (In the model the exterior aediculae on the ground story are closed, and the arrangement of the niches in the interior makes it certain that they were to remain closed.)

The difficulties encountered during construction of St. Peter's might account for the cautious engineering. San Gallo's building would have been solid but gloomy. Bramante had built with greater daring, and San Gallo's model is certainly a critique of his design. Bramante's rich creation of forms was destined to fail because of his inability to provide abundant light.

When Michelangelo took charge of St. Peter's in 1546, his first move was to eliminate the outer passages and so admit daylight from all four ends of the main cross (Fig. 11). He also braced the piers of the main dome by strengthening the enclosing walls. Since the arcades encircling the dome in San Gallo's project thus became superfluous, Michelangelo's dome might be much like that of Bramante's first project. Michelangelo greatly simplified everything. Most surprising in relation to the earlier projects is his removal of the outer cross arms from the ancillary centers. These, we remember, were excessively emphasized in Bramante's earlier design. There is no longer, in Michelangelo's design, any external indication of the independence of the ancillary centers. They are under-

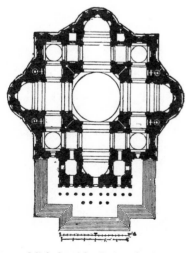

11. Michelangelo, Project for St. Peter's in the Vatican, 1546. Plan.

developed, and must submit to the absolute sovereignty of the principal system.

Circulation beneath each of the four ancillary domes is directed outward along two rather than four radii because the outer arms are absent. As the circulation turns a corner at each ancillary center, progression from ancillary center to small cross arm, to large cross arm, and so on, round the central domed space *approaches,* but does not quite achieve, a circular path. A true circular movement does not occur, because the ancillary centers retain their effect as focal spaces: they interrupt and halt the movement. Also, as the lower barrel vaults above the small cross arms are perpendicular to the higher barrel vaults above the large cross arms (the latter actually spring from a point above the crown of the former), the effect of discontinuity is enhanced. There is no continuous flow along a closed circular path. The present St. Peter's demonstrates this very clearly despite the seventeenth-century nave added to Michelangelo's crossing, and the narthex planned by Michelangelo would not have altered this effect. Similar halting points in the ancillary centers are found in the smaller versions of Michelangelo's St. Peter's, such as Sta. Maria di Carignano in Genoa, 1552, and Sta. Maria delle Vergini near Macerata. The Madonna della Ghiara in Reggio Emilia, 1597, is related to these.

Since I have established the fact that one spatial group of the second order has no circular movement, it must be clear that we have here a family of spatial forms in which a continuous peripheral movement is unknown and avoided. The four ancillary centers on the diagonals are completely independent. We must return to the focal space, the great cross, to pass from one of these ancillary centers to another, just as in a simple octagon with niches, we must return to the central space to go from one chapel to the next. As niches of the same zone are not connected, circular movement is excluded. The only exception to this rule is Sta. Maria degli Angeli in Florence (Fig. 3A), the earliest centralized church of the post-medieval period. Perhaps this exception occurred because the consequence of placing individual compartments of space next to one another had not yet been realized. Bramante himself faltered. He left a sketch for St. Peter's in the Vatican in which the piers of the main dome are opened to create diagonal circulation into the ancillary centers.[22] The most direct path would thus have been opened from the sacristies to an altar located in the center of the entire building, but the grandiose openings in the piers would also have made the ancillary centers equivalent to ancillary spaces of the first zone of the main space. The lack of clarity (to say nothing of the crucial problem of stability) would have been accompanied by an overlapping of several paths of circulation. The ancillary centers would have been just as accessible from the large central space as from its cross arms, and, conversely, a person standing in an ancillary center would not have found his path clearly prescribed, but would have had to make a decision.

Leonardo's method of adding smaller ancillary spaces, arranged in zones, to a larger central space did not lead to all conceivable centralized buildings, but to one kind only. The paths along which movement is directed radiate out from the central space, and when they reach the ancillary centers of the first zone, they again split off from one another. A diagram of this movement would show the paths branching off in a star pattern. All the spaces are closed entities, complete in themselves. Since one space is placed hard by the next, the joints between them are made as clearly visible as possible.[23] A radial composition of this type does not produce a continuous movement around a center. This explains the disuse of galleries in the first phase, for galleries provide uninterrupted paths of movement along the periphery of a building. It also explains the perfection of each space, complete in itself and tolerating no subsequent horizontal division by the insertion of intermediate floors. Such division has no place in the process of adding one space to another, if the principle of joining simple, complete spatial forms is strictly adhered to. And a parallel characteristic of this phase is the shying away from window lunettes. Lunettes carve up the perfect roundness, the unbroken completeness, of a vault. When they do appear, it is only as a last resort, as in the difficult problem of illuminating St. Peter's. The cross vault, composed of four such lunettes, directs movement outward instead of concentrating it; this is inconsistent with the idea that each space should be a focal point.[24] It does occur in this phase, however, not only in secular buildings but in churches as well (for example, above the choir of Sta. Maria del Popolo in Rome). The series of lunettes in a ceiling cove has the opposite effect: it concentrates rather than diffuses movement. The best known ecclesiastical example of this is the Sistine Chapel, 1473, in the Vatican in Rome.

A rush of movement in all directions might exist in the space beneath a cross vault, but the effect is essentially different in the case of the star-shaped, radial arrangement of the spatial groups so far discussed. Of course the ancillary spaces draw us outward from the central space. This effect is somewhat lacking in the ancillary centers in Michelangelo's plan for St. Peter's (Fig. 11), because the outer arms were amputated. But the individual spaces themselves contain nothing inhospitable: they draw us inward. A group of such spaces is a collection of focal points, of self-centered individuals. The schema of movement by which the essential effect of such a building might be graphically explained is not a star-shaped pattern of radiating arrows pointing into infinity but a *star-shaped group of separate, discrete points* lying on radial axes.

These points show only the network of construction, the framework, of such a drawing.

In spatial groups of the second order, the effect is dependent upon the sturdiness of the crossing piers. The earliest example of such a spatial group in this stylistic phase is S. Giovanni Crisostomo in Venice, 1497. Because the Venetian soil cannot support a heavy load, however, the crossing piers in this church are so thin that the primary effect is of one spatially coherent square into which the four piers were later inserted. The continuous space at floor level seems to break up into separate spaces only in the region of the vaults. This is because the arms are covered by cross vaults, whereas the center is covered by a dome. A similar effect can be seen in Sta. Maria di Campagna in Piacenza, 1522, and in Sta. Maria Nuova at Cortona, 1530, although in the latter at least the central dome is raised much higher than its neighbors, and there are barrel rather than cross vaults above the arms.[25] Even in this church, circular passage is impossible because of the four domed corner spaces and because of the orientation of the cross-arm vaulting at right angles to the direction of peripheral movement.

A group of Leonardo's sketches would form an exception to this rule if it were true, as Geymüller says, that they show "a dome resting on four pillars in the center of a square edifice, with an apse in the middle of each of the four sides."[26] But Geymüller is wrong. What he thought was the ground plan of four piers carrying a dome is simply one of Leonardo's characteristic graphic devices. It was Leonardo's habit to connect the opposite ends of the apses that he drew on the sides of squares or octagons (Fig. 2). Other draftsmen control such a drawing by projecting the center line of the sides across the square. In larger sketches (Fig. 1), Leonardo works from the generating, innermost figure, and we need only to copy such a sketch freehand to realize that his method actually makes his task easier. In some cases the points at which the construction lines intersect become small squares, because they are doubled to correspond to the outlines of the enclosing wall. But these squares do not represent piers. Perspective views of the exterior show that the dome does *not* rest upon these points of intersection. If it did rest upon the inner square, it would appear exactly as wide as the apses. In the perspective sketches it is clearly wider and therefore rests upon the outer square, that is, upon the arched openings between the central space and its apses.[27] These sketches represent neither spatial groups of the second order nor centralized churches in which a circular movement occurs, but the simplest form of centralized church with one zone of coordinated apses.

5. COMBINED GROUPS

The spatial compositions that are called centralized, although consisting of large and small centralized spaces

12. Florence, S. Lorenzo,
Old Sacristy, 1419. Interior.

aligned along a common axis, can form the transition in this systematic survey between the true centralized churches already discussed and the longitudinal churches to be discussed next. They are not developed on all sides but are formed by omitting all but one of the ancillary centers from the spatial formations already described in Section 3. The archetype of this family is the Old Sacristy (Fig. 12), 1419, in S. Lorenzo in Florence. In this composition, a smaller square, covered by a pendentive dome, is attached to the center of one side of a larger square (covered by a dome with ribs and arched severies, which is still Gothic). Variations of this type are the Pazzi Chapel, 1429, at Sta. Croce in Florence; the Portinari Chapel, 1462, at S. Eustorgio in Milan; the Sacristy, 1470, of Sta. Felicita in Florence; the Cappella Colleoni, 1470, at Sta. Maria Maggiore in Bergamo (this has an off-center entrance); Sta. Maria dell'Umilità in Pistoia, 1495; the choir, 1492, of Sta. Maria delle Grazie in Milan; Sta. Maria di Loreto in Rome, 1507; S. Eligio degli Orefici in Rome, 1509; the cathedral in Montefiascone, 1519; the Manna d'Oro in Spoleto, 1527; and the Madonna di Campagna in Verona, 1559. The fact that each of these examples has its own peculiarities is not important in this study.[28] The Canepanova in Pavia, 1492, can be included here; it has rhythmical chapels off the main space (Fig. 4B).[29]

6. THE SIMPLE SERIES

If we align along a common axis several, rather than just two, of the simplest centralized spaces (domed squares) of similar, rather than different, size and shape, we then produce the nave or side aisle of a longitudinal church of this stylistic phase. The spatial form of one of the side aisles of S. Lorenzo in Florence, 1419, with its series of pendentive domes (Figs. 13A, 14), is nothing other than that of the little choir of the Old Sacristy of this same church (Fig. 12) multiplied eight times. The first longitudinal churches of this epoch, which still show the influence of the Early Christian basilica, have domed bays only in the side aisles. The nave is covered by a flat ceiling and is thus an unarticulated unit. This inconsistency was corrected at the cathedral in Faenza, 1474, where the nave is also composed of a succession of square domed spaces (Fig. 13B). The circulation here cannot possibly be represented by radiating arrows either, but only by the isolated center points of the spaces; this produces a series of isolated, static units. Compare with this the church in the convent of the Osservanza near Siena, 1485, and S. Francesco in Ferrara, 1494. (S. Sisto in Piacenza can be mentioned here too, although it was probably erected mainly upon Romanesque foundations.)

7. THE RHYTHMICAL SERIES

The biaxiality characteristic of the fifteenth century is still present in the cathedral of Faenza (Fig. 13B) and related churches. By this I mean that one bay of the nave corresponds

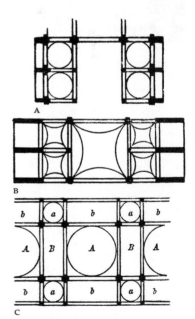

13. Longitudinal Churches of the First Phase. Diagrammatic Plans. (No common scale.)

A. Florence, S. Lorenzo, 1419.
B. Faenza, Cathedral, 1474.
C. Venice, S. Salvatore, 1507.

14. Florence, S. Lorenzo, 1419.
Interior.

15. Venice, S. Salvatore, 1507.
Interior.

to two smaller bays of the side aisles. In S. Salvatore in Venice, 1507, this becomes the triaxial rhythm *b a b* (Figs. 13C, 15), so that the principle of grouping spaces reaches its full development in longitudinal churches at the same time as it does in centralized churches (St. Peter's in the Vatican). But this rhythm is not produced by the juxtaposition of one nave bay with three side-aisle bays. Nave and side aisles have the same number of bays, and both are composed of transverse, oblong, barrel-vaulted bays that alternate with square domed bays. The nave begins with an oblong space, however, whereas the side aisles begin with square spaces; this produces rhythm in both lateral and longitudinal directions. The rhythm of these bays can be represented by the following diagram, in which *b* is the same size and shape as *B* but rotated 90 degrees:

$$
\begin{array}{ccc}
a & B & a \\
b & A & b \\
a & B & a \\
b & A & b
\end{array}
$$

The nave of the Annunziata in Arezzo, 1491, begins with a domed space, followed by an extended barrel-vaulted space, and then another dome (Fig. 16A). In the side aisles, however, three identical domed bays correspond to the second bay of the nave, thus:

$$
\begin{array}{ccc}
b & A & b \\
\left.\begin{array}{c} a \\ a \\ a \end{array}\right\} & B & \left\{\begin{array}{c} a \\ a \\ a \end{array}\right. \\
b & A & b
\end{array}
$$

The nave of SS. Flora e Lucilla in Arezzo, of about 1550 (Fig. 16B), begins with a barrel-vaulted bay, and the coordinated side-aisle bays *a a a* of the Annunziata in Arezzo are here replaced by the group *b a b*, thus:

$$
\begin{array}{ccc}
\left.\begin{array}{c} b \\ a \\ b \end{array}\right\} & B & \left\{\begin{array}{c} b \\ a \\ b \end{array}\right. \\
c & A & c \\
\left.\begin{array}{c} b \\ a \\ b \end{array}\right\} & B & \left\{\begin{array}{c} b \\ a \\ b \end{array}\right. \\
c & A & c
\end{array}
$$

(This spatial rhythm arises from the alternation of barrel vault and dome, and is derived from the Pazzi Chapel in Florence where it occurs twice in the transverse direction, once in the porch and once inside. It can also be produced by omitting two opposite arms of a Greek cross. It existed in this simplest form in S. Lorenzo in Damaso in Rome before its reconstruction. If the barrel vaults are of considerable length, the dome appears as an interruption in *one single* vault, as in

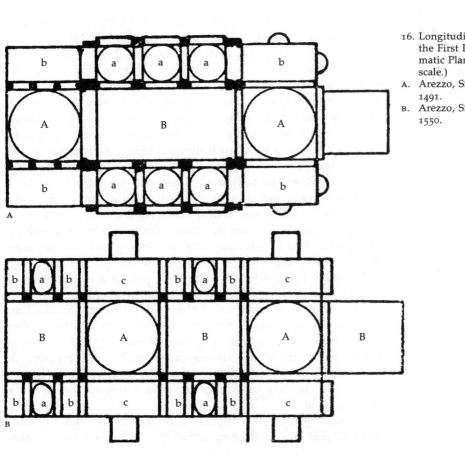

16. Longitudinal Churches of
    the First Phase. Diagram-
    matic Plans. (No common
    scale.)
A. Arezzo, SS. Annunziata,
   1491.
B. Arezzo, SS. Flora e Lucilla,
   1550.

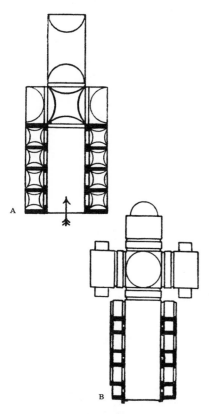

17. Longitudinal Churches of
the First Phase. Diagram-
matic Plans. (No common
scale.)

A. Fiesole, Badia, 1463.

B. Mantua, S. Andrea, 1470.

the cathedral in Padua, of about 1550, and in Bramante's earlier longitudinal project for St. Peter's in the Vatican.[30])

8. THE SERIES WITH COORDINATED ANCILLARY CENTERS

The side aisles of both S. Lorenzo (Figs. 13A, 14) and Sto. Spirito in Florence are accompanied by a series of isolated chapels. If these side aisles were removed, a longitudinal church of one nave and isolated chapels would remain. Examples of this type of church are Sta. Maria Maddalena de'Pazzi, 1479, and S. Francesco al Monte (with exposed rafters above the nave), 1499, both in Florence. Gothic churches become spatial formations of this type if transverse walls are inserted between the bays of their side aisles, as occurred in S. Francesco in Rimini, 1446, Sta. Maria Annunziata in Florence, 1451, and the Madonna del Monte in Cesena, at the end of the fifteenth century.

The following are all spatial forms of this type, in which the flat ceiling of the nave is replaced by a barrel vault: the Badia near Fiesole (Fig. 17A), 1463; SS. Severino e Sosio in Naples, 1490; Sta. Caterina a Formiello in Naples, 1519; and S. Tolomeo in Nepi, 1540.

9. THE SERIES WITH RHYTHMICAL ANCILLARY CENTERS

If the chapels in a longitudinal church with a single, barrel-vaulted nave are not coordinated but are rhythmically alternating, then the spatial schema of the Badia of Fiesole is transformed into the nave of S. Andrea in Mantua, 1470 (Fig. 17B). Rhythm was thus achieved in this family of forms even earlier than at S. Salvatore in Venice (Figs. 13C, 15). S. Giovanni Battista in Pesaro, 1543, repeats the schema of S. Andrea in Mantua, but its larger side chapels are expanded by three apses, that is, by ancillary spaces of the second zone.

It is characteristic of all the barrel vaults just mentioned that none is broken by window lunettes. In Sta. Caterina a Formiello in Naples, lunettes were *painted on,* characteristically, at a later date. Even the cathedral in Mantua, 1545, the outer aisles of which are covered with flat ceilings, has unbroken barrel vaults above the inner aisles. Galleries are rare enough to be conspicuous when they do occur; there is one (original?) in the Annunziata in Arezzo. They are unavoidable in monastery churches, and especially in those of nunneries, as for example, S. Maurizio in Milan, 1503. The nave here is a very long cross-vaulted space bisected into two churches by a transverse wall reaching up to the spring of the vault. Isolated chapels flank the nave, and above these runs a gallery. But the gallery seems to be broken into separate spaces by the transverse walls that buttress the ribless cross vaults of the nave. The buttressing could have been solved in a different way if the effect of a continuous upper movement around the nave had been desired.

The longitudinal churches show that even when the architects of this phase aligned rather than grouped spaces, their

sole aim was to achieve the combination of complete, undivided spatial units. They also show that the architects knew
how to give this alignment the character of a group by the use
of rhythm.

10. THE COMBINATION OF GROUP AND SERIES

A simple rectangular hall such as the Sistine Chapel
in the Vatican, whether covered by a vault or a flat ceiling, or
enriched by one or two zones of coordinated or grouped
ancillary spaces, is rare however—rare because the rectangular
hall does not have the appearance of something definitely
self-contained. S. Andrea in Mantua resembled such a hall
throughout one century because, until funds were available
for its completion, its nave was closed by a temporary wall.
When funds were in hand, the resumed construction allegedly
adhered to the original design, but it is certain that Alberti
never intended the radiant brightness of the *present* domed
space; this is a characteristic product of the eighteenth century.
What he intended remains uncertain, except that a dome *was*
planned to follow the nave, and the nave was to be the overture
to the dome. Alberti wanted to add to S. Francesco in Rimini
(Fig. 67) a circular building *wider* than the nave, and Michelozzo
did add one to Sta. Maria Annunziata in Florence. This space,
similar to the Pantheon in Rome, is not related organically
to the nave, although it does enhance our experience of the
space. The opposite experiment, the addition of a dome the
diameter of which is *narrower* than the nave, was tried at
S. Giobbe and at Sta. Maria de'Miracoli, 1481, both in Venice,
but the only obvious solution was to add a domed space *equal*
in diameter to the width of the nave. This had already been
done in the Romanesque period, but S. Lorenzo in Florence
(Fig. 14) is the first of this series in post-medieval architecture.
The crossing at S. Lorenzo is covered by a dome on pendentives; at the Badia of Fiesole (Fig. 17A) by a pendentive dome;
at Sta. Maria del Calcinaio near Cortona, 1485, by an octagonal
cloister vault above a drum (Fig. 18). The latter is repeated in
the Madonna delle Lagrime in Trevi, 1487, and in Sta. Maria
de'Miracoli in Castel Rigone, 1494.

Now Sta. Maria del Calcinaio at Cortona is a centralized
church with one arm three times as long as the others. It
could be thought of as a combination of a Greek cross and a
nave of just two bays, although this does not correspond to
the impression that the third bay belongs to the nave. Reading
the whole as a sequence of nave and centralized church is
justified if, as here, one arm of the cross juts into the nave, or
if it appears left out altogether. As much as possible of the centralized church is preserved. This is also characteristic of the
longitudinal projects for St. Peter's in the Vatican, which are
reflected in the new cathedral, 1514, and in S. Nicolò in Carpi.
The latter was first erected as a completely centralized church
of the second order, and only in 1518 was one apse demolished

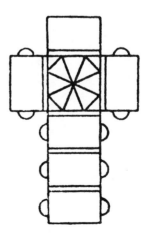

18. Cortona, Sta. Maria del
Calcinaio, 1485. Diagrammatic
Plan.

and a nave with side aisles added. The nave is composed of three bays that lead into the main space of the centralized church. The side aisles lead into its ancillary centers.

Such a combination of longitudinal and centralized spaces naturally produces a longitudinal church, but movement along its longitudinal axis stops in the center of the crossing. Radial axes branch off from this hub, and they in turn stop in the ancillary spaces. The focus in such a church lies in the crossing, not in the choir.

I have made a distinction between spatial groups with aligned ancillary spaces; spatial groups with grouped ancillary spaces; and groups of spatial groups, or groups of the second order. I can also make a distinction between spatial series with aligned and isolated ancillary spaces; spatial series with rhythmically grouped and isolated ancillary spaces; and parallel arrangements of such series (many-aisled churches), which I call series of spatial series, or series of the second order. On the basis of this system we can now discuss the combination of the series and the group.

Since, in their purest state, the series and the group are mutually exclusive, they can be combined only if one part of the centralized building is amputated. The pure series draws the spectator to a distant goal, to the choir and beyond. The effect of a Gothic cathedral with polygonal choir depends upon this magnetic longitudinal axis. The Gothic cathedral with flat choir points toward infinity. If an ambulatory encircles the polygonal choir, the entire movement within the space catches the spectator in an endless whirl. He has no thought of return, and the path forward pulls him toward an unattainable goal in infinity. On the other hand, the final result of the fully developed, symmetrical formation of the group is impenetrability, because its exterior of closed convex apses repels us. If doors break into the apsidal curve, they are necessary conveniences: they make it clear to us that even where rectangular spaces determine the contour of a church, or apses are hidden by rectangular exterior walls (as in the design for St. Peter's in the Vatican), all entrances are necessary evils. We are not supposed to enter such a church slowly and approach its center step by step. We are supposed, as if by magic, to arrive with one bound at this central point and to experience there the unique quiet, the secluded, serene independence that seems to be realized in such geometric formations. Just as the pure group permits no one to enter, it permits no one to leave: we must remain forever in this central point. The spatial group is formed by the juxtaposition of such isolated center points. Certainly there are continuous paths of circulation, but they are not present aesthetically. The person entering such a space remains an intruder, a guest of the church's true inhabitant, who is a Divine, Eternal Being.

The sequence of series and group is a totality marked by

tension and release. The series draws us to the group, to a spatial form in which we can find calmness and reassurance. The series is specifically preparatory. In it we gain a presentiment of the feeling of absolute freedom that we shall find in the group. The same space also leads us back from the group. We do not leave it with the feeling of having confronted for a brief moment, with inadequate strength, a superhuman force. Rather, it remains with us as a permanently available retreat in which we can be elevated to that ideal.

In combinations of two spatial systems of the second order, the effect of either the series or the group can prevail. If the flow of movement in the longitudinal direction is powerful enough to carry through the group, the series is supreme. A pronounced extension of the choir or shortening of the transepts will cause the group to appear swept away in the longitudinal movement. But it is characteristic of all examples of this family in the first stylistic phase that this is not the case. In Sta. Maria del Calcinaio at Cortona (Fig. 18), the cathedral in Como, Sto. Spirito in Florence, Sta. Maria della Passione in Milan, the cathedral in Faenza (Fig. 13B), Sta. Giustina in Padua, S. Nicolò and the cathedral in Carpi, and in the designs for St. Peter's in the Vatican in which a nave was planned (Fig. 28), the spatial group is completely balanced on all sides. The longitudinal church thus demonstrates clearly that, in the period from 1420 to 1550, the group is the form-determining factor in every case. But the expression "to group" is not entirely accurate, for this is a specific kind of grouping, which avoids unbroken movement in a circle and excludes any true sequential continuity or infinite procession. There is only the grouping that is characterized by the addition of whole spaces along axes radiating or branching out from one another. The preference for the group over the series, the rhythmical over the simply coordinated, is the result of the supreme principle of pure *spatial addition*.

11. SPATIAL ADDITION

No matter how rich or complicated a whole space thus governed by spatial addition might become, each of its members is, for the observer, a detachable, clearly defined entity, an addend. Each member that seems, from the exterior, to push outward is clearly accessible only from the center of the whole and clearly opens into the members of the next zone. Even in the longitudinal church, where this characteristic is not in fact present because of the nave and many aisles, a very strong suggestion of this same characteristic is present. No aimless wandering is possible in these churches: we advance briskly along a planned path with fixed halting points. From the requirement that space be set next to space, it follows that the spaces must differ in shape. The series suggests the creation of identical shapes. It also follows that the individual members of differing shape must be subordinate to a higher

community of spaces—a community that they freely create
without losing their own identities. Rhythm, which even the
series possesses, is the result of addition. For the same reason
that the ambulatory and the gallery do not fit in with this
principle, we can understand the lack of cross vaults and
window lunettes in this phase. The desire for the undisturbed
oneness of each entity permitted no interruption of the barrel
vault or dome. Every lunette has the effect of an interpenetration, a fusing together of two spaces, so that their bounding
surfaces cannot be determined with certainty. Of course, if
the lunette is very small, we can say that the boundary between these spaces is the continuation of the surface of the
larger vault or dome, but that is the response of a trained
geometrician, of a mathematically oriented mind. To the
average observer, space seems to penetrate the large barrel
vault and overflow that geometrical boundary. This causes an
uncertainty that cannot be tolerated. All the other spaces are
placed next to one another with visible seams, so that if we
wished to divide such a group into its natural components, we
would know immediately where to apply a knife.

Spatial addition characterizes all ecclesiastical buildings,
centralized as well as longitudinal, in Italy from 1420 to 1550.
It is the principle of style that characterizes the first phase.
We must now seek its polar opposite.

Second Phase (1550–1700)

The tidy survey of ecclesiastical spatial form that I have
been able to present, based on Leonardo's systematic study,
is heavily dependent on the nature of addition. What now
follows, or at least the major part of it, *could* be considered
under the same heading. Sta. Barbara in Mantua (Fig. 19),
1562, for example, could be discussed as a further development
of the form we have already seen in SS. Flora e Lucilla in
Arezzo (Fig. 16B). But such a discussion would no longer be
concerned with essentials.

Sta. Barbara has three aisles. The nave, composed of three
square bays, is extended by a square choir with semicircular
apse. The choir is attached to the nave by a shallow barrel-
vaulted space. The latter has the effect of a wide transverse
arch, so that we can forget it and read the nave as the sum of
four aligned squares. The first and third bays are cross-vaulted,
but above each of the other bays is a square drum surmounted
by a cove and ceiling. A series of lunettes breaks up the cove.
These drum structures are not original at all, but probably
date from the eighteenth century. We do not know whether
the bays were once covered by domes or by cross vaults.[31]
The remaining cross vaults in the other bays, however, permit
lateral openings into the galleries, which run above the side
aisles. The areas of the side aisles corresponding to the first
and third bays of the nave are broken into the rhythm *b a b*

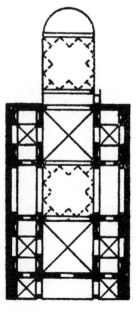

19. Mantua, Sta. Barbara, 1562.
Plan.

in which the spaces *b* are covered by barrel vaults and the spaces *a* by cross vaults. The lateral galleries are connected across the nave by a transverse gallery above the entrance and vestibule.

The cross vaults, the galleries, and the decisiveness of the nave sequence, which was probably even greater before the rebuilding, are new in this layout. It is of minor importance that the composition in other respects can be derived from SS. Flora e Lucilla at Arezzo.

Since these features are present in all the buildings that follow, I must change my method of analysis. I shall no longer consider an entire church as one of a family of related compositions but consider each of these features individually. A church that has many such features will reappear in the several paragraphs dealing with the different spatial forms.

1. LUNETTES AND CROSS VAULTS IN LONGITUDINAL CHURCHES

The church in S. Oreste sul Monte Soratte (near Rome), of about 1568, has *lunettes* that break into the barrel vault above the nave.[32] S. Giorgio Maggiore in Venice, 1566, has lunettes in the nave and *cross vaults* above the side aisles. S. Raffaele in Milan, 1575, has cross vaults over the nave (and pendentive domes over the side aisles). The Gesù in Perugia, 1562, has cross vaults above the side aisles (and a flat ceiling over the nave). The barrel vault above the nave of the Gesù in Rome (Fig. 23), begun 1568, is also interrupted by lunettes that are very pronounced and have an important effect upon the space. S. Vittore al Corpo in Milan, 1560, has cross vaults over the side aisles, but a barrel vault without lunettes over the nave (in keeping with the earlier taste). The University Church in Würzburg, 1582, is completely covered by cross vaults. The cathedral in Valladolid, 1585, has a barrel vault with lunettes above the nave and cross vaults over the side aisles (Fig. 20). Sta. Maria degli Angeli a Pizzofalcone in Naples, 1600, has side aisles broken into separate domed spaces, according to earlier taste, but its nave is unified by a barrel vault with lunettes.

The vault with lunettes is so common in the seventeenth century that I can spare myself the trouble of listing examples, except for two French ones. St. Paul-St. Louis in Paris, 1634, has cross vaults above the nave (Fig. 21), and the Val-de-Grâce in Paris, 1645, has a barrel vault with lunettes.

2. CONNECTED CHAPELS IN LONGITUDINAL CHURCHES

The wide nave of the Gesù in Rome (Figs. 22–23) is accompanied by individual chapels covered by elliptical domes. In contrast to earlier members of this family, such as the Badia of Fiesole (Fig. 17A), *these chapels* are *connected*. Since we do not have to return to the nave to pass from one chapel to the next, the possibilities of circulation have become complex. The passages between chapels in the Jesuit church of S. Fedele in Milan (Fig. 24), 1569, are hidden, but in S. Gaudenzio in Novara (Fig. 25), 1577, and in the Redentore in Venice

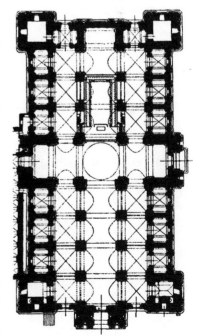

20. Valladolid, Cathedral, 1585. Plan.

21. Paris, St. Paul-St. Louis, 1634.
Interior.

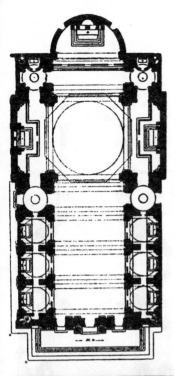

22. Rome, Gesù, 1568. Plan.
23. Rome, Gesù, 1568. Interior.

24 (left). Milan, S. Fedele, 1569. Plan.

25 (center). Novara, S. Gaudenzio,
1577. Plan.

26 (right). Venice, Redentore,
1577. Plan.

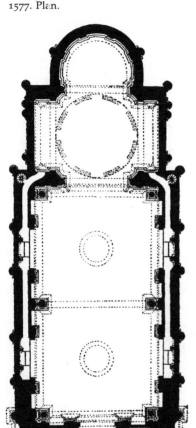

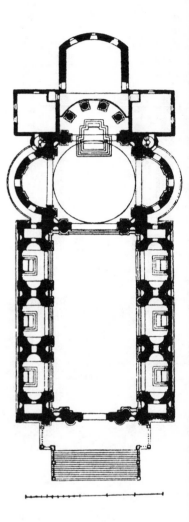

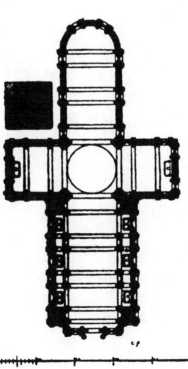

(Fig. 26), 1577, they are distinctly marked. As there are no side aisles to reinforce the longitudinal direction of the nave in these churches, the transverse direction—the relationship between chapels and nave—predominates, although each chapel is not set off as a separate entity with the *same* clarity as earlier. A church such as Sta. Caterina de'Funari in Rome, 1560, is a conservative laggard, because its semicircular chapels are isolated in the same way as those in Sto. Spirito in Sassia in Rome, which dates from the first half of the sixteenth century. Isolated shallow rectangular chapels also appear in the seventeenth century, as in Sta. Caterina da Siena (Piazza Magnanapoli) in Rome, 1638, SS. Domenico e Sisto in Rome, 1623, and elsewhere. But the proportions used in these churches rob the chapels of their individuality, and they become mere depressions for side altars. As a rule, side aisles were preferred instead of such chapels.

3. GALLERIES AND BRIDGES IN LONGITUDINAL CHURCHES

The fusion of the chapels forms an ambulatory round the nave, indicating that the feeling for peripheral movement was again respectable. The effect of something that is peripherally enclosed and that does not blossom radially is increased by the presence of *galleries.*

There are galleries above both side aisles of Sta. Barbara, 1562, the palace church of the Gonzaga in Mantua; they are connected by a transverse gallery above the entrance. Galleries almost invariably appear in Jesuit churches. The earliest examples are in the Gesù in Perugia.[33] The church in the Jesuit seminary (University) in Seville, 1565, has only a transverse gallery above the entrance. The Gesù in Rome has very low galleries (a person almost bumps his head on the ceiling) and no transverse gallery. The galleries in S. Giovannino, the Jesuit church in Florence, are also somewhat hidden. The first monumental galleries in Jesuit architecture appeared in the Michaelskirche in Munich, 1583, following the University Church in Würzburg, 1582. (The latter has two superimposed galleries.)

The chapels in the Michaelskirche in Munich (Fig. 27) are not connected but are isolated spaces opening frontally into the nave. The gallery that runs above them is broken up into separate spaces covered by transverse barrel vaults. These spaces are extraordinarily large in size and are connected only by small doors. At S. Maurizio in Milan, 1503, the galleries do not rise above the spring of the nave vault, but in the Michaelskirche in Munich the barrel vaults above the gallery cut into the large barrel vault above the nave like lunettes. (They are small because of the relative sizes of the two barrel vaults.) Closer inspection reveals that the isolation of the gallery bays is enhanced further by the beginnings of apsidal outer walls in each bay. If these had been completed, they would have continued the apses of the lower chapels, but they were altered

27. Munich, Michaelskirche, 1583.
Interior.

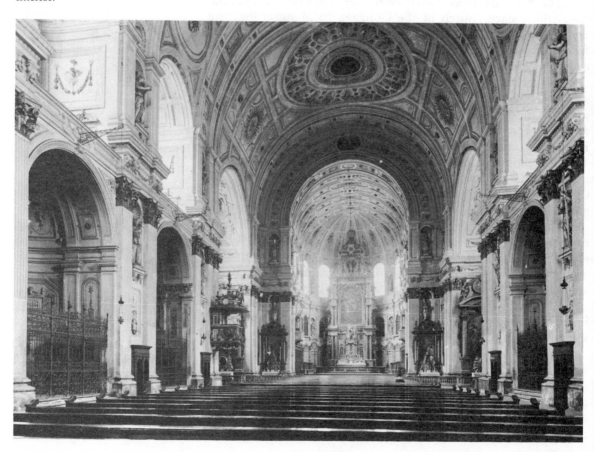

during construction. The gallery was closed in by a straight wall, and only the beginnings of the apsidal walls remain.[34] Thus the gallery is not a completely longitudinal space. It seems continuous to us because we assume that its bays are connected and that access is not only by separate stairs to each bay. This gallery is handled like a series of connected chapels. The transverse gallery above the entrance has just as decisive an effect in producing peripheral movement.[35] The space beneath this transverse gallery is not isolated from the rest of the interior like a vestibule, but remains a part of it. The railing of the organ gallery above is not continuous with the railings of the side galleries. This transverse gallery is thus a *bridge* across the nave: it is not added *to* the nave but placed *in* the nave. The effect of this principle of composition becomes clear when we compare the space beneath this gallery —it seems to extend across three aisles because its vaults rest upon two piers—with the outer passages planned by Bramante for St. Peter's in the Vatican. These added passages would have permitted a person to enter one whole space. The covering of the main space would not have extended over the vestibules but would have stopped at the dividing piers. In the Michaelskirche the main barrel vault extends over the organ gallery, which thus belongs entirely to the nave. In Bramante's church the complete separation of foyer and interior would have been noticeable immediately because it was to have been repeated on the opposite side of the centralized plan. When we enter the Michaelskirche, on the other hand, our glance is not contained by the space beneath the organ gallery: it travels immediately to the large barrel vault above the nave. Conversely, if we look back at this space from the choir, its division into three aisles suddenly appears to split the nave longitudinally into three smaller spaces.

I have waited until now to mention the existence, even in the first phase, of similar spatial formations, that is, of abrupt divisions of space, because only now will we see how exceptional they are there. Sta. Maria delle Grazie in Pistoia, 1452, has a single nave with a flat ceiling that abuts without transition against a three-aisled space—against transepts divided by a domed crossing that is narrower than the nave. The transepts extend halfway into the nave instead of projecting outward for their total length. Two square spaces with flat ceilings seem in plan to continue the nave beyond these transepts, but they are actually lower than the nave.[36] A second example is the choir of S. Domenico in Fiesole, and the church in the Foundling Hospital in Florence is a third. I do not know when the latter churches were built, but I judge from their corporeal forms that they belong to the *first* stylistic phase.[37] Finally, the transverse gallery in Sta. Maria delle Grazie in Venice, 1480, should be mentioned here.

The Jesuit church in Douai (then part of Belgium), contemporary with the Michaelskirche in Munich, was a replica of the Gesù in Rome, except that the space beneath the more pronounced organ gallery was divided into as many as five aisles. (The church was destroyed in the eighteenth century.)[38]

The organ gallery connecting lateral galleries now becomes a common spatial feature of Jesuit churches. The Gesù in Rome still lacks this gallery. The Jesuit church in Constance, 1604, had galleries even in the lunettes. They were removed in the eighteenth century, but the transverse gallery is preserved.

Even parish churches, such as S. Paolo in Bologna, 1611, take over these characteristic spatial features.

The longitudinal orientation of the lateral galleries was very marked in the Jesuit church in Antwerp, 1615. They were long continuous spaces with flat ceilings.

The Jesuit church in Innsbruck dates from 1615, although its present form is the result of rebuilding after a collapse of the old fabric in 1627. The third bay of the nave was transformed in rebuilding into transepts and domed crossing, which broke up the continuity of the galleries. Similar discontinuity was produced in the Michaelskirche in Munich, when its transepts and choir were added after a collapse in 1590. The galleries in the nave are not connected to those in the choir. In the church in Innsbruck, however, the interruptions are spanned by *bridges* across the transepts. Nor was this the first time that such transept bridges had been used, for they appeared in the church of the Clerecía in Salamanca as early as 1617. It is of no importance to us whether a direct influence between Salamanca and Innsbruck can or cannot be traced through the Jesuit order. Bridges spanning transepts are characteristic of the later Vorarlberg school. The choir and nave galleries in St. Paul-St. Louis, the Parisian Jesuit church of 1634, are connected by triforium galleries within the outer transept walls, and these even continue round the apsidal end of the choir (Fig. 21).

In the cathedral of Valladolid, 1585, galleries are placed above the chapels that open into the side aisles instead of above the side aisles themselves.

Jesuit churches without galleries are rare. S. Ignazio in Rome, 1626, has galleries in the choir but not in the nave. Such exceptions only show how characteristic these spatial parts are in churches of the second stylistic phase. Nevertheless, there are highly monumental complexes that manage without galleries. S. Andrea della Valle, 1591, and the nave of St. Peter's in the Vatican, 1606, are two examples in Rome. There was some discussion about placing an organ loft above the entrance in St. Peter's during the nineteenth century (a model of this is preserved), but nothing ever came of it. The lack of a transverse gallery above the entrance is conspicuous also in St. Kajetan, the Theatine church in Munich, 1663. This church has galleries in the choir and in the first and fifth

bays of the nave, which are narrower than the three bays between them. The galleries project into the nave like balconies.

4. BALCONIES IN LONGITUDINAL CHURCHES

Galleries take the form of *balconies* on consoles projecting into the nave as early as the Roman Gesù. They are not
present in Sta. Barbara in Mantua. A person sitting in the
gallery of Sta. Barbara feels isolated from the nave, but in the
Gesù he feels he is actually in the nave. The balcony swells
out from the gallery into the nave. We can say that we experience it twice, since it is simultaneously part of two different
spaces. It interpenetrates. The balconies in the transepts of the
Gesù project farther than those in the nave. A similar arrangement occurs in the choir and transepts of S. Ignazio in Rome,
1626; the nave of St. Paul-St. Louis in Paris, 1634; the church
at the Clerecía in Salamanca, 1617; and the Jesuit church of
S. Martín in La Coruña, 1693.

The organ gallery above the entrance is sometimes replaced
by an organ balcony, as in Sta. Maria della Vittoria in Rome.
There is an early and modest example of such a balcony (intended for the display of relics) in S. Lorenzo in Florence.

The wish to elevate the organ had long caused the installation of such balconies in churches, but in the first stylistic
phase they are not imposing. They are more like furniture—
like altars. There are organs elevated behind the altar in present-
day Florence, but these have no spatial effect. It is only in the
second phase that they are distributed equally throughout the
church, and are not intended for musicians.

5. OTHER FORMS OF INTERPENETRATION

There are other forms of spatial interpenetration besides
lunettes and balconies. The choir of the Redentore in Venice,
1577, ends in a semicircular apse defined by freestanding columns rather than by a solid wall (Fig. 26). These columns
stand within a rectangular space, the monks' choir. We perceive
the complete rectangle of the monks' choir, and the apse em-
bedded within it. This is interpenetration. The cross arms of
the Val-de-Grâce in Paris, 1645, terminate in apses that overlap
the rectangular space lying behind them. A smaller apse, that
of the Chapel of the Holy Sacrament beyond, pushes into the
center apse of the choir from a completely opposite direction.

6. REDUCTION OF ANCILLARY CENTERS AND TRANSEPTS

Interpenetrating forms and peripheral fusion now combine with an aversion to the balanced spatial group. This is
not the result of preference for the series over the group.
The series can be formed by addition, and the longitudinal
church of the first phase was an additive series. Rather, the
shift is away from addition as the principle of composition.
Extended hall-like spaces, which appear to be subsequently
divided, become more and more frequent. When a building is
formed by the combination of group and series, the group
now becomes more and more completely absorbed by the

longitudinal pull of the series. The *fate of the ancillary centers and transepts* is indicative of this.

A spatial group of the second order is clearly present in the Roman Gesù (Fig. 22), but the ancillary centers are smaller than the nave chapels. The principal center is not developed equally on all sides, because the longitudinal axis is emphasized by the extended choir and shrunken transepts.[39]

The transepts of the cathedral in Valladolid, 1585, are highly developed (Fig. 20), but the nave and choir are accompanied by side aisles, and these, by chapels. This longitudinal emphasis overwhelms the transepts.[40] The Michaelskirche in Munich (Fig. 27) received transepts but *no* dome in the continuation of 1593. The barrel vault above the nave carries through the crossing, and the choir also strongly accentuates the longitudinal direction. In S. Andrea della Valle in Rome, 1591, the transepts still project beyond the side aisles, and are nearly as well developed as the choir. There are also four ancillary centers present, even if they are smaller than the chapels off the nave. This church, which also lacks galleries, thus has almost nothing but the lunettes in the barrel vault to characterize it spatially as a work of the second phase. Nonetheless, the transepts do not radiate as independently as earlier. They are two bays long. The first bay is as wide as the connected nave chapels and ancillary centers, and itself opens into them. The effect of side aisles is thus produced. The second bay of the transepts, however, is significantly shallower than the first: it resembles a shallow chapel. This means that the transepts are stunted.

Ancillary centers can still be found at Sta. Maria degli Angeli a Pizzofalcone in Naples, 1600, but those *in front of* the transepts are identical to the domed bays of the side aisles. If I said earlier that these individual domed bays were characteristic of the first phase, I must now interpret them as repetitions of the ancillary centers. In any case, the impression is that the ancillary centers are completely drawn into the longitudinal direction of the nave and side aisles.

When St. Peter's in the Vatican received a nave, soon after 1606, such a fusion was impossible because of its unusually great size. In the design attributed to Raphael (Fig. 28), the axial alignment of the side aisles and ancillary centers was still possible because the piers sustaining the great dome were not as wide as they were to be made later. Serlio[41] shows them about a third as wide as the diameter of the dome, so that the nave piers could still be as wide as the dome piers. Michelangelo's existing piers, however, are almost as wide as the radius of the dome (Fig. 29). The side aisles as executed are not aligned with the ancillary centers but run into the dome piers; that is, they are aligned with the cross axis of the passage connecting the ancillary centers with the main cross. The closing of the side aisles against the broad piers also makes

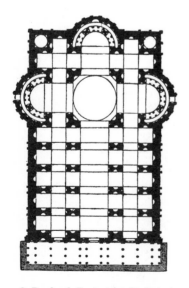

28. Raphael, Project for St. Peter's in the Vatican. Plan.

it conceivable that their longitudinality could not be permitted to be too pronounced. The added side aisles themselves are composed of individual bays covered by (longitudinally elliptical) domes.

Scamozzi's project for Salzburg Cathedral (Fig. 30) shows what this generation would have accomplished in such great undertakings, if it had had a free hand. The project is contemporary with the nave of St. Peter's. The projected church has a nave and side aisles of five bays each. Since the side aisles are broken up into individual square domed spaces, as in the Neapolitan church just mentioned, the fifth domed space corresponds to what earlier would have been an ancillary center. The transepts are each two bays long and terminate in large apses. They project boldly and are accompanied by side aisles, so that the first bay of the transept aisle coincides with the last bay of the nave aisle. Despite the highly developed transepts, the choir is overpowering. A square space, probably intended to be covered by a dome lower than that over the crossing, follows the first bay of the choir. Rhythmically articulated side aisles flank this domed space. We have no elevation for this design, but the stairs shown in plan and the present cathedral (executed after a later and much reduced design) indicate that galleries were intended for the space above the side aisles. They would have been connected by a transverse gallery over the narthex. The actual cathedral in Salzburg, finished in 1614, made use of extant Romanesque foundations. The three arms of the crossing are identical. The features that correspond to the spirit of the phase are the barrel vault with lunettes above the nave, the cross vaults above the side aisles, and the galleries with balconies projecting into the nave. The equal radiation of the three arms of the crossing is a vestige of the earlier taste and is a compromise resulting from the use of existing foundations.

Ancillary centers are totally absent from S. Ignazio in Rome, 1626. In St. Paul-St. Louis in Paris, the spaces corresponding to forward ancillary centers are fastened to the nave, and those corresponding to posterior ancillary centers are covered by cross vaults. Hence these four spaces can no longer be considered as balanced round the crossing.[42] Ancillary centers are completely eliminated from other contemporary monumental Jesuit churches, such as S. Isidro el Real in Madrid, S. Juan Bautista in Toledo, the university church in Innsbruck, and the university church in Vienna. All were begun in 1626.

7. DEMISE OF RHYTHM

The destruction of the group is paralleled by the demise of rhythm. Rhythm is still present in Sta. Barbara in Mantua (Fig. 19). The nave of S. Fedele, the Jesuit church in Milan, is still formed by the addition of two domed bays (Fig. 24), and its elevations are composed of side chapels flanked by

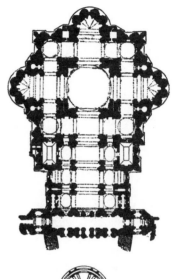

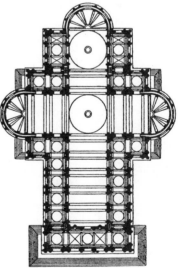

29. Vatican City, St. Peter's, with Maderno's nave, 1606. Plan.

30. Scamozzi, Project for Salzburg Cathedral, 1606. Plan.

confessional niches and surmounted by open galleries, all in the rhythm *b a b, b a b*. This is repeated in SS. Martiri, the Jesuit church in Turin (S. Carlo in Turin is similar), and in S. Filippo in Genoa. The Jesuit S. Bartolomeo in Modena belongs to this family, although it was constructed entirely by reusing Gothic material.

This sequence of groups in the rhythm *b a b, b a b,* and so on, is unquestionably the ultimate step in the systematic development of the principles of adding and grouping. It is a step beyond the simple continuous alternation *b a b a b a b,* and so on, but I leave open the question whether this most, highly developed form does not return to the simple series of coordinated members and, despite the rhythm, produce the effect of a series.

There are also examples within this phase of the simple rhythm *b a b a b,* such as S. Gaudenzio in Novara, with connected chapels (Fig. 25), and the Jesuit S. Isidro in Madrid. The latter is especially interesting because the rhythm, which is characteristic of the first phase, is combined with all the features characteristic of the second. For example, the connected chapels are covered by cross vaults; the continuous galleries pass through both *a* and *b* axes; and the transepts are stunted. The rhythm in S. Juan Bautista in Toledo is a secondary result of the width of the piers and of the niches let into them.[43]

In the eighteenth century, the rhythm *b a b a b* is found in the cathedral at Fulda, 1702 (we are uncertain how crucial the old foundations were in this building), and in the Jesuit church in Trent, 1708. The latter, which is related to S. Salvatore in Venice (Figs. 13C, 15), has a nave of five bays (*B A B A B*). The bays *B* are covered by barrel vaults that are cut by lunettes (one on each side). The square bays *A* are covered by cross vaults. The sequence in the side aisles begins with the small square cross-vaulted bay *a,* followed by the transverse barrel-vaulted bay *b.* Thus the spatial schema is:

a	*B*	*a*
b	*A*	*b*
a	*B*	*a*
b	*A*	*b*
a	*B*	*a*

as in S. Salvatore in Venice, but the effect is fundamentally altered not only by the lunettes in every barrel vault but also by the presence of galleries above the bays *a.* These galleries open as isolated loges, or *coretti* (as the Italians say), into *B* as well as *b.* We do not even need to notice the cross vaults over the *coretti,* which point toward the nave and in the longitudinal direction of the side aisles, to sense the continuity of the total space. This space is not an additive and rhythmical combination of separate entities, but was first conceived as one great parallelepiped and then subdivided (here rhythmically). Our awareness of rhythm disappears before this sense of forms placed within the space, or conversely, of inter-penetrating forms pulled out of a larger whole. Despite the rhythm, there is no break here between spaces but a broad continuous flow.

All these examples of rhythm are exceptions. The many churches built between 1550 and 1700—the number is very large—demonstrate that the sequence of coordinated parts was the preferred expression of the period's spatial perception.[44]

8. THE PRIMARY FORM

The relative height of the galleries has an important in-fluence upon the spatial effect. If they are entirely below the spring of the nave vault, they combine additively with the chapels below. If they extend *above* the spring, so that they break into the great vault like lunettes, then the higher they extend, the more closely the total spatial effect approaches that of a hall. The Jesuit churches in Poznań (Posen), 1651, and Wrocław (Breslau), 1689, and the Schlosskirche in Friedrichs-hafen, 1695, are good examples of this. The exterior rectangle—enclosing narthex, side aisles and galleries, transepts, and choir—appears as the primary form, and all the spatial parts I have mentioned seem to have been subsequently placed within it. Pure hall churches of the seventeenth century are the Jesuit churches in Luxembourg, 1611; Malines (Mechelen), 1670; Cambrai, 1679; and Bonn, 1686. The parish church of S. Salvador in Seville, 1680, is a triple-aisled hall for which part of an old mosque was used. Galleries were installed between the buttresses.

9. LUNETTES IN CENTRALIZED CHURCHES

The features I have mentioned are as characteristic of centralized churches of this period as they are of longitudinal churches. It would be unnecessary therefore to add a separate discussion of centralized churches, except that in the second phase they demonstrate the authority of the series and of fusion—the universal aversion to addition—just as in the first phase it was the longitudinal churches that demonstrated the author-ity of the group. The group persists in this phase, even in its most highly developed form, as a group of the second order, but it is deprived as much as possible of the characteristics of addition.

Lunettes are common in all the barrel vaults of centralized churches. A group of the second order, such as the new cathe-dral in Brescia, 1604, is identical to Sta. Maria di Carignano in Genoa, but its effect is completely altered by its lunettes and organ gallery. Not even domes remain pure. Windows are cut into the base of the dome, for example, in the Gesù in Rome (Fig. 23), in S. Andrea al Quirinale in Rome, 1658, and in the Theatine Church (St. Kajetan) in Munich, 1663.

10. AMBULATORIES IN CENTRALIZED CHURCHES

The church of the Escorial, 1574, a spatial group of the

second order like Sta. Maria di Carignano in Genoa, is completely surrounded by galleries. The gallery in the Bernardas Church in Alcalá de Henares, 1617, extends over the diagonally placed elliptical chapels and through the cross arms. It opens through rectangular portals into shallow balconies. This movement, encircling the core of the church, counteracts the radial force of the centralized space (here elliptical). It is repeated in the lantern above the dome. An *upper ambulatory* surrounding the oculus of the dome is produced by the marked recession of the lantern walls. This formation of an ambulatory by widening upper layers of space was used as early as the Cappella Pellegrini in Verona, 1553. Peripheral rings of space occur at the base of the drum as well as at the base of the dome in Sta. Maria della Salute in Venice, 1631, and these are brought into prominence by corner ressauts, or projections of the entablature.[45] An ambulatory also encircles the octagonal main space at floor level (Fig. 31). An ambulatory of this type was characteristic of Byzantine churches, but it reappears here for the first time in many centuries.[46] The radial effect of the main space is still present, however, and is played off against the peripheral movement of the ambulatory. The latter forms a concentric exterior octagon round the main space. The entrance is at one end of the building's main axis, and the other is marked by the opening into the choir. A shallow rectangular chapel is added to the center of each of the remaining six sides of the octagon. The ambulatory vaults above the corners of the octagon are awkward combinations of cross and cloister vaults, but the vault on the axis of each of the openings is a cross vault that reflects the intersection of peripheral movement around the ambulatory and radial movement into the chapels, choir, or entrance.[47] A similar opposition of radial and peripheral movements occurs in the Jesuit Collegium Regium in Loyola in Spain, 1681. The main space is a cylinder surmounted by drum and dome. It is surrounded at floor level by a circular ambulatory covered by an annular barrel vault. The vault is interrupted on the diagonals by radial barrel vaults, and these intersections produce cross vaults. The exits into the college are not placed on the axes of the spaces but behind the piers. There are balconies above them.

11. CORETTI AND BRIDGES IN CENTRALIZED CHURCHES

Individual *coretti,* generally with balconies projecting into the central space, are more common than continuous galleries in these central-plan churches. Diagonal *coretti* are especially characteristic. Perhaps those in the Cappella del Tesoro, 1608, in Naples Cathedral, are the earliest of these. I do not know whether those in S. Giuseppe in Milan date from the first campaign of 1607.[48] The introduction of *coretti* into the dome piers of St. Peter's in the Vatican, 1639, and the Val-de-Grâce in Paris, 1645, had a decisive influence.

In Sta. Agnese in Agone, 1652, and Sta. Maria in Campitelli

31. Venice, Sta. Maria della Salute, 1631. Plan.

(Fig. 36), 1663, both in Rome, there are *coretti* in the cross arms that project out next to the dome piers. Finally, galleries occur above ancillary centers, most noticeably in the Kollegienkirche in Salzburg, 1696. Even the lattice-enclosed galleries for clerics, such as those in S. Carlo alle Quattro Fontane in Rome, 1638, have an effect upon us. We immediately perceive the rectangle surrounding the entire layout, and not only at floor level. We project this parallelepiped to its full height on all sides. Thus every individual interior spatial form appears as if it were carved out of this extremely simple primary form.

Bridges in their purest form are found in S. Carlo in Modena, 1664, a Greek cross with central dome. The four corners are filled out with rectangular spaces to form a kind of over-all rectangular group of the second order, but these ancillary centers are covered by barrel vaults cut by lunettes. The bridges run transversely from each dome pier to the exterior wall; from them we can see both the transverse cross arms and the corner spaces. The bridges in S. Ambrogio in Genoa branch off at right angles from the organ gallery and abut against the nave piers. From these bridges we can see both corner spaces and nave. The bridges in Sta. Maria della Consolazione in Turin have a very decisive effect upon the interior space, and so do those that span the individual bays in the side aisles of SS. Apostoli in Rome, 1702.

12. EMPHASIS UPON LONGITUDINAL DIRECTION
IN CENTRALIZED CHURCHES

Lunettes, ambulatories, galleries, *coretti*, balconies, and bridges are all interior forms within the total space. The primary feeling for the total space does not lead to the creation of a group round a central point. It leads to the creation of a longish rectangle in which the longitudinal axis is overwhelming, or to the use of ellipses rather than circles in centralized churches. The latter first occurred in S. Andrea in Via Flamina in Rome, 1550 (the year I have mentioned as the dividing line between phases), then in Sta. Anna de'Palafrenieri in the Vatican, 1572, and then in S. Giacomo degli Incurabili in Rome, 1580. In the elliptical form the longitudinal or transversal direction is emphasized at the expense of symmetrical radiation. Equilibrium is completely upset.[49]

The longitudinal direction can be stressed by other means. The Gesù Nuovo in Naples, 1584, is basically a group of the second order, but its nave and choir are each two bays long, and the second bay in each is flanked by smaller repetitions of the ancillary centers (Fig. 32). This is not a group, then, but a triple-aisled layout bisected by transepts, each of which consists of only one bay plus a shallow chapel. Since the depth of this chapel is equivalent to that of the chapels off the double ancillary centers, the resultant form is once more the simple parallelepiped. The Jesuit church of S. Ambrogio in Genoa, 1589, is similar, except that there are no domed spaces flanking the choir. The longitudinal direction is stressed sufficiently by the forward pair of domes. As the choir is rectangular, the whole has the effect of the parallelepiped. S. Alessandro in Milan, 1602, has *no* galleries; it has lunettes *only* in the apse, and unbroken barrel vaults and domes. This is a group of the second order with overdeveloped choir. It is distinguished from similar spatial schemas of the first phase only by the emphasis upon the attached choir, which is a domed Greek cross with its forward arm pushed into the main spatial group, and by the repetition of the posterior ancillary centers as (isolated) chapels. Chapels off the domed spaces and transepts once again fill out a circumscribing rectangle.[50]

The equilibrium of the great octagon, ambulatory, and radiating chapels of the Salute in Venice is preserved by the autonomous formation of the choir as a second centralized building (Fig. 31). The choir does not have the effect of being a mere ancillary space of the great octagon, precisely because of the conservative, additive handling of the ancillary spaces. A complete fusion of the two spatial groups would have been achieved if the ambulatory or a gallery had continued uninterrupted from one to the other. I find such examples only in the eighteenth century, but the concept of longitudinal fusion characterizes the spatial form of Notre Dame d'Hanswyck in Malines (Mechelen), 1663. Here (Fig. 33) the domed space lies in the center of the predominant longitudinal axis, so that the nave and choir are of equal length. There are no transepts; in fact, there are even columns on the transverse axis. Cross-vaulted side aisles cling to the domed space, which extends beyond the width of the nave. There is a smooth flow of space. The church of the Sorbonne in Paris, 1635, resembles a less fluid version of Notre Dame d'Hanswyck. (I mean to imply by this no real connection but merely to stress similarities within the phase.) The dome of the Sorbonne church rises above the exact geometric center of the longitudinal axis (Fig. 34). The transepts are very stunted, but the four chapels that fill out the exterior rectangle are isolated. They share the direction of the nave, but the latter is bisected by transepts that do not radiate symmetrically from the center toward both sides. Rather, they cut through the nave in one direction: from the entrance on the north toward the funerary monument and altar on the south. This is a completely isolated case of spatial dissection, without the grouping of the first phase or the fusion of the second. Nevertheless, as a longitudinal, rectangular, centralized church, it is entirely a product of the second phase.

Sta. Maria in Campitelli in Rome (Figs. 35–36) was prevented from having the character of a group by slightly different means. Like S. Alessandro in Milan, it is a sequence of two rich groups, but there is no dome over the forward one. A barrel vault replaces the dome, so that the connected chapels

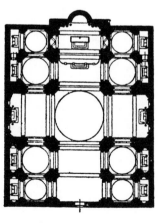

32. Naples, Gesù Nuovo, 1584. Plan.

b a b are no longer recognizable as ancillary centers and transepts. They are dependent servant spaces for the wide central space. The second group is altered by the curtailment of its transepts and by the accentuation of its longitudinal arm.[51] The space thus rolls forward comfortably in a broad tenacious flow toward the main apse. The undulating effect of the interior is due to the changing levels of the *coretti* and balconies.

13. THE UNARTICULATED HALL

The frequent appearance of individual spaces arranged within a simple circumscribing rectangle, that is, of the entire range of articulating inner forms existing within a hall-like, coherent, universal space, is paralleled by the frequency of unarticulated halls. These are exceptional in the first phase (Sta. Maria de'Miracoli in Venice, 1481, and the Sistine Chapel in the Vatican), but they appear with greater frequency after 1550: S. Giorgio de'Greci in Venice, 1550; S. Giuliano in Venice, 1555 (which Burckhardt angrily called a "parallelepiped crate"); S. Stefano de'Cavalieri in Pisa, 1562 (subtract the later side spaces); S. Moisè in Venice, 1668; and S. Marcuola in Venice, 1728.[52] Once we recognize that such primitive spaces were deliberately preferred in this phase, we shall begin to see the hall as the essential spatial form even of churches that seem complicated because of their elaborate interior articulation. This preference meant an emphasis upon the nave and a subordination of its attendant spaces to a longitudinal flood of movement. Indeed, the recognition of the simple unitary space that I call a hall leads us straight to the understanding of the spatial characteristic of the entire phase.

The less interesting the contour, the stronger is our perception of the space that fills the contour and of its continuity. The lack of emphasis of the spatial boundary also makes us aware of the continuity between the interior space and the open exterior space. All large hall-like spaces seem, as entities, to be sections of the infinite, formless, universal space. They convey this impression whether they are simple rectangles without interior articulation or rectangles with contours that can be seen only partially, because of the aisles, chapels, and galleries that seem to have been installed subsequent to their formation.

14. COMPLEX COMPOSITIONAL GEOMETRY

The desire to represent the *entire interior space* as a fragment, as something incomplete, now welcomes and justifies a much more striking method of composition that renders comprehension of the interior organization difficult.

SS. Trinità in Turin, begun 1598 and dedicated 1680, is a simple cylinder covered by a dome and expanded by radial ancillary spaces, which are arranged in the cyclic rhythm *b a b.* But as there are *six,* rather than four or eight, of these ancillary spaces, the choir is not opposite an *a*-axis of equal width, but

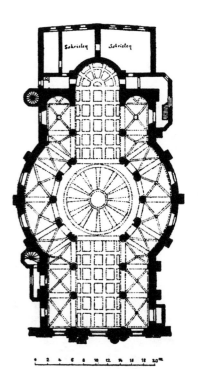

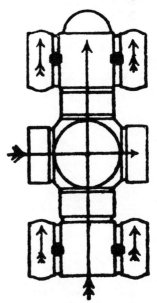

33. Malines (Mechelen), Notre Dame d'Hanswyck, 1663. Plan.

34. Paris, Sorbonne, Church, 1635. Diagrammatic Plan.

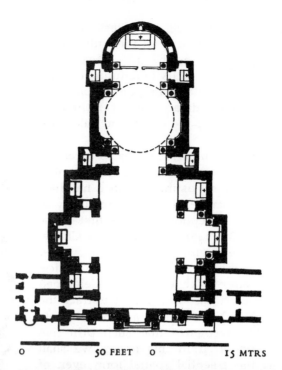

35. Rome, Sta. Maria in
Campitelli, 1663. Plan.

36. Rome, Sta. Maria in
Campitelli, 1663. Interior.

0   **50 FEET**   0   **15 MTRS**

opposite a *b*-axis containing the entrance beneath the organ gallery. There are confessionals on the two remaining *b*-axes, and above them are *coretti* with balconies.[53] Now since we are accustomed to equal spaces at opposite ends of a diameter, we are constantly surprised to find here the expected condition shifted by one axis. This is not simply a historically conditioned habit but corresponds to the invariable organization of the human body according to ninety-degree rather than sixty-degree angles.

The Cappella della SS. Sindone, 1657, at Turin Cathedral is more complicated. It has *eight* niches forming the rhythm *b a a b a a b A*, so that *A* is equal in width to the double axes *a a*. *A* is filled with a wall of glass that permits a view from this elevated chapel into the choir of the cathedral. The three *b*-axes form an inscribed equilateral triangle within the circular space, so that the sixty-degree angle is once more the basis of the composition. The small circular spaces on the *b*-axes, which flank the choir of the church, coincide with the chapel vestibules. The latter are reached by straight flights of steps leading up from the side aisles of the cathedral to the level of the chapel. Above these vestibules are *coretti* with balconies projecting into the chapel. The central altar and the very complicated dome are based upon a hexagon. The dome consists of a series of segmental window lunettes that taper round and round above one another and overlap syncopically.

S. Ivo alla Sapienza in Rome, 1642, has the effect of a six-pointed star or hexagram (Figs. 37–38), but if we look more closely, we realize that it is actually a triangular space with two rounded corners in which there are niches. The third corner, in which the main entrance is situated, is cut off by the exedra at the end of the University courtyard. I shall call these three corners *a*. What remains of each side of the triangle is divided rhythmically into a tripartite system, so that a large central semielliptical apse is flanked by short walls (*b*). The six points at which the three large apses intersect the wall of the triangle form an equilateral hexagon; above this central space rises a dome consisting of six ascending (curved) arched severies, all alike. As if this were not already sufficiently difficult to comprehend, the eye is taxed even more by a specific trick. The three large apses are subdivided into the rhythm *b a b* by pilasters and smaller niches, and this *b* is exactly similar in size and shape to the walls (*b*) that flank the large semielliptical apses. This gives the cyclic rhythm *b a b/b A b/ b a b*. We can grasp the group *b A b* easily enough, but *b a b* is very difficult because these axes are not on a continuous surface. Here *b* and *b* are placed at a sixty-degree angle to each other; *a* is not simply perpendicular to the bisector of this angle but a *convexly* curved wall that cuts off the point of the triangle. It is opened by the semicircular niche that rounds off the corners of the triangle. The fact that all *b*-axes are equal,

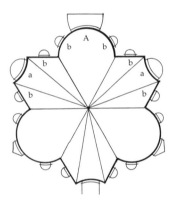

37. Rome, S. Ivo, 1642.
Diagrammatic Plan.

38. Rome, S. Ivo, 1642. Interior.

however, suggests that we are not to scan the walls in the manner just shown but as follows: *b b a b b*. On the other hand, we cannot read *A* by itself, and in the next instant we become aware of *b b A b b*. For example, if we attempt to orient ourselves by the first grouping and stand on the convex axis with niche below and gallery above, we find ourselves diametrically opposite the large central niche *A* rather than the expected *a*. This is due to the basic triangle. It suffices to deal with these principal difficulties, although they are sustained by lesser ones. Even when we have completely and rationally overcome the difficulties presented by this design, so that we can sketch its plan and any section by heart, we shall find that when we are in the space itself, this will be of no use at all. Our confusion remains.

The Mariahilfkirche at Innsbruck, 1647, is simpler because it has only six radii. The pilgrimage church at Kappl near Waldsassen, 1685, is an equilateral triangle covered by a dome that circumscribes the triangle, that is, a triangular pendentive dome or spherical triangle. On each side is a semicircular apse the vault of which flows directly into the spherical triangle.[54] Since each of these apses is divided into three parts, the rhythm *b a b b a b b a b* is formed.[55] Each pair of adjacent *b* axes is also pulled together by the openings for *coretti* located in the corner towers between the apses.

15. "UNEXPECTED" VAULTS

Finally, the effect of subsequent division within an ecclesiastical interior is produced by breaking up a vault that covers a *single* space into *several* adjacent vault shapes. Such a vault can be described as "unexpected."

St. Paul's in London, 1675, has a nave composed of rectangular bays, yet several forms of vaulting were used to cover these simple rectangles (Fig. 39). This covering is without prototype, and cannot be derived naturally from the plan, because the nave is homogeneous in plan, whereas the vaults might be said to correspond to a triple-aisled layout. In the center of each bay is a shallow circular dome resting upon transverse arches and lunettes. These occupy the area between the rectangle of the bay and the isolated inscribed circle in the center. The four corners are filled in with a kind of pendentive. The division of a simple nave bay into a tripartite covering is completely analogous to the division of a domed crossing into a three-aisled transept.

I have already referred to the surprising dissolution of the dome into rings of window lunettes that overlap one another syncopically in the Cappella della SS. Sindone in Turin.

The covering of S. Lorenzo in Turin, 1668, also belongs to this class of unexpected vaults. The convex plan of this church is converted by pendentives into a regular octagon at the base of the dome (Figs. 40–41). From each corner of the octagon, large semicircular arches span the space. The arches are so arranged that parallel pairs spring from adjacent corners and bind every third corner (thus two arches spring from each corner). These arches intersect one another to form a (spherical) sixteen-pointed star, that is, a regular figure with eight corners projecting inward and eight projecting outward. All the interstices of this star are open, and the arches themselves form the bearing ribs for the window lunettes that "close" the openings. Above the open star at the summit of this construction there rises a second, smaller dome formed also of a skeleton of arches that jump over every second corner. Arched window lunettes fill in this skeleton, and there are also lunettes (partly hidden by the arches) at the intersection of the large and the small dome.[56] This geometric formation was produced from elements that are still relatively simple, but it is far beyond the comprehension of the average visitor. He receives the vague impression of one large dome somehow divided at a point that is ill-defined: the two domes have the effect of *one*.

16. PROTESTANT LONGITUDINAL CHURCHES

We must now see whether contemporary Protestant churches exhibit the same characteristics as the Catholic ones.

No Protestant church—originally built as a Protestant church—has been preserved from the period before 1550. Prior to that date, Catholic buildings were used. The form of the Huguenot Temple de Paradis in Lyon, 1564, is known from old illustrations. It was a rectangle with semicircular apses on its short sides and an encircling balcony. It looked like an elliptical hall. The castle chapel at Augustusburg, 1568, is a hall with oratories in the form of separate chapels covered with transverse barrel vaults. Above these is a gallery, but there are still no lunettes in the vaults. The castle chapel in Szczecin (Stettin), 1570, is a hall covered by a lattice vault. The connected side chapels here are covered by transverse barrel vaults, and above them are *three* galleries. Before it was remodeled in 1602, the castle church at Kaliningrad (Königsberg), 1584, was an undivided rectangular hall with a shallow wooden vault and a choir on one long side. The chapel in Schloss Wilhelmsburg near Schmalkalden, 1584, has a central space three bays long covered by cross vaults. A cross-vaulted ambulatory encircles three sides, and above it are two galleries.

Various alterations were necessary when Catholic churches were taken over by the Protestants. The first monumental galleries were installed in the Marienkirche in Pirna, 1570. The purpose of these galleries concerns us no more here than in our discussion of the galleries in Catholic churches. For the moment we are interested merely in the presence of these spatial features.

Common to all Protestant churches of the seventeenth century is the simple, whole form, hall-like in character, with simple or superimposed galleries. These galleries seem to be built into the space, not added to it, especially when their parapets

39. London, St. Paul's Cathedral, 1675. Interior.

40. Turin, S. Lorenzo, 1668. Plan.
41. Turin, S. Lorenzo, 1668.
Interior of Cupola.

mount up, without supports, to the flat ceiling or vault, that is, when they are inserted into the space like balconies or bridges, such as the transverse gallery in the Michaelskirche in Munich. There are galleries of this type in the Marienkirche in Wolfenbüttel, 1604; the church in Bückeburg, 1611; St. Paul's Covent Garden in London, 1630; and in the Trinitatiskirche in Sondershausen, 1690, where they partially fill in the side aisles.

Spaces divided into three aisles of equal height are relatively frequent. Examples of these are the church in Fredericksborg, 1602; St. Mary in Wolfenbüttel; the Stadtkirche in Nidda near Friedberg, 1615; the Trefaldighetskyrka in Kristianstad (Scania), 1617; the Trinitatis Kirke in Copenhagen, 1637; the *old* Michaelskirche in Hamburg, 1649; the Altrossgärterkirche, 1651, and the Haberbergerkirche, 1653, both in Kaliningrad (Königsberg); and the Trinitatiskirche in Sondershausen.

17. PROTESTANT CENTRALIZED CHURCHES

There are no known sixteenth-century Protestant centralized churches. The earliest seems to have been the Dutch-Walloon church in Hanau, of about 1620, an octagon encircled by galleries.[57] The octagon with *ambulatory* is found again and again. Examples are the Marekerk in Leyden, 1639; the Salvatorkirche in Roda, 1650; and the Östermalmskyrka in Stockholm, 1658.

St. Paul's Cathedral in London would have been by far the most important octagonal church of Protestantism if the design of 1673 had been built. In this design the principal and diagonal axes of the domed central octagon open into domed square arms that flow together into a continuous ambulatory through intermediate triangular spaces (Fig. 42). One small side of each of these triangles joins a diagonal space; the hypotenuse joins a cross arm. The remaining small side opens into a large apse, thus orienting the triangle toward the cross arm. Some confusion in movement must have arisen because of these unbalanced triangles. The confusion would have been increased by the openings in the piers, which would have permitted circulation from one diagonal space to another through the central octagon. The possibilities of circulation here would have been significantly greater and more complicated than, for example, those in the Dôme des Invalides in Paris, 1680, where both the ambulatory and the diagonal path through the dome piers are present. The result in St. Paul's would have been a turmoil of movement.[58] Whether galleries were intended is unknown. The completely centralized space was supposed to have a slightly emphasized longitudinal axis marked by the vestibule (formed as a centralized space) and the opposite apse. The cathedral as erected is a longitudinal church.[59]

Besides the octagon with ambulatory, Protestantism created another archetype still more strongly opposed to the

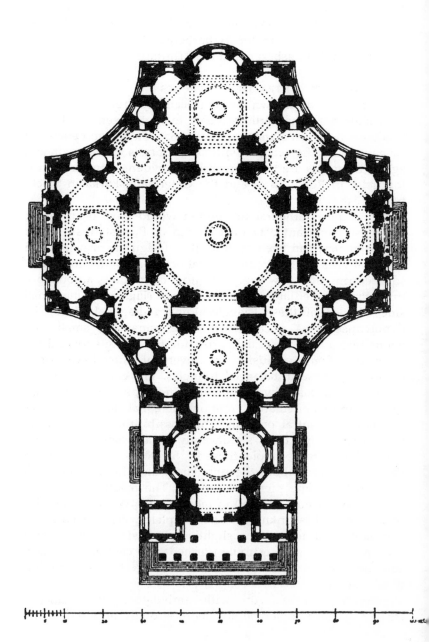

42. Wren, Project for St. Paul's
Cathedral, London, 1673. Plan.

principle of addition. This is exemplified by the Noorderkerk, 1620, and the related Oosterkerk, 1669, both in Amsterdam. The center of the Noorderkerk (Figs. 43–44) is a square covered by a cross vault the severies of which continue into the four cross arms. Each of these arms is two bays long, and the inner bays are connected by triangular spaces behind the corner piers of the central space. The piers are thus completely free-standing. We can say either that an octagonal ambulatory is formed by the triangular spaces and the inner bays of the cross arms or that the central square appears to have been inserted into a unified octagonal space. The Oosterkerk achieves the same effect by a square placed within a square ambulatory. It is a kind of four-centered group with thin crossing piers.

The choir of Kempten Cathedral (Bavaria), 1651, which is not dependent upon the Amsterdam churches, has the same form as the Noorderkerk, but it is enriched by galleries and bridges on the side toward the nave. This shows that without exception both Protestant and Catholic churches obey the same principle of spatial composition.

Once we have understood the Dutch churches, we can also understand a complicated form such as that of St. Stephen Walbrook in London, 1672. A square is staked out in the center of the space by twelve columns: one in each corner and two on each side (Figs. 45–46). The latter break the side into the rhythm *b a b*. Arches spring from column to column but miss the corner columns, thus forming an octagonal base for the central dome. The four triangles in the corners are covered by lunettes. Additional spaces enrich this relatively simple central form. The main axis (*a*) opens into a cross-vaulted arm, while the remaining sides of the central square open into rectangular or oblong spaces with flat ceilings. As the exterior wall is rectangular, the central space is split into three aisles on each side, and, as these aisles are flanked by two more, the entire space is a five-aisled hall. The domed space with its cross arms seems to have been placed into a five-aisled hall with flat ceiling, or conversely, the hall seems to perfuse the central space. This is a fusion of two spatial systems, which are in themselves already complicated.

18. SPATIAL DIVISION

In the period 1550 to 1700 the same characteristics appear in Catholic and Protestant centralized churches just as in Catholic and Protestant longitudinal churches. All these characteristics are special manifestations of a stylistic principle that is the opposite of spatial addition: *spatial division*. The components of spatial form are no longer complete, isolated addends, but fractions of a pre-existent whole. The space does not consist of many units; it is *one* unit divided into parts or fractions. These parts are incapable of independent existence. They are fractional interior forms suspended or floating within the total space. The clarity of the bounding surfaces of these

43. Amsterdam, Noorderkerk, 1620. Diagrammatic Plan.

44. Amsterdam, Noorderkerk, 1620. Interior.

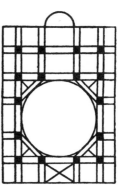

45. London, St. Stephen Walbrook, 1672. Diagrammatic Plan.

46. London, St. Stephen Walbrook, 1672. Interior.

fragmentary spatial parts is also diminished. A lunette, a balcony, or a bridge has something vague about it, and the possibilities of circulation can and should be vague too. All the spatial parts are connected. The space has a broad, flood-like movement with a pronounced recessional tendency. Whereas a group composed by addition can be broken into individual isolated static points, the schema of movement in compositions formed by true division is the row of parallel piers. These may give direction to a hall, like a broad phalanx urging us on toward infinity, or they may flow back upon themselves in an endless circle. And just as the individual parts are only fractions of the whole space, so the whole should appear as a mere fraction of the universal space. If it is a hall, its perimeter is uninteresting. If it is based upon the sixty-degree angle, the space has the effect of something constantly changing, incomplete, becoming.

In the first phase, the *development* consisted of ascending from simple additive compositions to ever richer ones, of accomplishing ever more consequent and exclusive rhythm, and of submitting the longitudinal church to the taste for addition by the use of groups and rhythms. In the second phase, the *development* consisted of recasting the completely transmitted spatial form according to the principle of division, of kneading the happily differentiated, radiating products of addition into units that gain their rich differentiation from the overlapping of interior forms, and of depriving the central-plan church of its grouped, rhythmic character. Gradually, every kind of spatial division and interpenetration had to be found and then combined. All vestiges of pure addition had to be eliminated to attain a whole that was again characterized by a *single* stylistic principle. But a detailed discussion of this development belongs in a descriptive work on the subject. My purpose here is simply to disclose the stylistic principle.

Third Phase (Eighteenth Century)

The principle of spatial division lasted into the eighteenth century, but was carried to its extreme consequences. We can therefore distinguish a third phase that has its roots in the scattered experiments of the seventeenth century. A spatial formation of the second phase is already far more difficult to understand than one of the first, but in the third phase the impression of an indeterminate form is even stronger.

1. CONVEX SPACES

The lack of clarity in many eighteenth-century churches is the result of the use of convex spaces, and particularly of convex whole spaces. The convex corners of S. Ivo in Rome (Figs. 37–38) lead us to believe that the exterior is pressing in upon us, and as a result the interior as a whole seems somewhat incomplete. As a *totality* it seems *fragmentary* in the same way as the interior spaces of the second phase. The convexity in S. Ivo is still moderate, but the more pronounced it becomes the more an interior takes on the appearance of a fortuitous, undefined fragment of universal space. This is of course the extreme opposite of pure addition, in which without exception an interior is a world in itself, set off as clearly as possible from the space of the outside world.

A plan in the shape of a violin case is produced by alternating convex and concave walls, as in S. Francesco di Paola, 1728, and Sta. Maria della Sanità, 1708, both in Milan. There is a similar effect in the Maddalena in Rome, although the wall between the two diagonal concave niches is straight rather than convex. Sta. Maria dell'Orazione e Morte in Rome, 1732, is a long elliptical space expanded on each side by two relatively small, shallow, rectangular chapels with flat ceilings. The entrance and the choir form two more openings on the longitudinal axis. (The choir is rectangular and covered by a cross vault. The organ balcony is opposite the choir, above the entrance, and in front of a shallow niche.) Between the six openings, the wall swells inward convexly. Churches with violin case plans are to be found in Upper Bavaria at Schwarzlack, 1750, and at Berbling, 1751.

Convexity is possible in churches of four axes as well as in those of six. The Piarist church of Maria Treu in Vienna, 1751, has four cross arms between which the piers press inward convexly. The arms appear to be squeezed outward by diagonal pressure at the corners.[60]

The S-curve in plan at the beginning of the choir of Cadiz Cathedral, 1722, was possible only in a period which permitted convex spatial forms.

2. CONVEX SPATIAL PARTS

Convex forms in the interior are more frequent in this period than convexity of the entire space. Galleries that project into the central space as S-curved balconies are very common. After 1700 they are the rule. Examples are the balconies in St. Peter's in Vienna, 1702, and in the Jesuit church of Sv. Mikuláš Malá Strana in Prague, 1703. The galleries in the Jesuit church in Lucerne, 1666, are the prototypes of these eighteenth-century examples, although the central part of the parapets of these galleries forms a comparatively straight balcony. If this broken line is made into a double curve, it will push convexly into the gallery itself.

An effect identical to that produced by convex forms is produced by concave galleries, as in the abbey church at Weingarten, 1715, and the Heiligkreuzkirche in Donauwörth, 1717. The nave of the latter church seems to swell into the side aisles. Even the straight galleries of the Jesuit church in Mannheim, 1738, have this effect because the parapets do not coincide with the forward plane of the nave piers but are located far back from it.

The central space of S. Lorenzo in Turin, 1668, is convex

(Fig. 40). The four chapels on the main axes make it into a full circle, except that the choir is a transverse ellipse fused to the main space. The chapels are formed of two segments of circles that meet at pointed corners. These are in turn subdivided and enriched with *coretti*.

3. VAULT FORMS

Convex spaces within the total space can also be produced by the form of the vault. The most prominent examples of this are the abbey church at Banz, 1710, and the pilgrimage church at Vierzehnheiligen, 1743.

If a barrel vault of the second stylistic phase was not fused into a unit by a large painting spread over its bays, it was divided by transverse arches corresponding to the piers below, as for example in S. Andrea della Valle in Rome. The boundary between bays is represented in plan by a straight line perpendicular to the longitudinal axis of the church and connecting the centers of opposite piers. In elevation the boundary is a vertical *plane* that forms a semicircular intersection with the barrel vault above. The individual bays in Sv. Mikuláš Malá Strana in Prague, however, are not rectangular, because the walls of the nave are undulating. The corners of the bays project into the nave, and the two pilasters flanking each of these corners are no longer in the same plane. They turn away from one another. The natural consequence of this arrangement would have been to bend the nave arches as continuations of the diagonally placed pilasters, rather than place them in the vertical plane between opposite corners. This possibility was first realized, not in Prague, but in Banz (Figs. 47–48) seven years later.[61]

One solution was to eliminate the transverse arches entirely and to replace them by other arches that joined diagonally opposite pilasters. Diagonal arches of this type would describe vertical planes standing at an acute angle, rather than perpendicular, to the longitudinal axis of the nave, but they would still be vertical *planes*. Their intersection with the vault above would be a semiellipse. Two of these ellipses would cross at the summit of the vault and would thus form a cross vault with the arches as broad diagonal ribs. The arches at Banz, however, do not join diagonally opposite pilasters. They are double curves that swing up to the summit of the vault (it might help to think of this as a cross vault) and then turn back in symmetrical arcs to the perpendicularly opposite pilasters. These spatial curves no longer adhere to planes. The boundaries between bays are no longer vertical *planes* but vertical cylindrical surfaces. Since each adjacent pair of these arches touches at the summit of the vault, the boundaries of the bays meet in the centers of the spaces. The placing of the pilasters in Sv. Mikuláš in Prague tells us that such a vault was planned above *every* bay there. The transverse axis of each bay of the vault would thus have been where we would

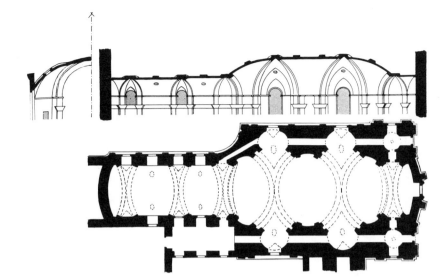

47. Banz, Abbey Church, 1710.
Plan and Section of Vaults.

48. Banz, Abbey Church, 1710.
Interior.

expect to find transverse arches, and the point where the arches would meet would occur where we would expect to find the transverse axis of the bay. There would have been a syncopic shift between the divisions in the vault and those in plan. It might help to pretend that the paired arches springing from adjacent piers are elastic and have been pulled away from one another until each touches the succeeding arch of the next pair. The area between these paired arches would no longer maintain a constant width but would increase in width toward the summit of the vault. The area of vault above the bay in plan would correspondingly become narrower in width and break into two separate parts. In the choir at Banz this is not the case in *every* bay but in *every other* bay. In addition, the barrel vault has already been given up for structural reasons. The arches were built as self-sustaining members that actually rest upon one another. A transverse line connecting the opposite edges of the soffit of such an arch is horizontal at the spring line. In a normal arch this line is horizontal at the summit too, but here it is bent soon after the spring of the arch and is inclined at the summit. The keystones of the two abutting arches are inclined like the planes of a gable roof. The center line of such an arch is a *three-dimensional curve,* and its soffit is a *warped surface.* Cylindrical severies would have no place between these arches. There are warped severies spanning between them, and I cannot say whether these belong to any geometrically defined class of surfaces.

I used the expression "pair of arches" to designate the two arches that rise above adjacent pilasters, but this relationship is destroyed when the two arches that meet above the center of a bay seem to belong together. Warped severies rise from both sides of the nave to fill in the area from spring line to summit within *one* pair of arches in the latter sense. At their base these severies have the width of a bay in plan. They also contain the windows and are therefore also cut through by large lunettes. *One* large continuous severy vaults between two adjacent pairs of arches. The nave at Banz is wider than the choir. Its vault is essentially similar except that the lunettes within the pairs of arches join the quarter-spherical vaults above the chapels (which are connected and have galleries). There are also lunettes in these apsidal vaults, and the galleries are bent into S-curves outlining a convex space that is not repeated in the vault above. The chapels beneath the galleries are covered by a kind of elliptical vault, which is cut by lunettes. The organ gallery is similar except that its ceiling is formed like the bays of the nave. Finally, since the vaults above the organ gallery and choir are lower than the vault above the nave, the large warped severies above the transitional bays must be inclined. Thus they differ from the severies over the center part of the nave. The summit of the vault (allowing for the internal curvature in each severy and the breaks where the arches meet) rises from the organ gallery to the center of the nave and then falls in a similar curve to the front of the choir. Despite all this enrichment, the interior has the effect of a continuous, cohesive unit to which the side chapels and the galleries belong, and which, as an undulating structure, seems to be in contact with the infinite exterior space. We must understand clearly here that these vaults cannot be predicted from the plan of the nave. They correspond to its outline, of course, but not to its divisions. The divisions in the vault are unexpectedly displaced: they do not correspond to the bays in plan. In Sv. Mikuláš in Prague, they were intended to be syncopically displaced, and this idea was carried through at Sv. Markéta, the Benedictine church in Břevnov (Breunau) near Prague, 1708. The idea was developed further at Banz because the three-dimensional arches occur only in every *other* bay, so that syncopic variety combines with rhythmic alternation. The severy of the intermediate bay is extended longitudinally to both sides until it reaches the apex of the next pair of arches. The chapels within the pairs of arches, however, are convex spaces of another kind. On the surface of the vault these spaces appear like triangular tongues pointing toward the center from both sides. Somewhere (it is impossible to say where) the space they suggest fuses with the homogenous part of the space below. This is an interpenetration of convex spaces.

Cross vaults that are formed by arches rising above pairs of oblique pilasters actually do occur, as for example in SS. Justo y Pastor (the present S. Miguel) in Madrid, 1739. They cover the first and third bays of the nave. The vault above the second bay oversteps its proper boundaries here also, for its shallow dome is tangent to the diagonal arches and is not confined between parallel arches. In the former Benedictine church in Legnickie Pole (Wahlstatt) in Poland, 1727, three-dimensional arches are used in a central-plan church (Fig. 49). The central space has an elliptical effect, but the ellipse itself is nowhere evident. Six spaces are set out radially and all are fused into an undulating unit by the three-dimensional arches. The longitudinal axis is accentuated, and the side chapels are shallower than the vestibule and the opposite passage into the choir. Vestibule and choir have the effect of centralized spaces, so that the whole seems to be a chain of centralized parts. This impression is not overwhelming, however. The whole is something between a centralized and a longitudinal church. The convexity of the whole space is echoed in the vault. The vault begins as a convex shape and gradually loses this shape to change into a concave curve.

At Vierzehnheiligen, 1743, syncopation occurs in the plan itself (Fig. 50). Three long, elliptical vaulted spaces are aligned along the central axis. The center space is larger than the others, one of which contains the organ gallery while the other forms the choir. These elliptical forms do not begin only in the region of the vaults, for the plan too is elliptical, that is, the usual circumscribing rectangle is missing, and elliptical and circular spaces can thus be placed tangentially between each pair of central ellipses. The extended transverse axes of the two small elliptical spaces coincide with the tangential line common to the first and second ellipses of the central axis. The line connecting the centers of the two large circular spaces is congruent with the tangent common to the second and third ellipses of the central axis.[62] Although there is nothing present that could be called a crossing, the two circular spaces have the effect of transepts, because all the vaults are intersected by lunettes extending so high that they create the impression of a continuous ceiling height (Fig. 51). The two small side ellipses form part of side aisles the remaining parts of which are complicated convex spaces. Comprehension of these spatial forms is made still more difficult by the galleries that pass through the side aisles. In the small elliptical spaces the vault withdraws back upon itself so that here too there is syncopation. The organ gallery is a little lower than the side galleries, which are interrupted by the transepts. They are continued in the choir by the *coretti* of one bay, which appear as extensions of the space above enclosed sacristies. Since the exterior enclosure is relatively very simple, enrichment of the interior is attained by division alone, as in the second phase. The vaulted spaces are placed into the total space and produce convex spaces. But since the boundaries of the seven vaulted spaces are completely dissolved, they have no clear definition, and all the vaults are fragments because of the predominance of the lunettes. Moreover, these fragments are fused by convex connecting spaces, so that the distinct form of the individual parts of space into which the plan ought to develop is present only by suggestion. (The five elliptical and the two circular spaces are clearly the generating factors in the design—all the rest being convex supplementary parts.) A second difficulty is thus added to that created by the complex total space, since the individual forms themselves are only suggested to the inquiring mind. The minds of more than ninety-nine per cent of the visitors to this pilgrimage church capitulate before such difficulty, and this is precisely the object: to appeal not to the mind but to the imagination that surrenders itself to the ambiguous and uncontrollable.

4. "UNEXPECTED" VAULTS

Unexpected vaults are present in the third phase too. There is no denying that those of the second phase were already very difficult to understand, but they were still basically simple because their components were forms of lower geometry. In the third phase even the components of unexpected vaults are very difficult to explain because they are ellipsoids or similar shapes that are sometimes not even the products of

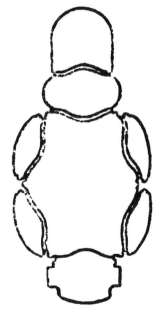

49. Legnickie Pole (Wahlstatt), Former Benedictine Church, 1727. Diagrammatic Plan.

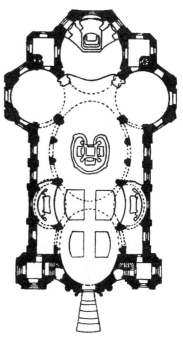

50. Vierzehnheiligen, Pilgrimage Church, 1743. Plan.

51. Vierzehnheiligen, Pilgrimage Church, 1743. Interior.

rotation. Warped surfaces and other such complicated forms, which have no technical justification but exist solely because of the period's delight in complication, are often so inconspicuous as to be overlooked by everyone but the person who wants to make a drawing of the building. Yet, no matter how inconspicuous they are, such vaults have a crucial effect upon a space. An example of the most complicated vaulting is that above the ambulatory surrounding the choir of the church in Günzburg. I shall spare the reader a description of it!

I describe it as "unexpected" when domes rest upon lunettes (as in the church of the Fraternity of St. Michael in Berg-am-Laim near Munich, 1737), that is, when there are openings in the pendentives that are not the usual horizontal barrel vaults but vertical cylinders covered by domes. In the parish church at Etwashausen, 1741, vaults that are customarily found above circular plans are used above rectangular ones, and vice versa. The apse of this central-plan church is formed by a segmental curve and separated from the choir by columns that abruptly split the choir into three aisles. The central aisle is covered by a cross vault, and each of the flanking spaces by a kind of quarter sphere. The end of the nave (in which the organ gallery is situated) opposite the choir is also segmental and is divided into three spaces. Thus the arms that have rounded ends are covered by cross vaults, whereas the flat transverse arms are covered by domelike, half-cloister vaults.

5. OPEN ABOVE CLOSED SPACES

Open galleries placed above closed sacristies, such as those in the choir at Vierzehnheiligen, especially tax our imagination. There are examples in the church in Diessen, 1732; Steinbach an der Iller, 1740; St. Peter in Munich, about 1750; and the Jesuit church in Landsberg-am-Lech, 1752.

6. CONSTANT CEILING HEIGHT

The drum, which is a vertically added space, frequently disappears because of the desire for continuous spaces. Pendentive domes replace the towering drum and dome. In the over-all impression these low domes collectively comprise a more or less continuous covering. The drum is lacking where it would have normally appeared earlier, for example, in the Dreifaltigkeitskirche in Munich, 1711 (which also has large lunettes in the dome). Other examples are at Krzeszów (Grüssau), 1728; Berg-am-Laim, 1737; Etwashausen, 1741; Ottobeuren, 1748; St. Gall, 1748; and Maria Treu in Vienna, 1751. Spaces such as the former abbey church at Legnickie Pole (Wahlstatt) also belong here in a certain sense. (There are isolated seventeenth-century prototypes such as the church at Kappl near Waldsassen, and the church in Waldsassen itself.)

7. THE HALL CHURCH

The striving for an impression of a constant ceiling height makes the hall church (a church with aisles of equal height) an expected feature of the third phase. Examples are the church in Schöntal in Württemberg, 1700; Unseres Herrn Ruh near Friedberg (Upper Bavaria), 1730; the Dominican church in Würzburg, 1741; and the Catholic church in Amorbach, 1752. The impression of a hall is also produced in a church of one nave flanked by chapels, if these chapels are of the same height as the central space. Examples of this are the churches in Diessen, 1732; Dietramszell, 1729; Gössweinstein, 1730 (all three in Bavaria); and Sta. Maria in S. Sebastián in Spain, 1743.

Many of these hall churches are identical in spatial form to those of the late Gothic in which nave and chapel vaults of equal height were also used. The ceiling of the Spanish church just mentioned is formed of ribbed star vaults. This return to late Gothic forms can actually be a Gothic survival in provincial districts that were late to receive the new style. Yet the essential quality of the hall is absolutely characteristic of the second and third phases. The hall church is not necessarily a reference to the past, but a development of a present that felt an affinity to the spatial forms of the late Gothic period. All this is shown by the appearance of the hall in the work of such men as Balthasar Neumann, who were not dependent upon fortuitous local traditions but belonged to the main stream of development and were aware of what the architecture of their time had achieved.

It is not surprising therefore if the hall church assumes a centralized plan: a central space surrounded by an ambulatory of nearly the same height, as in Steinhausen, 1728, or Die Wies, 1746.

8. INTERPENETRATION OF SPATIAL FORMS

The principle of creating a space by the interpenetration of two spatial forms is adopted from the second phase. An example is St. Nikolaus in Murnau, 1717, where a circle and the circumscribing square occur simultaneously, without the triangular spaces in the corners appearing as pendentives. Another example is Günzburg, 1737, where an ellipse within a rectangle is suggested at ground level but is only clearly developed in the space overhead.[63]

In this way even the narrow space of one aisle became a very complicated interior. This is true of St. John Nepomuk in Munich (Fig. 52), 1731, and the chapel in the Residenz in Würzburg is even richer in convex forms. The sixty-degree angle developed in the second phase recurs in the third, as in the chapel of Sv. Anna at Panenské Břežany (Jungfernbreschan) in Czechoslovakia, 1705; the Salesianerinnenkirche in Vienna, 1717; the church in Železná Ruda (Eisenstein) in Czechoslovakia, 1727; Clemenskirche in Münster, 1745; and the church in Skreyschov in Czechoslovakia, 1764.

These characteristics of the second phase, however, tend to be overpowered by those of the third phase. In this development as many effects as possible are piled one upon the other. They are used simultaneously in order to create the impression of spatial division in its extreme form. At Neresheim, 1747, the ambulatory produces the effect of a hall; there is no drum; high-reaching lunettes are present; the bounding surfaces are convex; the vault is as complicated as possible; and the gallery balconies are convex. The fragments of ambulatory surrounding the central space fuse with the elliptical transepts. As in Vierzehnheiligen, the seven tangential, domed, elliptical spaces are only hinted at in plan. Neresheim is much simpler than the earlier Vierzehnheiligen only because there is no syncopation. Another combination of characteristics is found in Die Wies, 1746: hall with ambulatory; unexpected vault above the ambulatory; open gallery above an enclosed space off the choir; projection of the gallery into the first bay of the ambulatory; and balconies at the base of a dome without drum.

9. THE PROTESTANT CHURCH

The spatial characteristics of the Catholic churches are reflected in contemporary *Protestant* churches to the extent that the latter have any aesthetic pretentions. As a rule, even in those that are aesthetically insignificant, the line of the gallery parapet is not concentric or parallel with the exterior wall. The kernel of space left open by the galleries cannot be read from the exterior. The galleries become convex rings. In this way, for example, a longitudinal dodecagon is formed by the galleries of the externally rectangular Huguenot church in Erlangen, 1692. Other examples are the ellipse within a rectangle with transepts in the Lutheran church in Leszno (Lissa), 1709, and the nearly circular ellipse within a rectangle (with transverse arms for choir and tower loges) of the Church of the Holy Cross in Poznań (Posen), 1776. Conversely, a rectangle within an elliptical outer wall is found in the church at Pokój (Carlsruhe), 1713.

The few Protestant churches that have artistic pretensions are much more complicated. From the exterior, the Ordenskirche in Bayreuth, 1705, looks like a Greek cross, but only three arms are apparent in the interior. The fourth is occupied by the tower. The interior is thus composed of transepts and a short choir, although the central square is preserved intact (Figs. 53–54). There are double galleries in the choir and in both arms. The galleries in the choir (for the pulpit and for the organ, which is above the altar) do not extend as far as the central square, whereas those in the arms extend precisely to its edge. On the tower side is a bridge bearing a court loge that projects into the central square. The kernel of space surrounded by these galleries is therefore displaced in relation to the central square in plan: it is shifted syncopically into the choir. Above the galleries is a cove with lunettes, and above this a cornice. The latter supports a final great oblong cross vault that encompasses the cross arms. Thus the plan of the

52. Munich, St. John Nepomuk, 1731. Interior.

53. Bayreuth, Ordenskirche, 1705.
Interior.

54. Bayreuth, Ordenskirche, 1705. Interior.

galleries and that of the vault do not coincide either. Their relationship to each other is syncopated.

The Frauenkirche in Dresden, 1725, is another example. We are concerned here only with the five galleries. The parapet of each gallery describes a somewhat different shape, and thus the spatial core of the church has a different plan at each level. The first gallery is approximately U-shaped—a horseshoe with convexly bent ends—and projects beyond the circular form of its eight supporting piers. The second gallery is similar in shape but does not project. The third is similar to the second. The fourth has a semicircular recession on its principal axes, and the fifth bridges over the openings in the fourth. The spatial core, with its form changing at each level, is an indeterminate shape; its various projections can be united only when we comprehend the continuous, arbitrarily divisible fluid of the whole space. The impression of a continuously shifting form is still more marked here than in the church at Bayreuth, for the individual parapets of the galleries are the discontinuous fragments of an implied continuous surface that would define the spatial core. The points of transition between one shape and another are undefined.

As a final example I examine the great Michaelskirche in Hamburg, 1750. The plan (Fig. 55), a Greek cross with four corner spaces, can be described only as an undefined layer of space above which develops an integral gallery. The great, continuous curve of the gallery's parapet describes a spatial core that is diagonally convex (Fig. 56). The four corner piers that stake out the central square of the Greek cross cut through the gallery and, ringed about by space, rise up to the spring of the transept vaults. These barrel vaults are of the same height as the vaults of the four corner spaces, so that there appear to be continuous side aisles, with openings through three arches toward the central space and the two longitudinal arms. These three spaces form a single, unified nave at the height of the vaults because they are covered by one shallow barrel vault with apsidal ends. The church is thus a centralized building in plan and a longitudinal building at the height of the vaults. Between ground level and vault floats a convex spatial core that is not clearly connected to either.

10. FORMS BASED UPON INFINITESIMAL CALCULUS

The following characteristics can all be brought together under one general principle: convex spaces; the fusion of simple spaces to produce three-dimensional curves; syncopation of convex spaces or even (as in the case of the Ordenskirche in Bayreuth) syncopation of simple spaces, giving the impression of a space that curves or bulges vertically. Each of these is primarily an aspect of spatial division, as in the second phase. In the second phase, however, all the spatial parts (even in such extremely complicated formations as S. Ivo in Rome [Figs. 37–38] or S. Lorenzo in Turin [Figs. 40–41]) can

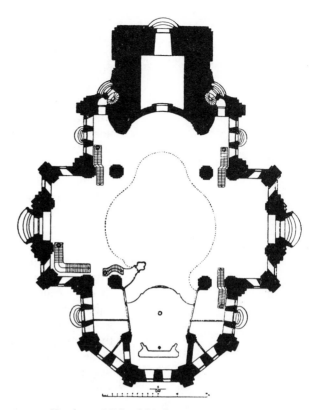

55. Hamburg, Michaelskirche, 1750.
Plan.

56. Hamburg, Michaelskirche,
1750. Interior.

still be established by lower geometry. In the third phase the whole space, or its subdivisions, or at least some of them, are *infinitesimal*. I mean by this that they are forms of higher geometry the calculation of which was possible only by infinitesimal calculus. Even if such calculation is not the observer's task, we can define the essential feature of ecclesiastical architecture in this third phase by saying that it could have been achieved only with the help of higher mathematics.

Fourth Phase (Nineteenth Century)

Forms based upon infinitesimal calculus in the third phase can be found in Spain, Italy, Switzerland, Austria, and Germany, but not in France, Holland, or England. Meissonier's design for the façade of St. Sulpice in Paris would not have affected its interior.

France, Holland, and England did not experience the third phase at first hand. In these countries the fourth phase directly follows the second. The third phase can therefore be considered, at least within the development of spatial form, as only an extreme or special case of the second phase. The third phase created no new polarity; it merely carried the idea of spatial division to its extreme consequences. In the same way the fourth phase created no new polarity but demonstrated a loss of feeling for both polarities.

The use of spatial forms based upon infinitesimal calculus lasted until about 1760. After that time we again find spaces that can be produced by lower geometry alone, but there was no dogmatic return to spatial addition. The fourth phase swayed back and forth uncertainly between the two principles of addition and division, and even permitted both to operate in one and the same space.

Ste. Geneviève (the present Panthéon) in Paris, 1754, is a Greek cross covered in the center by a large dome on a drum (Fig. 57). The arms, each of which has four short cross arms, are covered by smaller domes. An ambulatory, with flat ceiling, permits circulation from one ancillary space to the next, behind the great crossing piers, and encircles the cross arms of the second zone. The galleries are placed above the spring of the vaults so that lunettes are necessary. These cut into the barrel vaults of the short ancillary cross arms.

In the church of the Benedictine abbey at St. Blasien in the Black Forest, 1768, the desire for a stricter conformity to spatial addition is clear. The choir is set off as precisely as possible, but the galleries in it are above closed corridors. A narrow ambulatory surrounds the cylindrical main space, and the galleries are let into the thickness of the wall.

The simple cylinder is also the essential feature of the Elisabethkirche in Nuremberg, 1780. But the indecisive way in which the arms meet the circle; the segmental barrel vaults; the complicated arrangement of the organ gallery with its

57. Paris, Panthéon (Ste. Geneviève), 1754. Interior.

convex curves; and the meeting of the circle with the outer wall on the entrance side—all these are characteristics that cannot be associated with pure addition.

The Roman Pantheon became again, as in Alberti's day, the ideal and the prototype for many replicas.[64] S. Francesco di Paola in Naples, 1817, is the principal one. Others are the Gran Madre di Dio in Turin, 1818, S. Antonio in Trieste, 1827, and S. Carlo Borromeo in Milan, 1847. In the Neapolitan church, the cornices of both orders are developed into encircling balconies. A gallery and a large organ balcony with *baldacchino* are found in the drum. Rhythm is avoided.

Early Christian prototypes were also used in addition to antique ones, however, and so the continuity in the development of spatial forms was broken. It was now possible to return even to Gothic and Romanesque spatial forms and to mix forms of different stylistic periods. The Ludwigskirche in Munich, 1829, would be a Romanesque church, but its side aisles are covered by separate, shallow domes, and its choir is covered by a barrel vault with lunettes.

I need not thoroughly discuss the formation of ecclesiastical space in the fourth phase. It is enough to recognize that this phase is not characterized by marked recognition of *one* polarity, and that its connection with previous phases does not at all lie in the domain of space.

SECULAR ARCHITECTURE

The designations "ecclesiastical" and "secular" architecture refer to the purposes for which these spaces are created. Since I am excluding from this chapter all discussion of purpose, the separation of these two types here would be incorrect if it were not possible at the same time to establish a geometric difference between them. This is the case, although linguistic usage, which originates in purpose alone, does not exactly coincide with this separation. The ecclesiastical spaces I already discussed, whether they *appear* to be composed by the addition of many individual parts or created by the division of a whole or fragmentary space, are always *actually* a unit. They have a simultaneous and cohesive effect. The spaces I shall now discuss are, so to speak, agglomerations of spaces, that is, spaces *actually* perceived one after the other. They are separate from one another. Closed walls divide them; closable doors connect them. This distinction between simultaneous and successive comprehension, which is based upon the degree of openness or closeness of the surfaces defining individual spaces, coincides in the main with the difference between ecclesiastical and secular architecture. I can therefore retain this nomenclature without fear of being misunderstood, even when I discuss those spaces in ecclesiastical or secular architecture that do not conform to this geometrical distinction.

There are sacristies, stair turrets, and vestibules attached to churches that have no effect upon the interior as a whole. As far as their stylistic relationship to the interior as a whole is concerned, they are identical to the individual rooms, staircases, and vestibules in a palace. They can thus be included in the following discussion of secular architecture.

On the other hand, there are rooms in palaces and monasteries that are complicated spatial formations with open boundaries and yet are perceived as units. This is especially true of the third phase. For example, libraries become spatial forms with the same characteristics as ecclesiastical spaces when they contain convex galleries or, as in the Hofbibliothek in Vienna, 1722, when they are formed by the fusion of many spaces. Since their stylistic development parallels that of ecclesiastical architecture, I have not found it necessary to discuss them separately.

There is still the problem of whether the development of the rest of secular architecture parallels that of ecclesiastical architecture. Do addition and division play the same roles here? Even if the individual spaces that form a secular building are *actually* isolated, the question still remains, whether they can *appear* isolated at one time and fused at another. The opposite is certainly true in an ecclesiastical building that is *actually* composed of connected spaces but can *appear* to be formed, at one time, by the addition of isolated individual parts and, at another time, by division. The difference between ecclesiastical and secular architecture is therefore based upon actual adding and dividing, whereas the difference between stylistic phases is based upon apparent adding and dividing.

Since the geometric separation of all the rooms by closed walls and ceilings is fixed forever, stylistic differences cannot become manifest on these solid boundaries. Such differences cannot be based upon the clarity or vagueness of walls, upon the contrast between a radial and a peripheral arrangement of rooms, or upon the contrast between a star-shaped group of discrete halting points and a continuous unity of many rooms (which is a contradiction in itself). Yet a secular building of the first phase is essentially different from one of the second.

To understand a secular building we must get to know it as a whole by walking through it from end to end, from cellar to roof, through all its outstretching wings. The entrance, the vestibule or passage leading to courtyard or stair, the connections between several courtyards, the stairs themselves and the corridors leading away from them at each level, like the veins of our bodies—these are the pulsating arteries of a building. They are the passages that form the fixed circulation leading to individual rooms, to individual chambers, cells, or loges.

The organism of the house reaches as far as these arteries guide the circulation. Circulation between rooms through connecting doors plays a part, but this part is secondary when there is a corridor system. The stylistic maxims of spatial addition and division concern this network of circulation within a secular building. I can quickly demonstrate this, since my reader already knows these principles. Rather than lead him slowly toward an understanding, I think it is sufficient to give a few pronounced examples from each phase.

1. STAIRCASES

First Phase. The spiral staircase is a Gothic heirloom. If it has a closed newel, it confines our view as we ascend or descend to that which is immediately in front of us. Its minimum use of landings and its vertical continuation into infinity are no longer suitable in post-medieval architecture. If it has an open newel, it offers us a view through all the floors it joins, but the vertical pull is so strong that its space is unrelated to the floors. Even when landings are present at each floor for practical reasons, they are absent artistically. The spiral staircase rushes upward vehemently, and its open well has the effect of a flue. Yet its *isolation,* characteristic of the stair well as a whole, makes its appearance possible in the first phase. Bramante's spiral staircase in the Vatican, and the one in the Palazzo Farnese at Caprarola, are examples.

The spiral staircase is not typical of this phase, however. Existing as early as in the Foundling Hospital in Florence, 1419, the typical staircase is a dog-leg. It is composed of two straight parallel flights separated by a common, *solid* wall. Each flight is covered by an inclined barrel vault (without lunettes). We see a staircase of this type in relation to only *one* floor at a time and have no idea of the number of floors to come. Each floor is an individual halting point, and the flights of steps themselves ascend leisurely as separate entities. But our view is not confined immediately to the front as it is in the spiral staircase with closed newel. Our impression is not of incomplete, momentary, fluctuating segments of space. Each flight is a whole space and is clearly joined to its respective floor or corridor. There are easily accessible examples in the Palazzo Farnese (Fig. 58), 1534, and in the Palazzo Sacchetti, 1540, both in Rome.

The relationship between the staircase and the whole building is not essentially altered if the first flight begins within the arcade of the courtyard, as it does in the Palazzo Gondi in Florence. Here the first flight joins upper flights that again have the effect of individual spaces in the usual way.[65]

If secular buildings of the first stylistic phase contain staircases without a central dividing wall (that is, with cantilevered steps), or with a pierced dividing wall, or with three or four flights ascending round a rectangular open core of space, we can be certain that alterations have taken place in a later period. The only exception to this rule is the staircase in the courtyard arcade in Schloss Porcia at Spittal in Austria, 1527, and this was installed over a length of time. Here the effect of clearly isolated floors was abandoned. There may be other examples that have eluded me, but they will certainly be small in number.

Second Phase. The staircase connecting the vestibule with the higher reading room of the Laurentian Library in Florence (Fig. 59) occupies a special position. Although it was first planned and begun in 1525, its definitive design and execution date from 1558. In place of the present staircase, we must imagine one that exemplifies the taste of the first phase—simple, straight, and narrow, with walls on each side, and covered by an inclined barrel vault—like the one that leads to the vestibule on the upper floor of the cloister. We can then understand fully that what confronts us here is a *spatial* revolution. The present staircase is freestanding in the center of the vestibule. Michelangelo originally intended the ceiling of this room to be the same height as that of the adjacent reading room, but he was forced to raise it to its present height, which is greater than that of the reading room, to improve the illumination. Michelangelo wished to break with the principles hitherto in use. According to these, there should have been a difference in the ceiling height of the two rooms about equal to the difference in their floor level, the vestibule ceiling being lower than that of the reading room. These two characteristics—the equal height (in the original design) of stair well and space to be reached, and the position of the staircase as a divider of space—make the Laurentian Library the earliest secular building of the second phase. Although the staircase as executed in 1558 differs from the one first designed, these two characteristics were already established in principle early in the design process. The staircase could have been influential only after 1558, however, so that if secular architecture temporarily led ecclesiastical architecture in the use of division, this remained an isolated case. In fact, the isolated, additive staircase persisted even after 1550. There are examples in the Uffizi in Florence, 1560, and in the Palazzo Lateranense in Rome, 1586.

The exterior stairway, almost unknown in the first phase,[66] seems to have been the indirect source of the new form of stairs. The first and crucial design here was the double-ramped stairway in front of the Palazzo del Senatore on the Capitoline Hill in Rome, 1546. A stairway of this type (Fig. 65) visually connects all the floors into a unit; the ground and main floors appear as a unit in any case. To what extent this visible stairway appears to serve all the upper floors; to what extent the space in front of the palace belongs to it; to what extent inner and outer space are joined—all this would quickly become clear if we imagined a stairway in front of, say, the Cancelleria in Rome (Fig. 69). Not only would its ground and upper floors

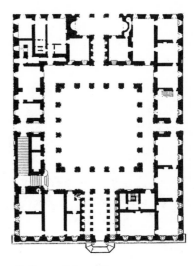

58. Rome, Palazzo Farnese, 1534. Plan.

59. Florence, S. Lorenzo,
Laurentian Library, 1524.
Longitudinal Section and Plan.

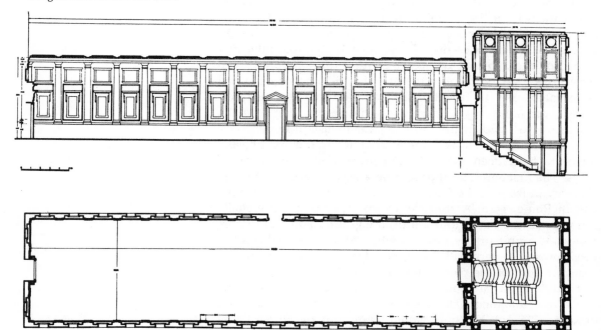

suddenly become fused together, but the palace as a whole would appear to be less self-contained.

One of the earliest examples of a stairway that follows the Capitoline design is that which descends from the ground floor *salotto* to the uppermost garden terrace at the Villa d'Este at Tivoli, 1566. The stairway, which is on the principal axis of the garden itself, is composed of two symmetrical semicircular flights. They represent a further development in keeping with the principles of the second phase. The stairway descending from the courtyard to the Nymphaeum of the Villa Giulia in Rome is similar.[67]

The staircase in the Laurentian Library, completed in 1558, prepared the way for the idea of fusing together the various parts of a building. The Palazzo Doria Tursi in Genoa, 1564, is composed in this way. The first flight of steps ascending from the vestibule to the courtyard is freestanding. At the rear of the courtyard, a double-flight staircase behind the arcade is visible because it is not enclosed. These staircases, placed at the beginning and end of the central axis (which itself seems to rise), fuse the palace into a continuous spatial whole. In *one* glance we sense the continuous flow of circulation that unifies the building both horizontally and vertically. Besides the copy of this at the Jesuit College (Università), 1630, there are a great number of similar staircases in Genoa.

The half-turn staircase, ascending in three flights round a rectangular or square spatial core, first appears in the seventeenth century. A good example is the one in the Palazzo Barberini in Rome, of approximately 1630. (In the same palace there are also an elliptical staircase and a symmetrical two-armed staircase, partly elliptical, partly straight, which is placed in a large vestibule. The latter staircase leads up to the garden, which is at a higher level.) A preliminary stage in this development is the dog-legged staircase with cantilevered steps. There is one in the Exchange in Seville, 1583. A forerunner of the staircase in the Palazzo Barberini is, perhaps, the one in the Clerecía in Salamanca, 1617. A similar staircase was designed for Whitehall in London in 1619. The staircase in the Louvre demonstrates how far behind France was in this development, although Bernini's design showed the Parisians what could be done in 1665. He placed a three-quarter turn, geometrical staircase in each corner of the courtyard. The open staircase designed for the Louvre by Cottard in 1670 remained unexecuted.[68]

The staircase in the Palazzo Altieri in Rome, 1674, is a reflection of Bernini's designs for the Louvre. Although Bernini's plan was rejected, the new type of staircase did find its way into the *hôtels* of Paris. There are examples in the Hôtel Lambert and the Hôtel Chevreuse, in the second half of the century. The staircase formed by doubling the type discussed in the previous paragraph is even more effective in producing the impression of spatial division. There are examples in the Palazzo Reale in Naples, 1651,[69] and in the cloister of S. Giorgio Maggiore in Venice, 1664 (now the Cini Foundation). In these examples symmetrical half-turn staircases ascend in the same space and meet at a common landing.

Finally, the Scala Regia in the Vatican, 1663, is not an additive composition despite its side walls and inclined barrel vaults. Its great length, the different angles of inclination of its steps and vaults, and above all the separation of its flights into three aisles are all consequences of spatial division. The steps extend the full width of the opening, and the columns seem to have been inserted into a composition that was already complete. There is another triple-aisled staircase ascending from the vestibule to the courtyard in the Palazzo Balbi Durazzo in Genoa, which was rebuilt at the end of the eighteenth century.

Third Phase. Symmetrical two-armed staircases such as those in the Palazzo Madama in Turin, 1710, or in the somewhat later Convent of St. Florian in Austria, are common in the eighteenth century. There is a faint suggestion of forms created by infinitesimal calculus on the upper landing of the Turin staircase, but these play a small role in the over-all effect of the stair well.[70] It is essential to recognize that only now was the way free for the invention of every conceivable arrangement of flights, for the common use of the stair well as an element that draws an entire building together. These open wells, which occupy the entire height of a building, make all floors visible at one glance. In Schloss Weissenstein at Pommersfelden, 1715,[71] symmetrical half-turn staircases ascend to a central landing connected to an elliptical space that forms the focus of the corridor system (Fig. 60). The corridors surround the whole stair well like galleries, and a second, higher gallery makes the next floor visible.[72]

In the Residenz at Würzburg, 1719, a central flight leads to a transverse landing and forks into two symmetrical flights that ascend in opposite directions to the next floor (Fig. 91). A peripheral corridor encircles the entire stair well.[73]

The so-called Riesentreppe in Schloss Ludwigsburg begins with a single, freestanding flight ascending from the vestibule to a landing. There it forks, midway in its ascent, into two symmetrical flights that are at right angles to the landing. One of the most complicated designs is to be found in the Palazzo Ugolani Dati (now Museo Civico) in Cremona, 1769. The staircase discharges into an upper peripheral passage with six flights pointing in different directions. Many designs for staircases that would clearly have expressed the period's spatial sensibilities were never executed or were considerably altered, as, for example, Allio's design for Klosterneuburg, 1730.

60. Pommersfelden, Schloss
Weissenstein, 1715. Interior.

The staircase in Schloss Bruchsal, 1731, is a perfect example of spatial division (Fig. 61). The elliptical landing cuts horizontally through the spatial core, which is formed by two semielliptical flights. As we ascend, we see *fragments* of a space that we are compelled to project into a *whole.* The curving of the flights here is not particularly new. This was present *in nuce* in the elliptical spiral staircase of the Palazzo Barberini in Rome and occurs in much more complicated form in the Palazzo Carignano in Turin, 1680. In the latter design the two flights, which ascend symmetrically from the vestibule, have a freehand curve and end in a hexagonal space. These staircases can be considered old-fashioned only because the flights are isolated, covered by barrel vaults, and enclosed by side walls.

The first curved staircase is found as early as the second phase, however: the stairway in the Cour du Cheval Blanc at Fontainebleau, 1634.[74] The exterior stairway follows the development just described. Examples are found at the Villa Valguarnera near Bagheria in Sicily, 1714; the pavilion in the Favorite-Park in Ludwigsburg, 1718; Monte di Pietà in Messina, 1741; Schloss Solitüde near Stuttgart, 1763; Communs near Potsdam, 1765. In addition to these there are the stairways in the great gardens of this period, especially those in Frascati and Wilhelmshöhe.

Fourth Phase. The fourth phase no longer aspired to greater complication, but even when it otherwise seemed to favor the isolation of parts, it retained large stair wells that cut through all the floors. But this phase had no sense of aesthetic value here either, as demonstrated by the main staircase in the Markgräfliches Palais in Karlsruhe, 1809. A staircase of the type in the Hof- und Staatsbibliothek in Munich, 1832, may have an effect upon the whole building, but since it is unrelated to the remaining space, it proves to be a form taken over ready-made and without understanding.

2. CORRIDORS

First Phase. The *ambulatory* within the coherent interior of an ecclesiastical building destroys the effect of pure spatial addition. The same ambulatory in a secular building, or a peristyle on the exterior of an ecclesiastical building, has an isolating effect of the highest order. Just as an antique temple seems completely detached from its environment because of its peristyle, so the circular colonnade of the Tempietto at S. Pietro in Montorio in Rome creates its own world (Figs. 62–63). We know from the design preserved by Serlio that Bramante intended to encircle this colonnade, which belongs to the Tempietto itself, by a narrow, concentric court bound by another circular colonnade. The surroundings were to face the spatial formation, which is completely self-possessed. In the deferential response of the environment we see the recognition

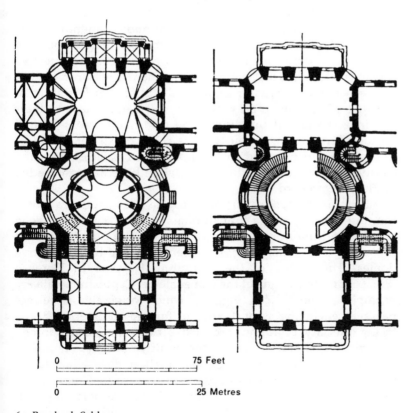

0   75 Feet

0   25 Metres

61. Bruchsal, Schloss.
Staircase Hall, 1731. Plans.

of an absolute independence. The same idea had been briefly in Bramante's mind during the design of St. Peter's in the Vatican. The centralized church was supposed to be encircled by a narrow, concentric court bound by buildings and colonnades, which would have given resonance to every projection or recession of its enclosing wall. The execution of this design was impossible because the buildings of the Vatican palace stood in the way. The single peristyle recurs once more at the Madonna di Campagna near Verona.

The most important secular buildings with peristyles are the Letohrádek ("Belvedere") in Prague, 1535, the Basilica in Vicenza, 1549, and the Banqueting House in Stuttgart, 1581, a later straggler.

The exterior peristyle has its interior counterpart in the colonnaded or arcaded passage that encircles a courtyard (Figs. 58, 64, 90). Such a passage convincingly creates the impression that all the rooms it connects are, floor for floor, a unit that is completely isolated from the adjacent palaces, which are self-contained units in their own right. The closed courtyard and the isolated blocklike form of the palace between four streets reflect the ideal of the first phase. When we enter such a courtyard, we sense the deep repose and seclusion of the entire palace and so recognize the marked contrast between this self-contained prism and the continuous, unending network of the city streets. The more the colonnaded passage appears as a unit—*one* continuous space—the more effective it is in creating this sense of isolation. There is no contradiction between the use of fusing cross vaults in secular buildings of the first phase and the aversion in this same phase to their use in ecclesiastical buildings. The continuous cross-vaulted passage surrounding a courtyard is characteristic of the additive phase and is found in the majority of palaces, from the courtyards of the Foundling Hospital and the Palazzo Medici in Florence onward.

Exterior arcades, or *porticoes,* that do not surround a building but create only a transitional layer of space between exterior and interior at the entrance were from the beginning broken up into separate compartments covered by pendentive domes. The arcade of the Foundling Hospital in Florence (Fig. 66) and the arcade of the Ospedale del Ceppo in Pistoia are examples. The Vatican loggias, which originally were not passages encircling a courtyard but formed an exterior façade facing the city of Rome, are also series of separate domed squares. In general, however, the additive principle is not so rigidly observed in porticoes, although it does characterize the portico of the Pazzi Chapel at Sta. Croce in Florence and the narthex of S. Andrea in Mantua. There are porticoes with cross vaults, with barrel vaults, and even with flat ceilings. Examples of porticoes with flat ceilings are found at S. Maria delle Grazie near Arezzo, 1449, and at the Loggia del Consiglio

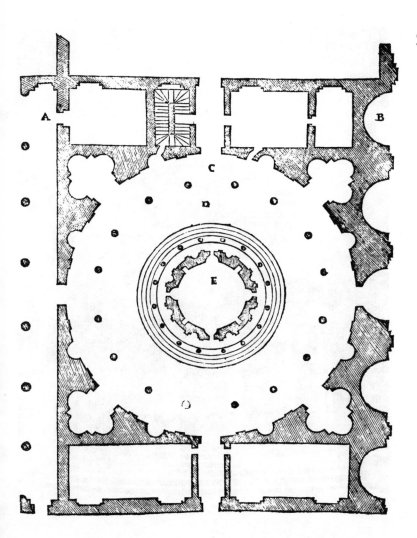

62. Rome, S. Pietro in Montorio,
Tempietto, 1502. Plan.

63. Rome, S. Pietro in Montorio, Tempietto, 1502. Exterior.

64. Rome, Cancelleria, 1486. Courtyard.

in Verona. On the other hand, isolated domes sometimes appear in porticoes. In the Palazzo Farnese in Piacenza, 1558, such a dome occurs in rhythmical alternation with transverse barrel vaults.

Pavilions and wings extending out from the main block of a building are rare in the first phase and modest when they do occur. It is even more important that these projections find no echo in the environment. The *Nicchione* of the Belvedere in the Vatican answers the segmentally curved façade of the old part of the Vatican palace, but since these two responsive motifs are connected by corridors (and indeed, corridors that do not serve individual apartments), the courtyard is enclosed. Despite changes in level it is an isolated unit. If the corridors were interrupted, if wings projected from each end of the courtyard without touching, then we would have a building type characteristic of the second phase. There are pavilions extending out from the main block of the Villa Farnesina in Rome, 1509, but there is no echo in the surroundings. All corresponding niches and grottoes at the Villa Madama in Rome are clearly linked together.

The semicircular court of the Villa Giulia in Rome, 1550, was perhaps suggested by the Villa Madama, but the semicircle of the Villa Giulia is not open to infinity, because the rectangular garden adjoining it is enclosed by high, articulated walls. Once again the old concept of a closed unit is preserved, although on the central axis the view over the deep grotto is lost in the garden.

Second Phase. The design of the Capitoline Hill in Rome, 1538, marks the first definite break with the principle of addition (Fig. 65). I must make it clear once and for all that continuity in secular architecture is something totally different from continuity in ecclesiastical architecture. The three palaces that form this piazza are set down individually and are totally isolated. But this isolation is not the same as that of addition, because the palaces form a unit around the piazza. Everything is of one piece *with* the piazza and with the stairway ascending from Piazza Aracoeli. It is all one unit that, so to speak, subsequently fell apart.

At the Palazzo Andrea Doria in Genoa, 1527, there are short colonnades perpendicular to the long main building that stands facing the sea. I do not know when these colonnades were added, but with the terraces and the groups of fountains they make a fragment out of the blocklike main building, which appears complete in itself. This fragment is made whole only by uniting with the sea; it is therefore infinite.

In the same way, the Villa d'Este at Tivoli, 1550, is an integral part of its garden. The main building of the Villa Lante at Bagnaia near Viterbo, 1566, is torn into two separate casinos; the central axis of its garden is unobstructed. The

65. Rome, Capitoline Hill, 1538.

garden of the Farnese on the Palatine in Rome offered a similar impression.

Even when there is no sea, park, or square, however, divisions of this type in a building are now possible. The Uffizi in Florence, first designed with a completely enclosed courtyard, was executed after 1560 as a pair of buildings. The courtyard became a cul-de-sac. The open arcade in the courtyard of the Palazzo Borghese in Rome, 1590, also suggests dissolution. The intention of the second phase was to replace the closed block by dispersed pavilions that form a unit by their symmetrical placing round a common center. This is clearly demonstrated by Palladio's villa designs, and we cannot be misled by the fact that these were executed only rarely, because of the cost, or by the fact that enclosed courtyards were still built, as at the Palazzo Lateranense in Rome, 1586; the Palazzo Quirinale in Rome, 1605; Schloss Aschaffenburg, 1605; and the Louvre in Paris. The stairs in *these* buildings are just as retrogressive as their courtyards and corridor systems. The persistence of such old-fashioned features only proves that some architects did not wish to follow the new taste. They stand out as conservatives in contrast to the multitude of progressive architects who made an open square out of a courtyard, replaced the enclosed corridor system by wings pointing into the distance, or thought of a building as a fragment. (These progressive architects thought that a fragment could become a whole only by uniting with another building or groups of individual buildings, or that a priori, as a mere locus of infinite, universal space, it would have to retain once and for all the character of a fortuitous fragment—the polar opposite of the Tempietto, with its projected circular courtyard.) St. Peter's, once to have been a centralized church surrounded by a wall of other buildings, now became a longitudinal church; it became a part of infinity by means of its colonnades, which are open on the central axis and are longingly awaiting the response of Castle Sant'Angelo. St. Peter's is still incomplete.

In France too, the open court or *cour d'honneur* replaces the blocklike château with enclosed courtyard. The Collège de France in Paris, 1611, and the Grand Trianon at Versailles, 1687, are examples of this process of opening the block. The development of French garden structures is a continuation of Palladio's villa designs. Circulation within the main building is never closed within itself. The corridor system is only the beginning of the radiating paths that continue through the garden and push toward the far distant focal point—if indeed that is not infinity itself.

Third Phase. The third phase carried to extreme the fusion of interior and exterior spaces by means of freestanding stairs, projecting wings, or other transitional features between the building and the garden or landscape, and by the dissolution of the block into a colony of pavilions distributed within a park. Examples are the Belvedere in Vienna, 1721; Castle Howard, 1699, and Blenheim, 1705, both in England; Schloss Bruchsal, 1720 (Fig. 92); the Hermitage near Bayreuth, 1715 (the Temple of the Sun); and the abbey at Weingarten, 1715. Spatial forms based upon infinitesimal calculus do not play a crucial role here either, although they do appear.[75] The aim of the third phase was to suggest rather than to make a clear statement, to produce fragments that need to be completed in our imagination.

Fourth Phase. The corridor system of the fourth phase permits neither of the two opposing principles of style (addition and division) to dominate. Schloss Ludwigslust at Schwerin in Mecklenburg, planned in 1763, still belongs as a whole to the third phase, but the main building, erected in 1772, appears as a rather isolated block despite its formal relationship with the church, 1765, across the square. The Madeleine in Paris, 1808, stands isolated behind its peristyle, but it is still connected to the civic composition of the Rue Royale, Place de la Concorde, Pont de la Concorde, and Chambre des Députés. But in addition to these examples of city planning in which individual buildings are caught up in a continuous stream, there are at least as many other monumental buildings standing like blocks between four streets. Growing stylistic uncertainty led to the detachment of buildings from their surrounding structures (especially churches) even when they did not profit at all by being detached. A building like Bramante's Tempietto (Figs. 62–63) is isolated, and even a pavilion of Schloss Bruchsal (Fig. 92), can be considered isolated, but there is a difference. The Tempietto is a unit; the pavilion, a fragment. The nineteenth century made fragments out of units, and, conversely, it sited buildings so that they have the effect of fragments. The Walhalla near Regensburg stands behind its peristyle in the landscape similar to the way in which medieval castles or eighteenth-century pilgrimage churches are sited, but its gigantic underpinning of terraces can neither fuse it with nor isolate it from the landscape.

Spatial addition and spatial division are the polar contrasts by which I distinguish the phases. In the first phase spatial forms are composed additively, no matter whether the problem is a centralized or longitudinal church or a secular building. In the second phase spatial forms are composed by division, no matter whether it concerns a Catholic or Protestant, centralized or longitudinal church, or a secular building. The separation of the third from the second phase is not marked by a change in the direction of style. Rather, the third phase stretches the given direction to its utmost conclusion. In ecclesiastical architecture this extreme position is expressed principally by the creation of forms based upon infinitesimal calculus. In secular architecture it is expressed principally by fragmentation, by breaking the building into individual pavilions, and by opening these fragments to the infinite exterior space. The fourth phase is characterized by its independence of both polarities.

2 Corporeal Form

First Phase (1420–1550)

1. THE ORDERS

The reintroduction of the ancient orders is the crucial factor in the elevations of the buildings designed by Brunelleschi and his followers.

Almost every building of the first decades demonstrated the reconquest of another variation in the use of the orders. The portico of the Foundling Hospital in Florence, 1419, is a columnar arcade framed by a superimposed entablature that rests upon the pilasters at the ends of the arcade (Fig. 66). The pilaster order is found in the Old Sacristy (Fig. 12), 1419, of S. Lorenzo in Florence (as well as in the side aisles of the church itself [Fig. 14] and on the facade and in the hall of the Palazzo di Parte Guelfa in Florence, 1420). Columns surmounted by their own isolated entablatures (corresponding to the pilaster order of the side aisles) occur in S. Lorenzo (Fig. 14). The column with straight entablature was used in the portico of the Pazzi Chapel at Sta. Croce in Florence. Arches on piers mark the side façades of S. Francesco in Rimini, 1446. The main façade here (Fig. 67) has arches on piers with engaged half columns. Pilaster orders (without pedestals) are piled one above the other on the façade of the Palazzo Rucellai in Florence, 1446 (Fig. 68).

We can make our survey of all these variations and combinations just as easy to understand as the survey of spatial forms in the first phase. An order consists of supporting and supported members. The supports can take the form of piers, columns, pilasters (with or without pedestals), or consoles[1] (and later even caryatids and herms). The form of the supported member is either the straight entablature or the arch. (The arch at first is always semicircular, except for the very rare, rudimentary use of the pointed arch; later, segmental and basket-handle arches appear.) Variation is achieved by changing the load, the support, or both. The façade of the Foundling Hospital, the first composition of post-medieval architecture, combines arches on columns with a pilaster order (Fig. 66). Compare the frame of Masaccio's "Trinity," 1427, in Sta. Maria Novella in Florence, and the tabernacle of St. Thomas, 1425, on Or S. Michele in Florence. The façade of S. Francesco in Rimini (Fig. 67) is a combination of arches on piers and a half-columnar order the entablature of which touches the archivolt of the central arch. Such combinations can be placed next to one another as well as above one another, so that the design of an elevation is no longer an exercise in imagination but a systematic, intellectual act. The basic elements of this process of combination, the "orders," therefore become the architect's most precious possession, his essential ABC.

66. Florence, Foundling Hospital,
1419. Portico.

67. Rimini, S. Francesco, 1446.
Exterior.

68. Florence, Palazzo Rucellai, 1446. Façade.

2. RHYTHMICAL SPACING OF THE COLUMNAR SERIES

Partly as a result of spatial rhythm, and partly independently of it, rhythm now appears in the spacing of supports. The wall on the choir side of the Old Sacristy (Fig. 12) of S. Lorenzo is the earliest example. The group *b a b*, there formed by concentric arches on pilasters, can be modified in many ways. What we call the triumphal arch motif and the Palladian motif are special cases of this. They can be derived from the individual variations and combinations pointed out in the previous paragraph. The rhythm *b a b a b,* and so on, is produced here, as in the development of spatial forms, by the sequence of groups. This rhythm is present on the façades of the Palazzo della Cancelleria, 1486, and the Palazzo Giraud, 1496, both in Rome. The rhythm on the Cancelleria (Fig. 69) is closed by projecting groups at the corners of the façade, whereas the front of the Giraud had an open, continuous, rhythmical series. But the Giraud had an odd number of bays, which meant that its main portal came in the center of the façade, while the front of the Cancelleria still has the even number of bays characteristic of the fifteenth century. In a sixteenth-century building, such as the Palazzo Bevilacqua in Verona, 1529, the presence of an eccentric portal makes it certain that the building was left unfinished (Fig. 74).

The desire for grouping also produced a stronger accentuation of the central bay in façades of five or seven bays. Examples are the designs for the façade of S. Lorenzo in Florence by Giuliano da San Gallo and Michelangelo in which the rhythm *B a b á b a B* occurs. It also produced an accentuation of the corners, and this resulted in a grouped center, as on the Palazzo Grimani in Venice, where the rhythm is *á/b a b/á* (Fig. 70).

The alignment of groups in the form *b a b/b a b/b a b* appears in S. Maurizio in Milan, 1503, in the Cortile del Belvedere in the Vatican, and then in impure form in the Palazzo del Te in Mantua, 1525. The principal example is the Basilica in Vicenza, 1549. Here again I leave unanswered the question as to whether in these sequences of groups the feeling prevails for the self-contained group or for the unlimited series of coordinated units.

The antique temple front was also used as a whole, as a central group, to give a central emphasis to an entire façade. This first occurs in the Villa Medici at Poggio a Caiano (Fig. 71) near Florence, 1480, and then in the upper story of the Palazzo Contarini in Venice, 1504 (as a transformation of the traditional Venetian loggia). It is true that in both cases the colonnade remains in the plane of the façade, rather than standing *in front of* the façade as its nature requires, but such examples demonstrate that the series of freestanding columns brought together into a unit by a common gable exactly corresponded to the artistic aims of this time. The unit, formed of discrete members, of freestanding round columns, which carry an

69. Rome, Cancelleria, 1486. Façade.

70. Venice, Palazzo Grimani,
1540. Façade.

entablature and above that a common gable, is the epitome of what we call an order.

The expression "order" must be taken quite literally. An order of supports is based upon a series of individual, separate (that is, discrete) points that become the determining factors of the whole composition. Certainly, the entablature forms a continuous band, and the arcade forms a continuous sequence, but the entablature and the arcade are not sustained by a continuous wall. They are sustained by individual, isolated supports. The order is a natural consequence of the selection of a regular or fixed spacing. We usually read each column from bottom to top, as it rises upward from the ground. But we can experience a columnar order in essence only when we have observed its formation from above downward, in contrast to the rising force of its shafts; that is, when we sense how the columns are placed as individual posts beneath the individual, discrete points of the entablature, whether they are placed at equal or rhythmically alternating intervals, or beneath the individual bases of the arches. In the Doric order this system is extended even into the entablature and gable: the entablature is divided into separate supporting elements, such as triglyphs, which are echoed in the gable. All its members, even the guttae, are therefore brought into dependence upon the regularity of the primary nodes (that is, of the axial spacing of the columns), so that we see the whole as an organism composed of easily disconnected members. The Doric became the favorite order after Bramante's Tempietto (Fig. 63).

3. THE ARTICULATED WALL

The column is the antithesis of the wall. The epoch that admired the orders, but still did not build outright open colonnades, could not entirely do without the wall, however, so that it was forced to debase the wall as such and to transform it visually into an order of supports. The wall became *articulated*.

The elements necessary for this desired articulation of the wall were found among the ruins of antiquity: the pilaster order, the engaged half column, the full column with its projecting entablature. But first of all, the Gothic tradition of regarding the wall as a continuous surface, which could be continued at will, had to be overcome. As a rule in medieval secular buildings the windows in each story are distributed according to its own needs. Vertical axes are not continuous. Nor did it seem necessary or desirable to Gothic architects to construct windows of the same height, width, or shape under all circumstances. Even in churches, where a regularity of spatial form forced a continuity of window axes and heights, this principle was avoided wherever possible. The limitless surface suggested by such irregular sizing and spacing was also enhanced by the lack of a clearly defined upper termination: the upper wall dissolved itself into spikes, turrets, and pinnacles.

Although traditional facade rustication was retained in the fifteenth century, it was controlled by two means: the axes of all openings were aligned,[2] and the façade was closed above by an emphatic horizontal cornice. The irregular distribution of vertical masonry joints is retained on the façades of the Medici, Pitti, and Strozzi Palaces in Florence but later gave way to a regular distribution. After the Palazzo Bevilacqua in Bologna and the Cancelleria in Rome (Fig. 69), it became usual to place the vertical joints in every second masonry course above one another. This led to the use of a consistent masonry length that was dependent upon the size and distribution of the windows. Certainly the wall was still a continuum but one that was built up of regular, discrete parts. The wall thus developed from its purest form into the symmetrically fenestrated wall and was now ready to become articulated. On the Palazzo Rucellai in Florence (Fig. 68), the moldings of the window sills are replaced by entablatures, which are carried on pilasters. Each pilaster is centered between two windows. The uppermost order carries the cornice. On the Cancelleria in Rome (Fig. 69) the moldings of the window sills are continuous, and the entablatures are placed below them, in the space between floors. This arrangement produces a common zone for the pedestals of the pilasters and the raised panels beneath the windows. The absolute isolation of the stories, which we have discussed in relation to stairways, characterizes the facade to the same degree. The over-all articulation, which begins with the separation of stories, is continued in the pilaster order and permeates the smallest details. A socle has its base and its terminating crown molding. Every profile is composed of members that form a beginning, a middle, and an end. The whole has become an airy skeleton instead of a mass of horizontal interconnected stone courses and arbitrarily placed window openings. Where rustication is used, its joints are dependent upon the windows and pilasters. On one of the façades of the Cancelleria, and on the Palazzo Giraud in Rome, the vertical joints are completely eliminated from the ground story, which becomes a unit, acting as a socle for the entire façade. Thus the accentuation of wall-like continuity, where it still occurs, also serves to isolate the stories.

If we examine façades that are built not of cut stone but of brick, incrusted with marble, or decorated with *sgraffiti,* we find the same result, although it is much more difficult to overcome flatness in these materials. But the orders break up the flat surface into individual areas that do not seem to be placed haphazardly within the surface. These areas are fixed; they are isolated panels filling in the framework. The pattern of incrustation and the painted *sgraffiti* conform to this given axial pattern. They do not arbitrarily spread out beyond their enclosed area but are confined by the moldings that produce the framework of the façade.

4. COMBINATION OF COLUMNAR SERIES AND ARTICULATED WALL

There is an analogy between the true, most consistent longitudinal church and the true wall, and there is a similar analogy between the genuine centralized church and the order, whether the latter is a columnar portico or an articulated wall. And just as within the development of spatial forms the longitudinal church was deprived of its essential character by the combination of the spatial series created by addition and the spatial group, so from the very beginning of the epoch, the possibility existed of combining the columnar series with the articulated wall. If all possible combinations and variations were developed for both, our problem henceforth would be one of organization: how to comprehend in a brief survey, with one stroke, the multitude of possibilities that lay within the scope of the first phase. In the nineteenth century, instruction in architectural forms was devoted to perfecting the architect's knowledge of this range of forms, and it proceeded in this systematic way. But the present-day architect has no great interest in such a complete survey, and the art historian is more interested in which of the possible combinations actually materialized. I shall confine myself to some striking examples.

The courtyard as well as the exterior of the Foundling Hospital in Florence has an open arcade on columns below an unarticulated wall (Fig. 66). The windows of the upper story continue the axes of the lower arches. The nave walls of S. Lorenzo in Florence (Fig. 14) have basically the same composition.[3] The effect of an open colonnade below an articulated wall is produced on the portico of the Pazzi Chapel in Florence by the use of paired pilasters on the upper, coffinlike story. An arcade on columns, a window wall, and a colonnade with straight entablature are superimposed in the courtyard of the Palazzo Medici in Florence, 1444. The courtyard of the Palazzo Ducale in Urbino, 1475, has an arcade on columns below a window wall articulated with pilasters. (There is a replica at Gubbio.) The wall opened by a colonnade is found on the exterior of this *palazzo*. A colonnade in the form of an antique portico occurs on the main floor of the Villa Medici at Poggio a Caiano (Fig. 71) and of the Palazzo Contarini in Venice (as mentioned earlier). Superimposed arcades extending from one corner pavilion to another were planned for the Ospedale Maggiore in Milan, 1455, and executed at the Villa Poggio Reale near Naples, 1487. (A series of arches on piers with engaged half columns was to have been placed in a similar way between rusticated pavilions on the Palazzo della Giustizia in Rome, 1512. It was never completed.) The Palazzo Massimi, expressly designated "alle Colonne," in Rome, 1532, has a true colonnade (with straight entablature and even a rather complicated rhythm) in the center of the ground floor. The remaining floors of this palace are enclosed by a flat, unarticulated wall, in contrast to its courtyard where articulated walls are combined in various ways with the colonnade. The Library of St. Mark's in Venice, 1537, has almost the effect of a double arcade (Fig. 72). Its ground floor is composed of a series of arches on piers with engaged Doric half columns. Its upper story is articulated, and the windows are handled in such a way that the impression of a series of arches is produced once more. On the villa at Sta. Colomba near Siena, 1540, there are superimposed loggias set into the articulated wall in such a way that the articulation carries through unbroken at each level (Fig. 73). Finally, the true double arcade occurs on the Basilica in Vicenza, 1549.

5. FRAMES

Frames, whether intended for paintings, statuary niches, doorways, or windows, conform to the requirements of this phase, because they too are composed of supporting and supported members, and create stable rectangular or circular boundaries.

Traces of the Gothic are very much in evidence in the windows and doors of the fifteenth century. The omission of wall to create voids and the use of arches with voussoirs, which occasionally interlock with the rest of the rustication, conflicted with the new spirit—as did the use of splayed jambs, which still occurred occasionally, and the inset central colonnette with its tracery arches. The Gothic feeling was only partially eliminated when the circles no longer overlapped (as they did in the Gothic), or when, as in the windows of the Palazzo Rucellai in Florence, an architrave divided the window from these arches (Fig. 68). The new spirit demanded that the center of the window be left open and therefore that either a simple rectangular opening topped with a straight lintel or semicircular arch be used, or the triple division in the rhythm *b a b*. The former occurs first as early as the Foundling Hospital (Fig. 66), and then in the choir of Sta. Maria del Popolo in Rome, in S. Eligio degli Orefici in Rome, and in the great hall of the Palazzo Vecchio in Florence. A stone cross set into a window, as in the Palazzo Venezia in Rome, for example, also seems rudimentary, and this effect is only partially altered if the center post is enriched by a half colonnette, or if the architrave is given the profile of, say, an entablature (as on Palazzo Bartolini in Florence, 1517).

The common type of surround was the aedicula, as it was preserved from antiquity in the Pantheon in Rome, for example, and the simple, compact frame with flat profile projecting from the wall. There are examples of the latter on the Palazzo Gondi, 1490, and Palazzo Pazzi, 1475, in Florence. The aedicula is found at the doors flanking the choir of the Old Sacristy (Fig. 12) of S. Lorenzo in Florence, round the niches of the

72. Venice, Zecca, 1536 (left), and
Library of St. Mark's, 1537 (right).

Palazzo della Fraternità in Arezzo, 1434, and at the cathedral in Pienza, 1460. The use of the orders in the composition of frames made possible an almost inexhaustible richness, especially in portals, tombs, and altars, which parallels the various combinations of the orders already described. Other combinations could be developed by using the rhythm *b a b,* where *b* corresponds to the frame, and *a* is the opening or center. It was also possible, in the case of an opening with semicircular top, to erect a basic order enclosed by a larger one with its entablature touching the archivolt of the first arch, or else to erect a second, smaller order on top of the basic one. The first describes the frame surrounding Masaccio's "Trinity" in Sta. Maria Novella in Florence; the second is found on the Brancacci tomb in S. Angelo a Nilo in Naples, 1427. The enclosing rectangle could be left without a gable, as on the Cancelleria in Rome (Fig. 69), or could support a gable, as on the cathedral in Pienza. If the frame is articulated in the rhythm *b a b,* then special crowning aediculae, with gables alternating rhythmically with segmental arches and pediments, could be placed above the areas *b* and *a,* as for example in the Piccolomini altar in the cathedral in Siena, 1485.

The gables above the windows of the same story of S. Francesco al Monte in Florence, 1499, alternate rhythmically,[4] as do those of both stories of the Palazzo Pandolfini in Florence, 1520. The latter arrangement gives rise to a chessboard rhythm because the sequence on the ground level begins with a round gable, and the sequence on the upper story with a pointed one.

Aediculae stand in the center of the area provided for them by a pilaster order or other articulation. The order is lacking on the Palazzo Pandolfini. Instead the entablature of the aediculae is carried across the entire upper story. The frames themselves form an order.

Every frame requires a developed socle composed of base, body, and crown molding. In the case of a window, this can be replaced by a balcony that, in the form characteristic of the first phase, projects as a separate unit for each window. The continuous balcony on the front of the Palazzo Pitti in Florence reflects the continuity of the wall. The isolated balconies of the Casa di Raffaello in Rome and of the Palazzo Pandolfini in Florence correspond to the principle of isolation we have discussed with regard to the orders.

A frame that is not composed of an order (that is, of supported and supporting members) extends round a simple geometric figure as a profiled band of constant width. Examples are the archivolts of an arch, the frame of a circular window, and the frames that surround the medallions located in the spandrels of arches and that rest their outer edges upon the archivolts and entablature. These are exactly like the medallions within pendentives, as in the Old Sacristy (Fig. 12) of S. Lorenzo in Florence.

6. COFFERING

Coffering has the same importance for the ceiling as have the orders for the façade. The coffering found in antique prototypes was immediately suitable, and generally accepted, for flat ceilings, barrel vaults, and domes.

Square coffers in flat ceilings are found in S. Lorenzo in Florence (Fig. 14), the Palazzo Medici, and the Palazzo Vecchio (Sala dei Dugento and adjoining room) in Florence.[5] Square coffers in barrel vaults and in the soffits of arches occur in the Pazzi Chapel, above the portal of S. Francesco in Rimini (Fig. 67) and the portal of Sta. Maria Novella in Florence, in the narthex of S. Andrea in Mantua (in this church there are also coffers painted on the barrel vault above the nave), and in the Umiltà in Pistoia. Octagonal coffers were used in the vault above the Altare del Crocefisso, 1448, in S. Miniato al Monte in Florence, and octagonal ones are painted onto the ceiling of Sto. Spirito in Florence, 1434. Circular coffers are found in the barrel vault above the main hall of the Villa Medici at Poggio a Caiano. At the tangent points and in the centers of these circles are smaller circles connected by flat bands. Variations of this pattern are found in the barrel vault above the vestibule of the Villa Medici, and in the barrel vault above the vestibule of the sacristy, 1489, of Sto. Spirito in Florence. A simple series of circular plates occurs above the vestibule of the Pazzi Chapel in Florence, and of circular coffers in the ceiling of the Sala delle Sibille, 1490, in the Vatican. More complicated coffers are combinations of circles and squares as, for example, in the chapel of the Palazzo Medici in Florence.

The coffers just described are coordinated with one another because they are of the same size and shape. Even the rosettes placed in their center are the same, unless some of the coffers on the central axis are emphasized by coats of arms, as in S. Lorenzo in Florence (Fig. 14). In S. Marco in Rome, large coffers (with coats of arms), equal to four normal coffers, are interspersed on the central axis (cf. antique prototypes such as the Arch of Titus in Rome). A ceiling with one single coffer occurs in the Palazzo Pandolfini in Florence.[6]

Rhythmical replaces coordinated coffering on the soffits of the arches at the crossing of St. Peter's in Rome, 1506. The rhythm is

a	*b*	*a*
b	*A*	*b*
a	*b*	*a*

in which *a* are small squares and *A* large ones, and *b* the complimentary oblong (according to the golden section).

Rhythmical coordination occurs next in the dome of the Cappella Chigi, 1513, in Sta. Maria del Popolo in Rome, and richer combinations of squares, hexagons, and octagonals are found in the Villa Madama in Rome. In a certain sense the ceiling of the Sistine Chapel in the Vatican can be included here too. Rhythm was transferred to a flat ceiling in the Laurentian Library in Florence; in detail, however, this already shows symptoms of the second phase.

Just as constant width was characteristic of all frames and archivolts, so was this true of the frames between coffers.

7. GENERATORS OF FORCE

The tectonic shell enclosing the spatial form of the first phase is, in its totality, a combination of these elements: columnar order, articulated wall, aediculae and frames of constant width, and coffering with frames of constant width. The tectonic shell, which forms a continuous boundary for the enclosed spatial form, a *skin* so to speak, is so thoroughly modeled that it is possible to sense tactually everywhere beneath this skin the solid skeleton with all its joints. Continuing this metaphor, I must add that it is not the skeleton itself that is present—not the prepared bones—but the firm articulated structure, including the muscles that are connected to the bones and that make the members actively movable. We cannot see the thin bones themselves; we can only sense them beneath the musculature.

In any system of supports, our estimate of the proportion is the result of the clear disposition of each member. Although proportion is present in every spatial composition, a definite, clearly intended proportion is visible only when the members that are in proportion touch one another at joining points so that they can be separated from one another piece by piece. However, our impression of musculature always corresponds to human musculature. In general and in detail, proportion has a family relationship to the proportions of the human body. Even a Gothic cathedral is a system of supports. In it, too, proportion plays a decisive role, but this is precisely the proportion of the skeleton, of the spidery members. Proportions adapted to the human body, in all its variety, range between the extremes of thinness and bloated fatness; between these is a mean that corresponds to the athletic, well-toned, fully developed human body. The first phase strove for this latter proportion and finally achieved it in its last stages, from the Tempietto at S. Pietro in Montorio in Rome (Fig. 63) onward.

The development of tectonic plasticity in architecture is paralleled in sculpture; in both, forms that are still rather fragile are followed by those that abound in vigor. The buildings of the first phase all adhere firmly to the ground; they are self-contained. They do not seem (as did Gothic buildings) to spread themselves out like a plant or to bend with every breeze. This quality of self-sufficiency is constantly increasing in the course of development during this phase, without there being an increase in massiveness. The Palazzo Pitti in Florence is at rest, but real repose—that combination of immobility and greater lightness of mass—first occurs in Bramante's buildings. I am not concerned here with exploring further the different experience of the human body characteristic of each successive generation within the first phase. I am concerned only with the fact that the entire apparatus of orders, frames, and coffering demonstrates a play of forces that, in the rising mass, strives for and achieves complete self-control. There is a play of forces outward from within. The Gothic cathedral takes root in the earth like a plant and spreads its upward surging forces out through thin stalks to its ribs. Its play of forces is rooted in its surroundings, like a vegetable. A building of the first phase of post-medieval architecture is rather like a man. It is not rooted to the earth but stands with its socle firmly upon the earth's surface. It is not inundated by a vertical force but is self-sufficient and self-contained, and endowed with movable, freely dismountable parts. This architecture as a whole appears to have a movable quality, like the "Doryphoros" of Polykleitos, standing at rest yet tense. This tension—this quality of potential movement—gives the impression of an easy elegance, a serene self-assurance, an alert fearlessness, peculiar to itself. This feeling of vigor sets off a building from others as a self-contained entity. It is independent—not part of a continuous association with other buildings. We now realize that the radial disposition of the spatial group and the total isolation of a building from its environment are also related to the building viewed as corporeal mass. But the difference between space and corporeality persists. In the concept of addition, space has its geometrically definable polarity. The polarity of corporeality can be only corporeal and psychological insofar as we regard all bodies as animated, as essentially related to our own existence. We believe that every molded object is capable of feeling (just as we feel in our own bodies) its own weight, the influence of exterior forces. Thus we also think of it as having the capacity to oppose its own strength against the force of gravity and other external forces. The common characteristic of all tectonic forms of the first phase is that they seem capable of withstanding external forces; they cannot be swept along or made to yield involuntarily; they do not passively resist a superior force but, on the contrary, stand triumphant and indestructible. They themselves form a center of force; from this every external assault rebounds, before it the surroundings humble themselves, and beside it other centers of force can rise untroubled without becoming mutually entangled. The tectonic forms of this phase are seen, as a whole and in part—even to the last profile—as *generators* of force.

The natural consequences of this one, ultimate principle of regarding the tectonic body as generator of force are these: the horizontal, not the vertical, now prevails; each part, like the whole, attains its individual perfection, its specific integrity; uniform proportions control the whole and its parts; there is sufficient room everywhere for the free development of each member; nothing is stunted or oppressed; everything is content, at ease, and serene.

Second Phase (1550–1700)

1. DEBASEMENT OF SUPPORTS

In the second phase the support remains but becomes debased. It was an exception—almost a great mistake—if on a building of the first phase the network of joints in the rustication was continued over the supports, as on the Palazzo Piccolomini in Pienza, 1459, and the Palazzo Fantuzzi in Bologna, 1519. We would be inclined to date the latter about a generation later, but the date 1526 is repeated many times in the ornament of its window frames. The rebuilding of the interior in the seventeenth century does not seem to have touched the façade. Elsewhere the supports of the first phase are usually smooth, fluted, or ornamented. A conscious debasement of the supports first occurs only when they are formed of rusticated pieces in such a way that (in contrast to Palazzo Piccolomini and Palazzo Fantuzzi) there are no butt joints on them; only the horizontal joints are visible. The base and capital peep out from this coarse shaft as if from a shapeless fur coat. These overlapping forms occur after 1530, and very soon they are varied by rusticated blocks that alternate rhythmically with the pieces of shaft visible between them. The columns appear to be bandaged. These can be seen on the Palazzo Bevilacqua in Verona (pilasters on the ground floor, Fig. 74), 1529; the Porta Nuova in Verona, 1533; the Porta di Terra Ferma at Zara, 1541; the Zecca in Venice (Fig. 72, left), 1536; and the villa at Sta. Colomba near Siena (Fig. 73). Compare also the building in the left background of Peruzzi's "Presentation of the Virgin" in Sta. Maria della Pace in Rome.

A second form of debasement is the clustering of supports, which thus partly conceal one another, as on Raphael's Palazzo Jacopo da Brescia in the Borgo Nuovo in Rome,[7] then on the Villa Lante[8] in Rome, 1520. The simple support sustains an isolated point; the clustered support sustains a whole continuous section.

Pilaster strips occur in place of or along with supports, as on the attic of the Palazzo Jacopo da Brescia, on the Palazzo Cicciaporci in Rome, 1515, and the Palazzo Maccarani in Rome, 1520.

The entablature also becomes debased. Architrave and frieze are no longer carried through between the ressauts. Only the cornice is continuous, so that frames can extend into

74. Verona, Palazzo Bevilacqua, 1529.
Façade.

the zone of the entablature, as in the aediculae above the doors in the Medici Chapel in Florence (Fig. 75), 1520, the door into the Laurentian Library, 1524, and the windows of the Palazzo Farnese in Rome (Fig. 76), 1546. And, since the ressaut is echoed in the gable, the latter also begins to suffer from the general debasing of the supports. Finally, it is completely torn apart in the center, as for example on the Palazzo Sanguinetti (Ranuzzi) in Bologna (Fig. 77), 1549, and in some of Buontalenti's sketches in the Uffizi.

The inner frames of the aediculae above the doors of the Medici Chapel demonstrate true interpenetration. They even take in the area of the gable (Fig. 75).

In the vestibule of the Laurentian Library, the *freedom* of the columns is constrained. They are squeezed into the walls in pairs (Fig. 59).

A necessary concomitant aspect of this debasing process is that the partial concealment of the supports, the interpenetrating forms, and the interruption of all the members makes these components appear incomplete. They seem to lack sufficient room, so that one seems to smother, or at least oppress, the other. Instead of a simple arrangement next to one another, they are placed one in front of the other. Thus an interweaving of members is now possible, as in the loggia of the Appartamento di Troia, 1538, of the Palazzo Ducale in Mantua, where the cornice above the small pilasters that flank the niches cuts across the larger projecting pilasters, and a console (intended to hold a bust) gives special emphasis to the point of intersection (Fig. 78). Spiral columns are also possible. Their contour no longer lies in one plane but is bent back upon itself with every turn, as on the façade of the Rustica, 1538, also at the Palazzo Ducale in Mantua.[9]

2. FUSION AND SPLITTING

The order persists in the form of the "colossal order"; that is, the supports draw the entire height of the façade together into a unit. The horizontal lines of the windows at each floor cut across, actually or by extension, the shafts of the continuous, colossal pilasters or columns. The feeling is created that the stories are no longer isolated but form the subdivisions of a total space, and this has its corollary in the conception of the exterior surface as a uniform, continuous fragment. The first essay in the use of the colossal order is found in Alberti's design for the façade of S. Andrea in Mantua, 1470, but the definitive development occurred on the palaces on the Capitoline Hill in Rome (Fig. 65) and on the exterior of Michelangelo's St. Peter's in the Vatican.[10]

When an order is carried across an upper story, the pedestals can be omitted so that the supports stand directly upon the cornice of the story below. Since the balcony remains, its balustrade abuts unceremoniously against every column, as for example on the Palazzo Iseppo Porto in Vicenza (Fig. 79),

75. Florence, S. Lorenzo,
Medici Chapel, 1520. Interior.

76. Rome, Palazzo Farnese, 1534.
Façade.

77. Bologna, Palazzo Sanguinetti
(Ranuzzi), 1549. Façade.

78. Mantua, Palazzo Ducale,
Loggia of the Appartamento
di Troia, 1538. Interior.

1550. This feature is almost inevitable in Palladian buildings. Another example is the Madonna dei Monti, 1580, in Rome. The opposite case occurs when the socle cuts into the windows, as at the Palazzo Uguccioni in Florence, 1550. The interruption of horizontal layers by vertical forces is only a special case of interpenetration in general or, to put it in still more general terms, of the fusing of originally isolated entities into a unit.

There is a similar result when the order is again abandoned and the wall predominates as a continuous surface. This surface is controlled only by the continuous vertical axes and by the horizontal cornice, which are now inevitable. The principal example of this is the Palazzo Farnese in Rome (Fig. 76).

As soon as this feeling for the entire building as a unit was once more appreciated, the balcony was either pulled together with the portal beneath, as in the case of the rusticated portal of the Palazzo Farnese (Fig. 76), the Palazzo Lateranense in Rome, 1586, and the Palazzo Borghese in Rome, 1590, or else it was carried across the greater part of the façade, as at the Palazzo Bevilacqua in Verona (Fig. 74) and the Palazzo Grimani in Venice (Fig. 70).

There were other equally effective means of fusing an elevation into a unit, which could then be subdivided, such as irregular spacing of the colossal order, emphasis of one story, or increasing the relief toward the center.[11] The skeleton as a whole declined in importance. The skin, pulled across everything, sometimes tightly stretched, sometimes richly folded, became the essential feature. The orders, which were retained and even recast as forcefully as possible, were made part of this skin through the manner in which they were used. They were no longer an airy framework with isolated panels filling in the mesh or the firm outlines of separate components joined together but the internal divisions of a continuous surface—the products of surface tension. Fusion is one characteristic of this; splitting, another.

The splitting of gables and entablatures in Italy led to many more striking results in the North. In Holland in particular, façades of this phase appear to be slit open because of their alternate courses of cut stone and brick. The cut stone courses themselves appear as mere inserts or intermittent scraps. Examples are the Stadhuis in The Hague, 1564, the Waagbouw in Alkmaar, 1582, the Raadhuis in Franeker, 1591, and the Vleeshal in Haarlem (Fig. 80), 1602. Northern Germany adopted these split forms, as for example in Schloss Hämelschenburg near Hameln, 1588; the arsenal in Gdánsk (Danzig), 1602; and the Hochzeithaus in Hameln, 1610. In France the best known examples are the houses of the Place des Vosges in Paris.[12] Paradoxical as it sounds, it is precisely this splitting of forms that introduces continuity. Each of these façades is like a torn jacket beneath which a continuous inner fabric appears.

79. Vicenza, Palazzo Iseppo Porto
(Colleoni-Porto), 1550. Façade.

80. Haarlem, Vleeshal, 1602. Façade.

The North did not retain the horizontal upper cornice either. High roofs took away the role of the eaves line as the upper termination of the façade. The principal gable, the gables of the separate dormers above the eaves, and the diffusion of dormers, chimneys, and turrets produced a complicated silhouette in which the individual parts acted more or less effectively as terminations. Some of these lay in the plane of the façade; others became separated farther back. The volutes common on Italian church façades were carried over to the gables of both churches and secular buildings of the North. They were then multiplied, fused together, permeated with other forms, interwoven with one another, and finally split apart again. In Italy itself this disintegration of the silhouette was also possible, as at the Villa Aldobrandini in Frascati, 1598. Towers were joined to the main body of a building in this new way, as at the Villa Medici in Rome, 1544, and Trinità de'Monti in Rome, 1595. In the first phase a tower stood isolated (as at Madonna di S. Biagio in Montepulciano). If it was connected to a church, as in Bramante's design for St. Peter's in the Vatican, it was multiplied fourfold; this had the effect of isolating the building from its surroundings (with its accented corners visible from any direction) rather than of fragmenting its silhouette.

By about 1600 this process of fusing and splitting all the corporeal forms handed down from the first phase had already been completed. The seventeenth century helped itself to these newly created components; it varied, combined, and modified them but did not change the principle in any way. But it is not the purpose of this book to examine this development or to study the occasional creation of new corporeal forms (especially those of Borromini).

3. FRAMES

Frames were attacked very early by rustication. The first examples are on the Palazzo Vidoni-Caffarelli in Rome. Later they were almost completely swallowed up by rustication so that only their corners looked out. The ground-floor windows of the Villa Giulia in Rome, 1550, are good examples.

The width of the frames used in this phase is no longer constant, as it was in the first phase. They acquire "ears," or unexpected extensions in width at their upper or lower corners or ends. At first these are modest and have square corners, but they soon become more and more complicated. Simple ears appear on the frames in the attic of the Palazzo Jacopo da Brescia in the Borgo Nuovo in Rome, on the upper windows of the Palazzo Branconio dell'Aquila in Rome, 1519, on the Palazzo Linotte in Rome, on the inner frames above the doors of the Medici Chapel in Florence (Fig. 75), and on the upper windows of the Palazzo Massimi alle Colonne in Rome, 1532. Volutes are now stretched between the ears, or a row of windows has frames that are partly composed of curves, as on the later upper windows of the Palazzo Del Monte-Contucci in Montepulciano. The mezzanine windows of the Library of St. Mark's in Venice, 1537, represent a further development. As their inner and outer contours are basically different, the frames do not maintain even an approximately constant width (Fig. 72). Here the separation into supporting and supported parts is absolutely impossible. (The attendant volutes here have been transformed into dolphins.)

Frames are doubled. One frame is stuck into another of different shape, and the two then collide with each other. Examples are the niche frames, again, above the doors of the Medici Chapel (Fig. 75), the portal of the Laurentian Library, and the main portal of the Gesù in Rome (Fig. 81).[13]

The further development of frames belongs to the history of ornament. This would discuss how the double or multiple frames begin to unravel at the edges; how these separate projections curl up and pierce through slits cut into their neighbors, or wrap around them; how figures are interwoven between them; how, finally, not only the outer contours but also the inner ones lose their simple geometric shapes, and the frame becomes a fantastic garland of entangled volutes. A thorough study of this development is still lacking. It had its origins in Italy. Germany and Belgium with northern imagination brought the simple elements to their most complicated form.[14] The history of the frame becomes united with the history of the cartouche; neither has any longer a solid skeleton. They are leatherlike formations. Their plastic, pliable, cuttable, shriveling, and puckering pulp becomes a strange, soft paste that changes by viscous trickles into scrolls.

Ornament now has greater influence upon the total appearance of a building than it had in the first phase. In both phases ornament obeys the same rules as the tectonic body. It is important for our impression of the architecture of the first phase that ornament is also perceived as generator of force. It is confined within its own area and possesses within that area the completeness, unvarying animation, and resilient strength that makes it a harmonious attendant of the tectonic body. But ornament is a great deal more decisive for our impression of the architecture of the second phase. It is not merely inserted into the framework but becomes an active force in the amalgamation of the whole. The luxuriant growth of cartouches and frames on the surface often destroys the last vestiges of the skeletal impression created by the remaining orders.

The last step in the liberation and debasement of the frame is its animation by figural sculpture. The frame competes with its filling and finally becomes more interesting. Examples are (1) the figures on the inclining planes of the gables above windows and doors (with their origin in the prototype of the Medici Tombs at S. Lorenzo in Florence), numerous examples of which are found in Palladio's work; (2) the figures in the

81. Rome, Gesù, 1568. Façade.

center of a divided gable, as in the Palazzo Doria Tursi in
Genoa; (3) the Atlantes supporting the frames, in the interior
of the Palazzo Spada in Rome (Fig. 82); (4) figures arranged
symmetrically in pairs, such as cartouche bearers (going back
to the *Ignudi* on the Sistine Ceiling), as in the Palazzo Spada
again, and in the Sala Regia in the Vatican; and, finally, (5) the
increasingly frequent herms. Herms appear early, as in the
first design for the tomb of Julius II (also in the final version
of 1545 in S. Pietro in Vincoli in Rome). Small herms appear
in the corners of the vaults of Raphael's loggia in the Vatican,[15]
then as a row of supporting members in the Casino della Grotta
at the Palazzo del Te in Mantua, 1530, and soon afterward
(in 1543) in S. Matteo in Genoa. They are numerous in the
garden grotto of the Villa d'Este at Tivoli (*after* the installation
of the Juluis tomb) and on the Palazzo di Giustizia in Mantua,
1550. The further development of this decoration, which
interweaves figural sculpture, herms, and tectonic scrollwork,
can be pursued in the Palazzo Marino in Milan, 1553; the
Palazzo Imperiale in Genoa, 1560; the Palazzo del Podestà
in Genoa, 1563; and the Palazzo Pallavicini in Genoa. This
type of form reached full maturity as early as 1557 in the choir
stalls of Sta. Giustina in Padua. The difference between frame
and filling is almost abolished by this metamorphosis. Decoration is spun as an unbroken web over both the frame and its
filling.

4. COFFERING

The ceiling of the Laurentian Library already shows symptoms of the second phase. On the whole, its subdivision into
three rows of coffering that run along next to one another as
in a nave and side aisles (in the rhythm *b a b*), is still characteristic of the first phase, but the frames set into these coffers
are without precedent, and their treatment is also new. There
are ellipses with ears in the center coffers, and the four corners
of each are filled out with fragmentary frames and ornament.
The side coffers are filled with pairs of rectangles with triangular ears, if I can so describe them, which interweave
where they meet. These rectangles have "gables" on both short
sides, and thus the meaning of the gable is invalidated. The
ornament sits between the frames rather than within them.

Interweaving in the true sense of the word occurs next.
The bands between the coffers alternate above and below one
another in many ceilings of the Palazzo Ducale in Mantua and
the Palazzo Spada in Rome. At Sta. Barbara in Mantua this
even occurs in a vault.

Coffers of the first phase had another characteristic that
I have not yet mentioned: they are so interlocked that either
there is no negative area at all (as in the case of the addition of
squares or hexagons) or there is complete regularity (as with
the addition of octagons and circles). The addition of octagons
leaves small square negative spaces; the addition of circles

82. Rome, Palazzo Spada. Interior.

leaves regular figures composed of convex quarter circles. The principle is the same when more complicated forms are joined. But the character of a ceiling is altered as soon as there are irregular spaces left over (as in the Palazzo Spada), that is, when the regular coffering is widely and unequally spaced. The negative spaces in the ceiling become figures of irregular width; they become uninteresting, merely a part of the continuous surface into which the regular coffering is arbitrarily distributed. It is now possible to design irregular coffers too, as the width of their frames need no longer be constant. The coffers are given ears and are enriched with ornament; they are changed into frames that float or swim freely side by side in the surface of the ceiling, supported by figures that are standing, flying, or stuck to the ceiling. The development of the ceiling from now on parallels the development of frames. The continuous surface, or the area within the frames, or both, are filled with a painting, so that the impression of the ceiling is more strongly determined by the details of the painting than by the tectonic elements that still remain. Obviously the painter will abolish altogether the space-enclosing function of the ceiling. He will construct his picture not as he would a mural, not as a projection of objects standing horizontally opposite the beholder, but rather as a ceiling painting, as a projection of things floating vertically above the beholder. He thus opens a vista into the heavens, which are filled with allegories, or with mythological or Christian scenes. Mantegna's ceiling in the Camera degli Sposi, 1469, of the Palazzo Ducale in Mantua already simulates a partial opening between painted coffers. Correggio's painting in Parma Cathedral, 1526, takes over the entire dome for an open sky. Michelangelo's Sistine Ceiling in the Vatican follows the principles of the first phase in its over-all arrangement. Its center is a series of simple, rectangular coffers alternating in the rhythm *b a b a* between the thrones that rise up from the sides. The *Ignudi* occasionally cut across the coffering frames. The Carracci Gallery, 1597, in the Palazzo Farnese in Rome has a richer juxtaposition of painted frames (partly grisaille and partly gilt, with figures in natural color). In the corners are painted balustrades, which do not accentuate the groins of the vault, and behind them is a painted sky. This splitting apart of the framework to create a vista was further developed in the seventeenth century in the ceilings of S. Bartolomeo and S. Paolo, both in Bologna, and SS. Domenico e Sisto in Rome. The framework is thought of as located in the center of space, with the represented objects floating in front of and behind it. The clouds and the figures, individually and in groups, swell over the frames, partly concealing them, and sometimes even continuing beyond them.[16]

5. TRANSMITTERS OF FORCES

The debasement of the entire skeleton—the reinterpretation of all individual corporeal forms as components of a continuous skin, stretched or hung round the spatial form—results in the triumph of two-dimensionality. The play of forces on the continuous surface becomes more important than the musculature, which is still present. The passivity of a skin that is folded, of a hide that is stretched, of a membrane that is torn is the common characteristic of the corporeal forms of the second phase. Certainly the accumulation of force is usually disproportionately greater now than in the first phase, but this is not an active force. It does not prevail against the still greater masses hemming it in. The over-all impression created by debased supports, interpenetrating forms, the colossal order, the unarticulated wall, the concomitant, characteristic design of frames and ceilings, and the uncontrolled ornament is always of an upward movement hemmed in by massiveness, of torment and defeat, of a passionate defense against external forces, or of resigned suffering. Instead of the triumphant, free, elastic resistance that characterizes independent centers of power, there now appears the constrained fragment, defeated, dependent upon and threatened by external forces. In itself it is incomplete and transitory. It exists as a momentary state—be it a state of the greatest precipitation and agitation or of idle flaccidity. The corporeal forms as individual units, the heavily oppressing cover that extends as a whole over the entire spatial form, and the whole building mass (which is perceived resting motionless beneath this cover) become *transmitters of forces*. They become transmitters not only of gravitational force but of all the arbitrary forces that the form-giving architect conducts through this totality to create those splits and bends and, in a few places, those one-sided displacements of the load.

The antithetical qualities of activity and passivity, independence and dependence, are only reflections of this all-embracing polarity: *generator of forces and transmitter of forces.*

The indescribable feeling of happiness radiated by the tectonic forms of the first phase is a result of their appearing to us as happy. They confirm the naïve belief that it could be given to man to determine his own fate, to move effortlessly through this world, to be unoppressed, to be in control of himself without effort. They embody this ideal because they form a harmonious whole, because they are proud, alert, dispassionate, guiltless and are created to endure for all time. And since each self-governing tectonic form is a king, almost a god, in its own realm, the juxtaposition of several of them produces a really strict coexistence. Their spheres of influence do not cross or merge.

The indescribable feeling of torment engendered by the works of the second phase is caused by the seeming unhappiness of their tectonic corporeal forms. They are not in a position to assert themselves freely. They are incomplete fragments of an unending association of physical forces. The volition

that works within them is always so controlled that it is opposed to a stronger force. They groan under this burden or
seem to be thrown into a passionate rage against it. We face
these corporeal forms as men who are incapable of controlling
our fate, dissatisfied with our lot, but unable to alter it.

I do not want to be misunderstood when I allude to
things tormented and tormenting in this phase, for I intend
no value judgment. Happiness and torment are ethical values.
Both are equally necessary for the life of man, and their emphasis upon two entirely different kinds of longing is not
carried over to the works of art that reflect these polar values.
Happiness and torment are values in human experience, but
in art they are forces of expression and are valuable to the
extent that they are artistically effective. Their resonant ethical
overtones are inappropriate in the characterization of the
polarities that distinguish the two phases. Objective characterization is concerned with the physical forces of which we are
aware in the corporeal forms.

I do not think it superfluous to repeat that these polarities
of corporeal form cannot be grasped geometrically like those
of spatial form. It is true that I have often described this change
in geometrical terms. For example, I spoke of the juxtaposition
of clearly defined bodies that softens into the overlapping of
bodies when outlines become partly obscure or uncertain.
When I speak of planarity in the second phase, I mean something quite different from that of the first phase. The planarity
of the second phase has a purpose similar to the overlapping
pilasters that partly conceal one another. The same flow of
forces that fuses objects in depth, depriving them of their
individuality, also fuses objects that remain on a common
plane. A description that confines itself to geometrical prop-
erties will miss the essential point. Juxtaposition also becomes
something different here, because the flow of forces penetrates
everything. It is precisely this that permits overlapping, interpenetration, and interweaving of parts. Spatial transformation,
when it occurs, is therefore only a phenomenon parallel to
physical transformation.

Third Phase (Eighteenth Century)

The principle of regarding the body as transmitter of forces
also continues into the eighteenth century, but a distinct
third phase can be discerned here just as in the history of
spatial form. I shall discuss only a few characteristics.

An analysis of the central pavilions (Fig. 83) at the ends
of the long axis of the Zwinger in Dresden, 1711, shows that
the supports are still present but have only a very slight
relationship to the spandrels above the voids between them
on the ground floor and none at all to those above the voids
of the upper story. On the upper story the three tightly com-
pressed pilasters carry an entablature and, above that, an attic

83. Dresden, Zwinger, 1711.
Wallpavillon. Façade.

with figures. This vertical body is unrelated to the arches of the central and side bays. The central arch is carried by pilasters consistent with this order, but they lack an entablature. The upper cornice floats high above the arch, higher than the attic figures. The area defined by curves and consoles between the arch and this cornice is filled with a cartouche and its attendant figures (here symmetrically placed). A similar situation prevails in the side bays, and the same tendency is recognizable on the ground floor. The fruit baskets and vases carry the vertical lines of the herms over the cornice, which is placed between stories; they obscure the bases of the upper pilasters and tie the piers together vertically. Door and window frames are loosely located between these piers. The same effect is obtained in the southeastern gate tower by different means. The forms are the same, but their functions are altered. There are supports, but they carry nothing. What they should carry floats free beside them. Compare the façade of the abbey church at Krzeszów (Grüssau) in Poland, 1728.

The uppermost cornice above the central bay of the pavilion at the Zwinger is an arch composed of two symmetrically curved arms. Each arm begins horizontally, rises convexly like a "curtain stay," becomes concave, and then rolls itself up into a volute. This convexity is characteristic of the third phase to the highest degree. It has its seventeenth-century prototypes but becomes widespread only in the eighteenth century. The source of this "curtain stay" form can probably be found in the corresponding transformation of the great volutes that connect the higher center section and lower side sections of Italian church façades.[17] Convex arches occur as early as the seventeenth century, for example, in the portals of the Residenz in Munich, 1611, and in the works of Bernini and Borromini in Rome, such as the court portal of the Palazzo Barberini, 1630; the tabernacle of St. Theresa, 1645, in the Cornaro Chapel at Sta. Maria della Vittoria (Fig. 84); the tower of S. Andrea delle Fratte, 1653; and the Porta del Popolo, 1655. In the eighteenth century the convexly mounted arch is found everywhere. Examples of different kinds are found on the façade of Sv. Mikuláš Malá Strana in Prague, 1709; the west portal of the palace in Berlin, 1707; the Belvedere in Vienna, 1721; the Dalberger Hof in Mainz, 1715; the Hôtel de Saxe in Dresden, 1720; the Residenz in Würzburg, 1719; and Schloss Werneck near Würzburg, 1733. It is used in three different ways on the façade of St. John Nepomuk in Munich, 1731: above the doorway, above the window, and above the entire façade (Fig. 85). It occurs at the monastery in Langheim, 1750, and above the gateway of the monastery at Banz, 1752. A simple building such as the old City Hall in Copenhagen, 1730, is characterized as a building of the third phase by the typically convex gable. The same form occurs, of course, on altars and organs, as for example on the altars in the transepts

84. Rome, Sta. Maria della Vittoria,
Cornaro Chapel, 1645. Interior.

85. Munich, St. John Nepomuk, 1731. Façade.

of S. Ignazio in Rome, 1730, and on the altar and organ in the Frauenkirche in Dresden, of about the same date.

The convex arch combines with ressauts and volutes and is often even split apart in the center. In this phase both this and older gable forms float as window coverings high above the straight or arched openings. They are usually supported by consolelike volutes placed into the surface of the wall. Examples are the windows in Schloss Ansbach, 1713; the Palais Trautson in Vienna, 1720; the Residenz in Würzburg, 1719; and the Catholic Hofkirche in Dresden, 1738. There are several different varieties on the Palais Preysing in Munich, 1727. These volutes are designed in such a way that we do not credit them with any real supporting strength. For the most part they incline obliquely toward one another, and it appears as if the heavy gables would crush these delicate brackets, except that the gables themselves seem to float unsupported. The convex form always gives the impression of resting upon its supports but at the same time of having its own upward-springing force. It is this floating or fluttering upward—not the convexity—that is its essential characteristic. The convexity is only a means of achieving this effect. If I speak here of convex forms, I do not mean that there is an essential connection between the convex arches and convex spatial forms. They are entirely independent of each other.

Convex spatial forms obviously have their consequences in the corporeal forms, for the spatial form is indeed determined by its corporeal boundaries. The façade of St. John Nepomuk in Munich (Fig. 85) is slightly convex as a whole, but the complicated "convexly attached" gables must then be convex in another sense. The window and portal gables of this façade are curved slightly forward, and their outer ends meet the convex plane of the façade. The characteristic of forms based upon infinitesimal calculus is thus carried over from space to mass, if it does not already have this character itself. St. John Nepomuk swarms with examples, such as the herms that support the interior gallery (Fig. 52). As a whole they wave back and forth, concave and convex, like the façade, the gallery balustrade, and the volutes in the cove.

The ornament that is modeled onto such complicated surfaces now reaches also the highest degree of complication. Occasionally it even frees itself from these surfaces, hangs in space as a garland, or flies completely free, as the angels in the choir of St. John Nepomuk (Fig. 52). The framework, generally loosely put together of thin moldings, gradually changes into foliage, especially in corners. The corporeal forms, now deprived of their tectonic function, are assimilated by the ornament, so that the final effect is of blossoming vegetation penetrating the building. The complexity of the frames of ceiling paintings, the blurring of the transition from ceiling to wall, and the veiling of all joints and articulating points by ornament are carried to such a degree that most scholars see this as an ornamental style. But of course this is an error. It is true that ornament now becomes even more decisive in the total effect than it was in the second phase. It now performs to the extreme limit its function of fusing all the individual forms into a continuous unit, or of splitting them up to an even greater degree than before. Altars, pulpits, organs, pews, the furnishings for public and private rooms in secular buildings—all become part of the architecture and completely fill the spatial shell. In the church at Ottobeuren, for example, the altars appear like a flourish of certain accented positions. Our eyes are drawn to them and thus perceive the complete disruption of the spatial continuity of the interior.

Ornament has entirely the characteristics of the corporeal forms of this phase: it has the same quality of suspension, of vegetable germination, of facile cohesion, without resting firmly upon anything. For this reason alone it has an architectural importance because, added to the floating image, it serves to heighten the feeling of suspension. The shell cartouche, the end product of this family of forms, now reaches the highest degree of fusion and splitting for which the second phase had striven. This would mean only a distinction of degree and would not justify a separation of the phases. But ornament now achieves more: it scatters rather than splits unity; it actually dissolves itself. In the church at Zwiefalten there are confessionals built of stalactites. They seem to represent the momentary stage of a continuous transformation. But the most extreme example I have found is a design for a cartouche by Feichtmeyer. It is on fire and is disappearing in smoke.[18]

Ornament is certainly the most flexible aspect of this phase, but it merely obeys the same stylistic principle as window and door frames, and fluttering fragments of cornice. There is a uniform restraint throughout all the corporeal forms. They are still transmitters of forces, but they no longer oppose those forces. They exploit them. They no longer suffer tragically; rather, they bend with every breeze.

We do not at first think of man in the midst of such corporeal forms. We think of petals flying pell-mell in a spring breeze, of hissing fireworks, of fountains, of smoke and the flicker of flames driven by the wind. As a metaphor for the corporeal forms of the first phase, let us imagine a hero who stands alone and happy on a small island. He smiles no matter whether the sea around him is as smooth as a mirror or is surging with a roar. For those of the second phase we can envisage a Herculean swimmer fighting against overpowering tides. He must finally succumb. But for those of the third phase we must think of a butterfly that partly lets itself be supported and partly flies on its own. There is, then, a greater difference between the corporeal forms of the second and third phase, one that concerns their divergent reactions to the permeating forces: the corporeal forms of the second phase resist them; those of the third exploit them.

This is the objective physical difference; there is a corresponding ethical one. The corporeal world of the third phase seems to be endowed with the most cheerful frivolity. It seems characterless, unprincipled, and given to every caprice, dancing gracefully over every pitfall. Man's dependence upon higher and greater powers, once considered a fearful torment, is now accepted as the self-evident system of universal rule, so that absolute irresponsibility follows. The most joyful acceptance replaces resistance to assault. Frivolity is the extreme consequence into which the original pathos is transformed.

But once again this ethical meaning is secondary to the simple feeling in response to the physical process. Architecture has changed into a loosely linked structure: its parts float and lean, and every puff of wind seems to threaten them (no matter how structurally solid they are). It is like a bouquet that is too loosely bound and so threatens to fall apart or a house of cards, unstable, ephemeral, infinitesimal in time. This impression of instability, of transitoriness, of spurting, of scattering, is at the opposite pole from the impression of permanent immutability of the first phase.

We can say therefore that the first phase is distinguished from both the second and third phases together by the polar opposites of generator of forces and transmitter of forces, and that the second phase is distinguished from the third by the subordinate polarity of resistance to the permeating forces and of exploitation of them.

Fourth Phase (Nineteenth Century)

The extreme development of the body as a transmitter of force is achieved about 1760, and the fourth phase sets up its first stage by rehabilitating the orders. The entablature becomes straight and travels an unbroken course above the supports. The gable is once more a closed triangle. All the members receive their natural integrity. Ornament is held in check in simply circumscribed enclosures, mostly in rectangles, and in general is greatly diminished. Antique Roman and, later, antique Greek forms become decisive in the total effect. It appears on first glance as if the corporeal forms of the first phase had been re-established and corrected by a more strict imitation of the antique, for the exterior form of the antique temple is now taken over as a whole without essential changes, as for example at the Madeleine in Paris, 1808, the Walhalla near Regensburg, 1831, and the small Theseus Temple in Vienna, 1821. But these are exceptions. More common is the portico with straight entablature, with or without uniting pediment; it is used as an articulated feature in front of an unarticulated wall. The Odéon, 1779, and the Bourse, 1808, both in Paris, and the Théâtre in Strasbourg, 1810, are examples

without pediment; the Royal Palace in Koblenz, 1778, Schloss Wilhelmshöhe, 1786, the Chambre des Députés in Paris, 1800, the Neue Wache in Berlin, 1816, the Glyptothek in Munich (Fig. 86), 1816, and the old Exchange in Amsterdam,[19] 1845, are examples with pediment.

Stark contrast between the rigidly articulated portico and the blocklike compactness of the remaining structure and lack of articulation in the details are features that essentially distinguish the buildings of this phase from those of the first, where uniform articulation was sought. I forego an investigation of the separate varieties. There is less variation than in the first phase, for now the only juxtaposition tolerated is that of the articulated wall or portico and the unarticulated segments of wall (Fig. 86). The windows in an unarticulated wall are always aligned vertically, and the wall always has a horizontal upper cornice. The fact that the Doric order is widely used does not mean that it has the same appearance as in the first phase; it is now heavier and, like almost all the corporeal forms of the early fourth phase, can be charged with being immovable.

The model for this phase is not the first phase of post-medieval architecture but Palladio—the Palladio who already belongs entirely to the second phase. Composition as a whole is either based upon or stimulated by his villa designs, and the details are corrected by elimination of everything that deviates from the norm. But the norm is that which the ordering intellect has constructed through intensive work as—for him—the most immediate, most primitive: the norm in architecture is something only apparently primitive. Although it is easily comprehensible, it is the product of laborious abstraction. This return to the corporeal forms of the second phase, together with the exaggeration of the rational ordering of all axial relationships characteristic of the first phase, produces the confusion of polarities that from now on, in general, becomes increasingly marked in the corporeal, as in the spatial, forms.

The sudden revival of medieval spatial forms results in the development of Romanesque, Gothic, and Byzantine corporeal forms. The development then follows a different path and cannot be understood as a continuity within the sequence of corporeal forms any more than within the sequence of spatial forms. The continuity is in fact broken here. The architecture of the nineteenth century as a whole is linked to the first three phases only by threads of quite a different nature.

The *radiation* of inherent forces, the *channeling* of external forces—these are the antitheses that differentiate the corporeal forms of the first and second phases. The third and fourth phases are not determined by new polarities. Rather, the third transforms the conception of the body as a channel of force into the *subordinate polarity of companionship* with the external forces. The fourth begins with a confusion of polarities and then, determined by completely different stylistic principles, follows a path along which the question of the polarity of corporeal form no longer has any meaning.

3 Visible Form

Differences of light and color are primary factors in the effect produced by a completed building. This specifically optical impression, that what is *merely* visible is a two-dimensional image, assumes that we see with one eye in fixed focus.[1] Physiological experiment demonstrates that in the course of everyday affairs, as we approach a building or walk through it, we always experience the merely visible aspect of architecture as a continuous series of shifting, complementary images. But binocular vision and the movements of our eyes, head, or entire body do not turn two-dimensional images into conceptions of corporeality. We have become accustomed from early childhood to interpret two-dimensional optical differences three-dimensionally. This is why we can recognize solids and voids in a painting. The difference between a two-dimensional painting and all three-dimensional objects is that congruence within a painting remains constant, even if we change our viewpoint. A painting as a whole becomes distorted when seen from the side, but its internal relationships are unchanged. As we walk round a building or any three-dimensional object, however, not only does it become distorted or altered as a whole, but its internal relationships also are constantly shifting.

We interpret as three-dimensional every single image of an object that we receive from any one viewpoint, but what is essential in viewing architecture is that we accept these isolated images as merely preliminary arrangements, not as ends in themselves. To see architecture means to draw together into a single mental image the series of three-dimensionally interpreted images that are presented to us as we walk through interior spaces and round their exterior shell. When I speak of the *architectural image*, I mean this *one mental image*.

First Phase (1420–1550)

1. COORDINATION

The unconditional demand for completeness, which in the first phase is produced by spatial addition and the radiation of force, means that differences of light and color must permit easy and absolute comprehension of this completeness. They must not hinder or disturb this effect. The intensity of light must be as uniform as possible throughout the interior. Gradations of light, when present, are subtle, as in S. Lorenzo (Fig. 14) and Sto. Spirito in Florence. There is no sharp contrast, and the darker areas are always bright enough to allow clear vision. But the colors are at the service of the corporeal formation because they bring the structural lines—the skeleton—into sharp relief against the remaining wall. It is certainly incorrect to assume that the sharp contrast between the dark stone members and the whitened walls in the interiors of Tuscan churches is the result of the subsequent whitewashing of polychrome frescoes (whether narrative or ornamental).[2] This severity is throughout a characteristic of the first phase, and a wealth of color, as in the Portinari Chapel at S. Eustorgio in Milan, is exceptional. Transverse striation in black and white or red and white horizontal bands is a vestige of medieval architecture. The stone chosen in this phase is always monochrome (usually a gray-green) and free from noticeable spots or veins. The polish is dull. Strong light reflections are avoided even when the material is bronze or gold. Painted colors are similarly always strong and clear and spread evenly as uniform surfaces; the individual colored areas of surface or articulating elements are sharply juxtaposed. The color detaches ornament from its background, sets off a panel from its frame, and separates a capital from its shaft. Coffered ceilings are convincing examples of this treatment. In the painted decoration of ceilings derived from coffering, especially that of the Raphael school (Perino del Vaga, Giulio Romano), colors are displayed in broad bands surrounding isolated geometric areas as strong dividing lines or in uniform backgrounds against which figures and decoration are silhouetted. The colors are set down separately next to one another, usually in many small areas, and the harmony of this gay polychromy is due partly to the compatibility of all these colors and partly to the repetition of the same colors on either side of a given axis of space and surface.

2. CLARITY

The coordination of colors, their pure severity, lack of brilliance, and their distribution in such a way as to accentuate the tectonic skeleton and to separate the individual components —this use of color, combined with the uniformity of light, results in the increase of clarity. Light and color are so chosen that the stable forms of space and mass are easily recognized, even when as a result of deep shadows or a lateral view there are impediments to recognition. In other words, the stimulus of the optical appearance has a right to exist only insofar as it does not prejudice the actual form. The object itself is more important than its appearance.

3. FRONTALITY

The coordination of individual optical values and their subordination to objective clarity are characteristics of the individual perspective image produced from any single viewpoint; to this extent the individual image enters indirectly into the architectural image. It must be understood from the beginning that this architectural image is obtained as we walk through the whole building and round the exterior, scramble up onto the roof, and ascend the towers. But such an examination is of a scientific nature, and it is in this way that the architect and art historian studies, with the concentrated interest of the specialist. The artistic image by no means presupposes such a thorough tour of inspection. In the first phase it suffices for us to view a building from surprisingly few points to gain a complete architectural image. The architectural image here is unique; it is always the same no matter whether it is seen from many different angles. It is identical with the actual complete form.

A cylindrical central-plan building like Bramante's Tempietto in S. Pietro in Montorio in Rome looks the same from every side (Fig. 63). Although the overlap of the freestanding columns of its peristyle shifts with every step we take, this shift is such that the same relationships always return at regular intervals. Only the background changes, and even this change would have been eliminated by the proposed circular court and its surrounding colonnade (Fig. 62). The eye takes in the situation at a glance. The image—the architectural image—is complete from all viewpoints. There is no temptation for us to walk round the building because we realize at once that it can offer us no surprises.

In Bramante's design for St. Peter's in the Vatican (Fig. 5), the overlap would have appeared different from every viewpoint because of the four corner towers. But the instability of the silhouette would not have destroyed the uniqueness of the architectural image. The very fact that there were to be four towers, one at each corner, would have enabled us to take in all four sides at a glance from any given point. We would not actually have seen them, but our imagination would have had no difficulty in supplying what was temporarily hidden from view. The image would always have been the same. Although each side would have existed as a separate image in its own right, it would have been sufficient to be in front of only one side in order to obtain a total image, because all the sides are of equal value. They are coordinated. The great apses that extend beyond the cube marked out by the towers in this design would have had an effect akin to that of the Tempietto.

It is clear that a unique architectural image is necessarily produced by every freestanding, additive, central-plan church or blocklike secular building, but the unique image is not restricted to these most convenient forms. The exterior appearance of a longitudinal church, even if it is partly attached to other buildings and therefore not isolated (like S. Lorenzo in Florence), conforms in principle to the ideal of an equal development of all four main views, which, in their original form (excluding later additions), always have the effect of self-completing, mutually explanatory images. Examples are S. Francesco in Rimini (Fig. 67) and Sta. Maria del Calcinaio at Cortona. Cornices surround these buildings at the same level. The main façade is often a heightened version of the sides, but it is nonetheless a continuation of them. The designs for the façade of S. Lorenzo in Florence by Michelangelo and

Giuliano da San Gallo are the first to show a slight independence of the front of the building from the sides.

Coordination of the individual images and simplicity of
the total image—these are the characteristics produced in the
interior by the radiating lines of circulation. Here too it is
superfluous to try out all viewpoints. We take in the situation
at a glance and perceive that no surprises are waiting round
the corner, that the new images that appear as we walk can
complete or elucidate the architectural image but not essentially alter it. In the domain of optics this quality of uniqueness and simplicity forms the analogy to the repose of the
isolated centers of space and force. We can stand anywhere
and yet feel ourselves in possession of the whole.

Individual images are frontal. Because of the radial branching outward of all the spatial axes, we always turn to face
every surface, and in a reciprocal manner every surface seems
to be turned toward us. Just as the individual soldier stands
erect, eyes front, without turning or bending, so here the
pilasters, piers, columns, consoles, and balusters stand erect;
and just as soldiers are not only drawn up in straight ranks
but also stand with foreheads and chests level, so too the orders,
frames, and coffers are arranged in planes, in full width and
parallel alignment. This is true of articulated walls and ceilings,
even if they form curved cylindrical or spherical surfaces,
for in an interior view of an apse, everything is turned toward
its center point, and in an exterior view, as for example of the
apses of Bramante's St. Peter's (Fig. 5), all the pilasters form
planes tangential to the radii. They demand our constantly
renewed orientation *perpendicular* to the curved surface.

The importance of the sagittal plane for every part of the
building of this phase makes us conscious that the axial plane
perpendicular to it is also a form-determinant. We see these
members from the front because they are always arranged
prismatically, because a circumscribing four-sided rectangular
prism is always so apparent that we can perceive its axes
immediately. We might see the members of a building obliquely
or in profile as we pass them, but we accept all these separate
perspectives as temporary and predict the frontal view from
each. The immense number of separate images again and
again reverts to the principal views. The principal viewpoints
are identical to the isolated central points of the spaces. Just
as we are psychologically compelled to complete for ourselves
the frontal view of a pilaster, even from a diagonal position,
we are also compelled to complete the perspectives for the
remaining positions as we stand in a spatial center. Everything compels us to see in terms of orthogonal parallel projection.

4. ONE IMAGE

There is an interaction between optical and corporeal
form. Frontality demands the possibility of circumscribing

rectangular prisms round the columns and of the parallel alignment of their complementary planes. On the other hand, these
conditions produce the frontal image. But the independent
variable in this equation is corporeal form; the dependent
variable is optical form. In other words, optical form is dependent upon corporeal form. Certainly, in the first sentence of
this chapter it is stated that optical appearance is primary.
This is still correct: it is always primary with regard to effect,
but in the genetic sense it *can* also be secondary. Optical
appearance can be simply the function of the masses and
spaces formed independently of it—formed in the dark, so
to speak. It is characteristic of the first stylistic phase that
optical appearance is *genetically* secondary.

Not only the frontality of all individual views but also
the character of their synthesis—what I call the architectural
image—ensues from this. The architectural image is not
conceived from fixed viewpoints but remains the unique
three-dimensional conception of the whole. The viewpoints
are coordinated. No matter how many we try out, they continually complement one another. The diagonal views refer us to
the principal viewpoints from which we see objects frontally.
The principal viewpoints are planned. *One* of these viewpoints
suffices to enable us to recognize all the others and to predict
their perspectives or frontal images. My statement that there
are many arbitrary viewpoints but one single constant architectural image is to be understood in this sense.

The architectural image is a unity in contrast to the multiplicity of the separate images. It is unified in the sense of
artistic unification. But I am concerned here only with the
fact that it is *unique*. This one architectural image has nothing
fluid about it; in the end it always leads to the same indestructible, fixed unity. In short, the architecture of the first phase
presents only *one image*.

Second Phase (1550–1700)

1. CONTRAST

In the second phase uniformity of illumination gives
way to increasing contrast of light and dark areas. I am referring to the horizontal juxtaposition of very dark chapels and
bright main spaces as well as to the vertical juxtaposition of
radiantly bright vaults above darker lower spaces. The Gesù
in Rome (Fig. 23) is still relatively moderate in this regard;
the Cappella della SS. Sindone in Turin and S. Lorenzo in
Turin (Fig. 41) are highly developed examples. The introduction
of lunettes is a result of the need for light on the vault. There is
also a correlation with ceiling painting, for as framed paintings increasingly replace coffering, so the need increases for
a ceiling that is a bright, unfolding zone of light rather than
a dark enclosure.[3] It is a symptom of the second phase that
skylights were considered for the ceiling of the vestibule of

the Laurentian Library in Florence. (They were not executed.) The subsequent addition of skylights to buildings of the first phase occurred occasionally, as for example in S. Salvatore in Venice (Fig. 15). The distinction here does not lie in a different degree of intensity of light—for both phases created very bright and rather dark spaces—but solely in the way light is distributed. The side niches off the radiantly bright space of the Cappella Sistina, 1585, at Sta. Maria Maggiore in Rome are so dark that the paintings they contain must be illuminated by floodlights.[4]

Such sudden transitions from bright to dark to bright are also characteristic of the individual details. Cornices now project farther and are occasionally designed so that part of the lower moldings nearly disappears in shadow. Projection becomes uneven, however: the gables above niches, aediculae, windows, and doors produce heavy masses of shadow, whereas the vertical jambs are rather flat. The unevenness of the shadow is also connected with the splitting of members, already mentioned, and in turn enhances the effect of splitting. Finally, in the Cattedra Petri, 1657, in St. Peter's in the Vatican, light becomes a material component of the composition.

The lack of color, or monochromy, replaces the clear coloring and gay polychromy of the first phase. Michelangelo still used the contrast between dark articulation and white walls (for example, in the Medici Chapel [Fig. 75] and the Laurentian Library [Fig. 59]). Palladio composed the interior of the Redentore in Venice and his other churches in a uniform tone. But when color is still used, its effect is changed. Marble with pronounced veins is now preferred. Red marble with large white blotches, reminiscent of Veronese salami, is now common, as well as brown, violet, and yellow marbles with vigorous, warm tones and permeated by a conspicuous, glowing, and very animated pattern of veins. The main examples of the use of such luxurious marbles are the Cappella Gaddi, 1574, at Sta. Maria Novella in Florence, and (to an even greater degree) the Cappella Niccolini, 1579, at Sta. Croce in Florence; the Cappella dei Principi, 1604, at S. Lorenzo in Florence; Sta. Maria della Vittoria in Rome, 1605; the Gesù e Maria in Rome, 1640; Sta. Caterina da Siena in Rome, 1638; Sta. Maria degli Scalzi in Venice, 1646. (Exceptions can be found in Florence where tradition remained on guard.)

Marble incrustation is also a decisive factor in the final appearance of St. Peter's in the Vatican. The simplest and most restful marble is found in the right anterior ancillary center, decorated under Gregory XIII about 1580 (including the pavement). The left anterior ancillary center, decorated about 1601 under Clement VIII, is richer and more complicated. The incrustation of the entrance to the crypt, 1614, is more colorful and has very agitated veins.

The polish of the marble on flat areas produces undefined,

constantly changing reflections, which overlie the pattern of the stone itself.

The incrustation of the lower surfaces in Sta. Maria della Vittoria in Rome is continued by the gilded stuccowork in the vault, which is so interrupted by the floating white angels with their ribbons and drapery that the result is a confusion of white and gold in which details are scarcely distinguishable. The very agitated white figures do not stand out in clear relief against the gold background because both figures and background are of equal chromatic value.

2. LACK OF CLARITY

A partial reduction or removal of objective clarity is the result of the unevenness of light and of the independent role of color, which is now free from all structural significance and spreads out like a speckled, wavy, and mottled coat. Some areas remain bright and clear; others are dim and hazy. Thus are formed on one hand sharply defined images, which have great attraction for the eye, and on the other hand subsidiary areas over which our glance slides, or in which—even if it wants to tarry—it is unable to achieve full understanding of the details. In both the clear and the vague images, our ability to grasp outlines is very much reduced by the clustering of supports, interpenetration, and fusion and splitting. These features are combined with a general exploitation of shadows, especially deep shadows, and of colors that lead a life of their own. Even the strongly illuminated areas remain unclear in comparison with the impressions of the first phase.

3. THE DIAGONAL VIEW

This extreme lack of clarity gives to the whole composition a quality of restless allure. We hope to understand it better by becoming familiar with it. The uneven illumination subordinates the vague, isolated vistas to those that are clear, the optically dull to the optically interesting.

On the exterior the main façade is now an independent image, freed from the appearance of the lateral façades as well as from that of the interior. The diagonal view now becomes a principal point of reference, because the dull lateral façade is a foil for the main façade. The view of any separate elevation does not satisfy us, since the others cannot be deduced from it.

In the interior, however, that intriguing quality of the unequal images is linked with the principle of spatial division. The great flood of movement that urges us round and through the building does not by any means permit us to look about us with equal comfort in every direction. We are always turned in the direction of the current, and the images to right and left become uninteresting in themselves and are only fleetingly comprehended (as long as we surrender ourselves to the effect of the space, without wanting to consider the individual details such as altars and epitaphs). The subordinated images are seen diagonally in passing. It is true that they can usually be seen frontally too, but in the second phase this frontal view is just one among many and quite the least important.

Where we are concerned with the impression created by divisions that have been subsequently introduced into the space (such as galleries, colonnades, and bridges), confusion occurs because of the large number of interpenetrations and the obscuring of significant boundary lines and planes. Even if we place ourselves frontally toward the side aisle, chapel, and gallery of each bay, we usually see the adjacent bays at the same time. We see them diagonally, and this is how we are supposed to see them.[5]

This preference for the diagonal view is manifested in the individual details, because the symmetrical parts of the frame turn slightly away from or toward one another. The tabernacle of St. Theresa, 1645, in Sta. Maria della Vittoria in Rome (Fig. 84) and the altar in S. Tomaso da Villanova in Castel Gandolfo (near Rome), 1661, are examples of this. Wavy façades, such as S. Carlo alle Quattro Fontane in Rome, 1665 (Fig. 87), obviously demand diagonal views. So indeed do spaces that are composed according to the sixty-degree angle.

4. MANY IMAGES

Optical appearance is now primary not only for the impression (receptively) but also genetically. The corporeal forms exist only to carry the visible phenomenon. They serve light, not the reverse as in the first phase. And even if the corporeal forms are characterized by the idea of force transmission, in the sense of mechanical forces, they also appear to suffer under the influence of light and shadow, reflections and colors, and the distortions of the perspective view, insofar as they might be separated; and they appear to be torn apart, insofar as they belong together. Finally, the architectural image itself is destroyed. Not only does the individual image, viewed from a fixed point, in one direction, disintegrate into something irregular and diverse, but the total conception of the optical image becomes multiplex.

In the first phase the corporeal forms all appear transparent, as if overlap, which is a necessary occurrence, played no role at all. We believe we can see every column, every pilaster simultaneously and continuously from all sides. We believe we can always fully comprehend, from the outside so to speak, each of the spaces that are thrust together by addition. The forms of the second phase become optical obstructions. Masses and spaces are pushed into one another, and since they always seem to be incomplete, we cannot imagine how they would be perceived from another viewpoint. The individual perspective is no longer the preliminary to the architectural image but has its own significance. It exists together with the other separate images as a partial representation.

If we yield to this optical fascination, or if, as students of

87. Rome, S. Carlo alle Quattro
Fontane. Façade, 1665.

architecture, we pace the building, investigating every detail and peering behind every corner, we finally gain an exact knowledge of its form of existence. But this does not in the least change the impression we derive over and over again from every viewpoint. We know that as a whole this image is caused by something invariable, but this invariable is only of scientific interest. Knowledge of it is gained only for the sake of artistic pedagogy; artistically only the impression of change has value. It is unnecessary here also to explore every viewpoint. We immediately survey the situation and perceive that this first image is unstable, momentary, accidental. From a second and third viewpoint the building becomes something we had not expected, and what we have already seen will now seem entirely different. These separate images cannot be reciprocally explained. They are interlocked; they interpenetrate; they fuse into a unit of multiplicity. The compulsion to view objects in gnomonic projection (in perspective) entirely replaces the demand to see them in orthographic projection (in elevation). The architectural image—our conception of the total optical appearance of the building—certainly remains a unit, but it now contains a multiplicity of partial images. *In order to sense this, a view from one spot is sufficient.* We know that what lies before us is a stable entity, but we see it not as a unique phenomenon but as a recurring one. We divine from its intriguing aspect that something new is always awaiting us. Even the individual perspective evokes a profusion of images.

The architecture of the second phase presents *many images.*

Third Phase (Eighteenth Century)

1. AN INFINITE NUMBER OF IMAGES

The character of the spatial forms of the third phase, which are based upon infinitesimal calculus, reduces the number of frontal views to a minimum. If we stand frontally before a spatial part or corporeal form, we see everything else diagonally. The breaking up of the continuity in a secular building, its disintegration into wings and pavilions, means that we never see these fragments as isolated, independent masses but view them in relation to the spaces between them: the court, park, or square (Fig. 92).

The external architectural image is viewed in the same way as the internal one. Even if we traverse the interior of each pavilion, we do not obtain a unified image of the interaction of spaces and spatial complexes but, rather, a profusion of partial images. It is true that these belong to one artistically unified object, but they yield only a part of the whole, so that no single view of it can be optically exhaustive. The most precise knowledge of every stairway, corridor, hall, and room, such as perhaps the inhabitant himself possesses, does not change this at all. The lord of the palace and his household know the existential form, but the optical appearance does not always produce a single total image.

The corporeal forms do not have the character of transparency that they had in the secular buildings of the first phase. In the second and third phases they yield always new, unforeseen discoveries. The third phase is distinguished from the second only because in the later period the number of partial images is increased as much as possible to create the effect of *infinitely more* images.[6]

This effect is reinforced by the fact that the reflecting surfaces exposed to light are scattered as much as possible and emerge from the deepest shadows. The incoherent reflections from gilt and bronze are intended, by means of their optical effect, to heighten the sense of discontinuity in the corporeal forms. They glitter and sparkle. A highly reflective polish is still more generally employed than in the second phase. Mirrors partly cancel out the wall. Placed opposite one another as purely optical phenomena, they completely destroy the effect of spaces bounded by masses. The Galerie des Glaces at Versailles and the Spiegelkabinett in the Residenz at Würzburg (Fig. 88) are good examples.

Perhaps the extreme development in the increase of images was reached by the wrought-iron screens that divide church choirs or vestibules from the nave of many eighteenth-century German churches (Fig. 89). They are themselves highly complicated in design and, when seen against the ecclesiastical space behind them, have the effect of a veil. Neither the veil nor the space it conceals can be clearly distinguished, and when we attempt to clarify the image by moving closer to it or to one side, the complexity of the overlapping forms only increases. (There are screens in the churches at Zwiefalten and Amorbach, and in St. John Nepomuk in Munich.) Confusion reaches its highest development here. Especially in churches such as St. John Nepomuk (Fig. 52), we shall find that if we walk to the choir and then turn to look at the entrance, we shall believe that we have entered a different building.[7]

2. A SINGLE VIEWPOINT

The diagonal disposition of symmetrically balanced columns, pilasters, consoles, and of ressauts in entablatures and gables is quite common in the third phase. They no longer stand in rank and file, and even when they form a common straight line in plan, they face in different directions. Nonetheless there is no arbitrary confusion. We do not think of them as a military company that has been dismissed, so that each man turns where he pleases. There remains an orderly interplay that is best compared to a ballet. The essential thing is that we are not seated *before* a stage on which the ballet is being performed but are encircled by the dance.

89. Zwiefalten, Abbey Church.
Interior.

I am no longer thinking here of the effect of the corporeal forms themselves and of their play of forces, which were dealt with in the preceding chapter; I am thinking exclusively of the restlessness of the optical impression. The impossibility of guessing from one view the appearance of the next and the feeling of confronting a crowded succession of surprises become characteristic of the architectural image. One glance from one spot is sufficient to detect this. But the consequence of the infinite number of individual perspectives is that now *one* definite point is prescribed from which the entire architectural image appears complete and without distortion. Ceiling paintings are designed for this *one* viewpoint. The clouds and figures projecting plastically, or painted on cutout sheet metal, appear from this one point only to overflow the picture frame. Standing in this spot, we have the impression of an infinite number of images confronting or encircling us, although we see only one.

In these extreme cases the third phase is the absolute polar opposite of the classic examples of the first phase. In the first phase we always see *(cum grano salis)* the same architectural image from an infinite number of viewpoints; in the third phase we see an infinite number of partial images from *one* viewpoint. The impression of many images of the second phase is here augmented into the impression of an infinite, inexhaustible number of images.

Fourth Phase (Nineteenth Century)

The fourth phase begins with a very decided return to the single image. The frontal view and tonal flatness again predominate. Precise, harsh color contrasts replace the imprecise colors of the third phase. But inasmuch as the colors retain some delicacy, this phase does not manifest a complete return to the first phase. The legacy of the second and third phases is still preserved. The heavy, deep shadow is not entirely overlooked; it occurs in the colonnades in contrast to the delicate relief of the rest of the exterior (Fig. 86). Polished surfaces often coexist with rough ones, as on floors or wooden furniture. The lack of color in Palladio's buildings, which was considered genuinely Hellenic, becomes standard in many cases, and "white halls" in palaces appear side by side with delicately toned, polychrome ones. The mirror is no longer used to confuse form, as it was in the third phase, but it does not entirely vanish from the architectural context.

As soon as medieval buildings, in addition to Greek and Roman antiquities, become prototypes, the architectural image, like the spatial and corporeal form, is dependent upon these. The nineteenth century has no simple, fixed relationship to the polarity of optical appearance. It tolerates both poles.

I can say in summary that the optical appearance of post-medieval architecture is in the first phase composed of *one image;* in the second, of *many images.* In the third phase, the impression of many images is augmented to an impression of an *infinite number of images.* The fourth phase begins half-heartedly with a return to the concept of one image and in its further development loses any definite relationship to the two poles.

4 Purposive Intention

Spatial form is crystallized round center points and center lines (vertical, horizontal, and diagonal) which, in a schematic but concentrated way, indicate the prevailing movement—movement in the general sense, including repose as a special case. When the space is composed by addition, this network of movement disintegrates into isolated static points strung along connecting, quiet, intermediary axes, and on the other hand, when the space is composed by subdivision, it becomes the arterial system of a continuous flow. This network of movement is not entirely a creation of ornamental fancy because it is involved with actual purposes. The center lines become paths through the space. They direct circulation between places equipped to serve appointed purposes. The movement infused into a space has thus a double effect: insofar as it derives from the contrast between addition and division, it applies to intuition; insofar as it derives from purpose, it applies to intellect. It is apparent, therefore, that the effective lines of movement are not exactly the same. Rather, two different networks appear to lie one above the other, partially covering each other but always standing in a reciprocal relationship to one another. In a church of the first phase, for example, the schema of movement is reduced to a series of isolated center points only as long as we overlook the purpose of the space. Circulation between the furnishings distributed within the space (altars, organ, pulpit, confessionals, baptismal font, choir stalls) produces a second network of movement, however. The first network forms the soul of the building; the second, its mind.

There exist within every space something that appeals to emotion and something else that appeals to reason. We are concerned with the latter here. The meaning of a space derives solely from its furnishings, and thus it is a grave error to attempt to explain architecture aesthetically or historically without them. The church in Neubirnau on Lake Constance, 1746, for example, is particularly characteristic of the spatial, corporeal, and visible forms of the third phase, but because it is now empty, it resembles a blown egg. And every space that has lost its original furnishings has the same plundered, lifeless effect. Most of the objects customarily treated separately in the history of decorative art belong entirely to architecture. They alone give it its emotional and intellectual existence.[1]

When I speak of purpose in architecture, I mean that architecture forms the fixed arena for actions of specific duration, that it provides the path for a definite sequence of events. Just as these have their logical development, so the sequence of spaces, and so too the principal and secondary passages existing within each space, have their logic. The clearly prescribed circulation, which leads us through the different spaces in an opera house, through the vestibule to the ticket office, or through the corridors and up steps to a cloakroom, presupposes a definitely ordered activity, and the spatial form is completely dependent upon the particular type of activity.

In churches, concert halls, and lecture halls there are within the whole arrangement two groups confronting one another, one giving and one receiving: there are both tension and relaxation. Even when the action is one-way, so to speak, as in the case of a collection of inanimate objects in a museum, gallery, exhibition, or store, the arrangement of these objects, on pedestals, along the walls, in niches, in showcases, or on racks, determines an ordered procession of thoughtful spectators. Whether there is just one person or a file or group of people walking through, absorbed in the objects on display, there is always this human activity—this viewing or shopping—that infuses something logical and conceptual into the crystalline, inanimate, geometric space.

The words "purpose of architecture" readily bring to mind the suitability of construction, mechanical strength, and durability of a building. They as easily bring to mind such reasonable requests as, for example, the avoidance of a broken gable, since the purpose of a gable is to shed water. We also think of the need for suitable illumination, which will certainly be somewhat different in a picture gallery and in a church. I am referring not to the requirements of mass or light, however, but solely to the purpose of the spatial form. Nor am I talking about the most commonplace purposes, nor about purpose in its narrowest definition. I am discussing it in a more general sense: insofar as purpose is the essence of architecture, architecture is its material manifestation.

Today buildings are erected for common purposes in which we ourselves are involved. We understand without explanation the spaces created for these purposes. But now the variety is so great that not everyone understands every building. A person who is at home in archives, libraries, universities, and museums probably needs special instruction about the operations governing factories, hospitals, prisons, and lunatic asylums. If we study the buildings of older cultures and find one lacking its original fittings because, for example, what was once a monastery is now a courthouse, then our need *to know* something becomes still more conspicuous. The spectator who is without historical knowledge has even greater need for the right reference when confronted by a building designed for an obsolete purpose. He sees a great display of artistic forms but does not perceive why they exist. For him they are mere ornament. As his historical knowledge grows, he can begin vaguely to reconstruct the essence of the building, but the exact reconstruction of its essence is a matter of very special study. Many people can surrender themselves to poetic or sentimental moods in a well-preserved medieval castle, but only the few who have a vivid conception of the weapons and the conduct of war in that period will *understand* it.

This interpretation of architectural monuments as molded theaters of human activity, then, is a parallel to iconography, which names the figures and explains the events represented in painting and sculpture. A painting and a piece of sculpture remain merely ornamental unless we understand their content; even if we are satisfied by a rather general recognition of a tree or a rock, an animal or a man, our understanding of the image is incomplete if by means of these objects it is intended to narrate a specific incident, such as the angel appearing to Joachim. When a generation ceases to have a vital interest in a certain content, the image becomes unintelligible to the multitude. But the visible surface remains, and to the historian it is a sign that a new epoch is beginning, when he sees a certain subject matter becoming obsolete. The variety of interpretations of one and the same scene represented many times within a period, however, is a key to the development of intellectual values. A series of iconographical studies of different contemporaneous themes will, therefore, always lead to the same result, explain the same intellectual development from different angles, and see the same moving force manifested in different materials.

Little has been done hitherto for the history of architecture in this area, perhaps because it is precisely here that the difficulties are so great. Buildings may last mechanically and chemically longer than pictures, but their life span as living works of art is often much shorter.

It has frequently been said that the theater of the Residenz in Munich, filled with the court society of 1753, was not the same then as it is today. People are part of architecture. This too distinguishes architecture from both painting and sculpture, for we do not stand in front of a building but are surrounded by it. Architecture and people interact. The general purpose of the theater in the Munich Residenz has at least remained the same; it is still in constant use as a theater. But the convent in Kempten is now a courthouse. Legal proceedings are now held in the Fürstensaal (about 1740), and the equipment necessary for these proceedings has been installed. The convent at Ebrach has become a prison. But even when an eighteenth-century palace retains some or all of its furnishings, and tourists are guided round its rooms, it is still a mummy. Such a palace is incomplete because festivals are no longer celebrated in it. There are no more theater and ballet performances held before a tipsy audience, which has been driven up to the door in light carriages, with liveried servants, and which has amused itself in the evening with a splendid fireworks display in the park. The one integrating element in all these palaces was destroyed forever in the French Revolution. A painting can be interpreted and brought to life again, because the figures remain in it always. A building dies as soon as the life within it has vanished, even if we know the customs of the people who once belonged to it.

Nevertheless, a trace of this vanished life remains behind in a building to the extent that the purpose is incarnated in the form of the space. This is purpose in a very general sense and does not include specific incidents. It is unnecessary to know what sort of compliments were paid at those festivals or how people laughed and lied, for these are details that never affect architecture. More influential are the meaning of the festival in the life of the patron and the predominance of artistically decorated state rooms over work spaces. Detailed knowledge of the course of such festivities will deepen our appreciation of a palace, just as an understanding of the conduct of war will deepen our appreciation of a castle. We must know how a society entertained itself, whether it favored tournaments or tilting at the ring on horseback, whether the court included jesters and dwarfs, whether music and dance were more common than conversation and cards, and how people dined. Each of these aspects of life forms part of the building program and, indeed, modifies that program according to the significance that each enjoys.

A history of building programs is therefore part of cultural history, and my task would be easier if studies in cultural history were more advanced, although I am concerned only with a *part* of these studies. It has long since been observed that a connection exists between the two disciplines; only the nature of this connection has been disputed. It was once customary to sketch a picture of a civilization as a grand backdrop for the period of artistic development under consideration. But the fault of this method was that the background contained a great deal that had no influence upon artistic development, or that the influential factors were either lacking or were not brought into sharp relief. The bridge between art and life remained undiscovered. This bridge is nothing other than the building program, the purpose in general, and for that reason it is difficult to begin with the cultural image, to go from the infinite number of bridges to all aspects of life. The opposite path is easier. We must begin with art itself and there seek the threads that bind it to civilization in general. Cultural history is not to be understood as a mere collection of data from public and private life. It is, rather, the ordering of these data round centers of thought that imply change in social expression.

It is true that those broad historical and cultural backgrounds also sought the mood of a period, the all-pervasive hue that colors even the art. Since this hue is hardly anywhere else as evident as it is in art, however, art history can do without those backgrounds.

It is clear therefore that I do not need to write in this chapter a cultural history from the fifteenth to the nineteenth century. I am concerned exclusively with finding the few or the most important bridges connecting the dead spatial forms with contemporary patterns of life and showing that in each phase the patterns of life were fundamentally different.

I still have not reached the heart of the problem however. If purpose, to the extent that it exists as a space-determining factor in the building program, is the spiritual core of architecture and forms the bridge between architecture and culture in general (of which architecture is only one aspect among many), then the history of purpose is a longitudinal section through one branch of cultural history, a longitudinal section cut, not along the central axis, but, so to speak, along a side aisle. A history of this kind, however, will always contribute to our knowledge of *cultural* history rather than to our knowledge of *art* history. This longitudinal section will also offer an explanation of artistic development only if it shows that a constant and fundamental relationship to art is expressed in a whole series of building programs, no matter how much they might differ in detail. The program of any building, even those without artistic pretensions, is a document of cultural history. There is thus a second, higher factor underlying the building program that approximates what Burckhardt (for architecture) and Wölfflin (for painting and sculpture) called intention. It is the practical and material certainty of purpose that determines the building program and hence the spatial form, but only intention gives to purpose its artistic character.

In this chapter I shall discuss the history of purposive intention. Not much more can be expected than that I state the problem clearly. The necessary preparation, which still remains to be carried out, would have delayed the completion of this book for years.

First Phase (1420–1550)

1. THIRST FOR GLORY

Sigismondo Malatesta built the church of S. Francesco in Rimini (Fig. 67) "to honor himself and the beautiful Isotta." Pippo Spano donated Sta. Maria degli Angeli in Florence (Fig. 3A) "so that a monument and a memorial to himself might be present at his homecoming." Among the motives imputed to the architectural undertakings of Pope Nicholas V were "the honor and glory of the Apostolic Chair, and the promotion of Christian devotion and the preservation of its special glory through immortal buildings." Nicholas, of course, said something quite different in his last testament: "We have not begun all these buildings out of ambition or love of splendor, or from a vain thirst for glory or inordinate longing to immortalize our name." He is obviously referring to the reproach provoked by his activities. We expect him to continue by saying that these works were begun *in maiorem dei gloriam,* but instead he adds that they were meant for

"the elevation of the reputation of the Apostolic Chair throughout the whole of Christianity, so that future popes might no
longer be banished, taken prisoner, besieged, or otherwise
oppressed." The number of similar remarks preserved from
the first phase is very great and is supplemented by the testimony of the works themselves. The donors of chapels in
churches vied with each other in their decoration, permitted
enormous sums to be spent on them, and saw to it by the display of coats of arms and portraits that their fellow citizens
for generations to come remembered their family name. But
we should not conclude from this custom that these men were
sacrilegious. They erected monuments to themselves, but not
in quite such an obvious manner, for they remained within
the framework of the Church. They honored God by what
seemed to be most artistically perfect and placed themselves
very conspicuously close by: personal thirst for glory and
concern for salvation were coordinated.

2. SUBORDINATION OF RELIGIOUS TO ARTISTIC INTERESTS

This intention now corresponds to an occasional contempt
for liturgical requirements. The fully developed central-plan
church demands an altar in the center of the main space. If the
altar is pushed against the wall, as in Bramante's Tempietto,
the meaning and form of the space do not exactly coincide.
In the Tempietto the focus is on the spot where St. Peter suf-
fered martyrdom; thus the circular latticed opening in the floor,
which provides a view into the crypt, is also a spiritual center.
St. Peter's in the Vatican marks the saint's grave. The steps
descending into the crypt are the focal point, and the high
altar stands behind them. The altar in this church is thus freestanding. This placing of the altar is badly suited to the Catholic
liturgy, for there are very definite gestures prescribed for the
priest celebrating Mass, some of which are directed toward the
altar and others toward the congregation. The congregation
should be on one side of the altar; it should not surround it.
Nonetheless, the architects of this stylistic phase were determined to have freestanding altars, even in longitudinal churches
with a choir. The center point beneath the dome that covers the
crossing was esteemed for purely aesthetic reasons the most
worthy location for the altar. Examples are the cathedral and
Sto. Spirito in Florence. The congregation had to be content
with a view obscured partly by the superstructure of the altar
and partly by barriers.[2]

But when the center of the centralized church was left
free and altars were placed against the walls of all the available
niches, the problem arose of adequately emphasizing one high
altar intended for the most solemn Masses, for as a result of
the over-all coordination, it remained spatially unaccented.
With the exception of the baptistry and the memorial church,
there was no place within Catholicism for the central-plan
church. Baptistries were no longer erected, and memorial

churches were very rare. Nevetheless, the preference for the central-plan church is characteristic of the first phase insofar as it develops out of the principle of spatial addition. Thus the erection of centralized sacristies, chapels, and parish churches proves that this phase was prepared somewhat to neglect the material claims of the liturgy in order to satisfy artistic ideals.

The sacraments were tolerated, and their sanctity as a whole was certainly increased by the perfection of the house that sheltered them, but this perfection had nothing directly to do with the Christian religion. It is of course Christ who is honored in these churches, who is imparted in the miracle of the Host to the multitude of the faithful, but the feeling of complete independence produced by spatial addition, radiation of force, and the concept of one image is opposed to the idea of sin and redemption.

It is true that a Christian service takes place in these churches, but they seem to have been destined for a divine service of a different kind and to be inhabited by a different deity—by an Epicurean deity perhaps, or by the ideal of absolute perfection. These churches bear no resemblance to antique temples, and the ancients would certainly not have found it easy to use them for their cults. We thus realize that the paganism of the first phase is still rather relative.[3] Christianity remained a vital force among the great majority. A church had to be the molded theater of the unchangeable Catholic liturgy. The real alienation of its innermost content, however—its approximation to the antique—originated in the Humanistic movement, which had to a considerable extent altered the religious ideas in the circles that furnished the patrons: the highest princes of the church and the secular authorities.

Architecture does not reflect the detailed aspects of Humanism, its grammatical niceties, its precise linguistic teaching or antiquarian knowledge, or the rude quarrels of jealous philologists. But it does reflect the liberalism and freedom of the ancients—never openly stated but everywhere implied—in all problems of science, ethics, and religion that flowed from the antique writers toward the Humanists, releasing them from unquestioning subjection to dogma and to the sacraments. Through the living ideal of Humanism, the freedom of the ancients was spread in wider circles.

Perhaps a consistent paganism is extremely rare, but a consistent Christianity is equally rare: a mixture of both cultures appears in a thousand variations. A liberalism based upon antiquity predominated in the leading social classes. Alberti, Leonardo, and Bramante designed churches, it is true, and certainly gave thought to the Catholic liturgy, but they demanded that it comply with *their* ideals of form and made it subordinate to unchristian concepts of architecture.

The equipping of sacred buildings with ecclesiastical furnishings was a concession to the multitudes for whom Christianity still prevailed. The church in which the Humanist feels the presence of a Platonic ideal, and in which at the same time the faithful receive the sacraments, is the result of a juxtaposition of antique liberalism on the part of the Humanists and Christian subjection on the part of the people. This is not at all surprising, since the faithful were also often in contact with Humanism. This personal union was projected into the architecture.

We can say, therefore, that the ecclesiastical building of the first phase makes room for every liturgical act; that its spatial form is determined by purpose, to the extent that its use for a different purpose is inconceivable; and that it cannot be thought of as a place for assemblies and popular festivals. The meaning of the liturgy is, however, so deeply affected by Humanist thinking that a pagan spirit, in which purposeless harmony and artistic perfection reign supreme, decides the form of the church to a much greater degree than Christian needs.[4] This subordination of the interests of religion to those of art indicates that the society of this period, which aspired to the harmonious expression of all its talents, certainly did not place religion foremost in intellectual life but considered it as *one* aspect among many of equal importance.

3. COORDINATION OF PURPOSES IN ECCLESIASTICAL ARCHITECTURE

If for the moment we set aside this equalization of the importance of purely artistic and religious interests and compare the liturgical determination of the churches of the first phase with that of the churches of other phases or epochs, we shall realize that in this phase no one aspect of the divine service, no one specific function, is especially predominant.

We cannot say that the clergy is given visible prominence. It is true that it has its own special area in the church and, unlike the laity, its own pews (as in the Middle Ages), but the choir is still not spatially emphasized more than the other arms. We cannot say that the church is considered primarily for the importance of the sermon. The period idealized great spatial dimensions without regard for acoustics. Nor can we say that the size of the space is really determined by the large congregation. The crowds of pilgrims certainly had an effect upon the building of St. Peter's in the Vatican, but its vastness has its own aesthetic meaning, which goes beyond practical purpose. Nor can we say that it is a processional church: its spatial form was not determined by the moment of highest solemnity.

The rite as a whole is secondary, and all its separate manifestations are coordinated with one another. The role of *these* purposes in the spatial form betrays the fact that the essential purpose of the church is something different. The church is the house of God, His throne room, but not His audience hall. Both clergy and laity are guests in it. They are actually superfluous, or at least unimportant, because that Supreme, Perfect, Independent Being enthroned within it does not trouble Himself about the worshiping crowd. He exists whether there is divine service or not. He is so independent that He needs no one dependent upon Him in order to feel the highest freedom. Man and God confront one another as separate powers.

I can thus say in summary that the first phase permits none of the individual liturgical functions to predominate in the ecclesiastical building. They become of little importance because they are basically meaningless to the Being who dwells within, aloof and eternal. The purpose of the church is to be a monument to God and, insofar as He Himself does not erect it, a monument to the donor or donors who, according to the medieval way of thinking, perhaps, hope for benefits for their salvation, but for whom earthly glory is absolutely of prime importance.

4. COORDINATION OF PURPOSES IN SECULAR ARCHITECTURE

Courtyards, corridors, and staircases provide for the main circulation in secular buildings. Their only purpose is to connect the rooms that are the setting for the private lives of the master of the house, his family, his servants, and his guests. If we ask about the uses of the individual apartments in, for example, the Palazzo Medici in Florence (Fig. 90), we shall learn that there is a clear coordination of purposes here too. The palace has private living rooms, rooms in which the patron conducts his business, guest rooms, housekeeping rooms, stables, store rooms, chambers for the servants, and a private chapel. The ground floor is so arranged that the house can be defended. But not one of these uses is predominant. It was absolutely necessary that the palace be defensible because of political uncertainties and the continuing family feuds, but it is not a fortress. The house is hospitable; it was not planned to amaze the guests by a show of wealth. Even the private family rooms are not artistically accented. All the individual purposes appear to be equal aspects of the main purpose. The building is intended to absorb evenly the life of the patron in all its complexity, and there is nothing to prevent us from seeing this coordination of purposes as a result of the desire for uniform development of personality, as long as we confine ourselves only to those aspects of personality that really are reflected in the building.

The complexity and harmony of material and intellectual refinement, which is the ideal of the leading social classes, cannot be expressed exactly in a dwelling, nor can it be found in a palace of the *Cortigiano*.[5] This book is no substitute for a palace, but a palace is nonetheless the consequence of the ideal of life that is verbally preserved in the *Cortigiano*: all the rooms in the house should be equally and continuously

90. Florence, Palazzo Medici, 1444.
Plan.

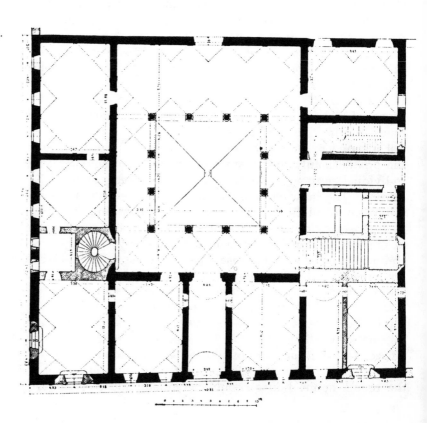

used; the purposes of the individual rooms should correspond to the actual activities of the inhabitant; the reality of life—not its mere forms—is most important. Art enhances every aspect of life, just as the lord of the house himself feels enhanced by his independent personality, by the vigorous use of all of his talents, and by his great abilities. Art and life advance on all fronts, and just as personality acquires a certain clarity and roundness, so too the dwelling has its dignity, as if the proud owner had nothing to conceal but at the same time nothing special to emphasize. He displays his whole self, because he knows how to maintain all aspects of his existence at an equal level.

A dwelling is not the literal expression of all its owner's talents but on the whole a monument to his aspiration to harmony for its own sake. Individual purposes all have equal importance for the master of the house, and for him alone. He has no desire to impress outsiders. He does impress them by the perfection of each separate purpose, but he perfects these for themselves, for domestic consumption so to speak. To the extent that all palaces of the first phase have something about them that is noble and distinct, they are preoccupied with themselves; they soliloquize; they are undramatic; they stand as independent entities in a world completely dissolved into similar independent entities.

The palace is a monument to power, to wealth, to taste, to ability, to a refined way of living. As a whole it is a monument to its owner's glory, his self-acquired glory. The palace is the concomitant result of glory; it is not erected through affectation for the purpose of creating glory or merely through blatant emphasis of one especially preferred aspect of life.

In this sense the first phase is characterized by the authenticity of its purposes. The patrons may have been treacherous in political battle against their rivals. They may have been vain, but on the whole they were not petty. They felt their worth without the testimony of others, were true to themselves, and lived in reality the role they played.

5. PURPOSES CONCEIVED CENTRIPETALLY

In secular as in ecclesiastical architecture of the first phase, purposes are coordinated. The building is a monument to an independent personality to whom alone are linked all the purposes united within it. These purposes are conceived centripetally: they surround an intellectual core that seeks to mold its existence in complete independence of the external world.

I am not referring here to the geometrical isolation of spatial form or of the mechanical freedom of the corporeal forms as centers of force. I am talking about intellectual freedom. This is analogous to the independence of space and mass and can be metaphorically applied to them, but the two concepts are not identical. The purposes considered for themselves alone detach the building intellectually from the rest of the intellectual world.

For the present, then, I can say that the purposes of the first phase are conceived centripetally.

Second Phase (1550–1700)

At the moment it is impossible to define precisely the boundary in time between the first and the second phases of the history of purpose, because there are too few preliminary studies in this area, which is not directly perceptible to the senses. What I say here, then, makes very little claim to completeness. I give some provisional hints and a very general solution to the problem.

1. THE JESUITS

First, I am unable to identify any change in attitude on the part of the patron toward personal glory. Cardinal Alessandro Farnese named himself very conspicuously on the frieze on the façade of the Gesù in Rome (Fig. 81), and the popes, like all other patrons, mounted their coats of arms on all their buildings or secured their share of earthly immortality by the use of inscriptions. It is true that no subsequent pontif planned such an extensive tomb as that of Julius II, but a decline in monumentality cannot be detected in later papal tombs. It would require a special study to determine whether a change in attitude is betrayed in the inscriptions and allegorical figures on tombs.

Thirst for glory remained a principal motive for great architectural projects, and yet we now sense a different emphasis upon religion than existed in earlier churches. According to Burckhardt,[6]

The Counter Reformation provided a new stimulus for church building about the middle of the sixteenth century. Not much was said, but important new buildings appear immediately. Only shortly earlier (about 1540), Serlio had complained in his fifth book about the loss of interest in church building. There is an especially noteworthy increase in building after 1563, that is, after the publication of the conclusions of the Council of Trent. Armenini (*De'veri precetti della pittura*, Ravenna, 1587, p. 19) says that "all over the Christian world people vie with one another in the building of beautiful and costly temples, chapels, monasteries."

But the Council of Trent gave no new rules, in fact *no* rules at all, for ecclesiastical architecture.[7]

The Jesuits had the decisive voice in the Council of Trent, and at that time they had not yet concerned themselves with architecture. They had many other concerns in the beginning: missionary work at home and abroad, preaching, rules for the efficacy of confession and for moral teaching, instruction, conquest of the order's extraordinary privileges, and the establishment, extension, and government of the order itself. They were always on the move and frequently did their preaching on street corners, especially in the beginning. Wherever they went, they utilized parish churches or the churches of other orders. If they settled in one place to found a school, they were assigned a certain altar in one of the local churches. Choral singing was forbidden to them by Ignatius Loyola. Thus for the first decade of their existence there was a lack of interest in an architecture appropriate to their dignity. In the beginning they were oriented so exclusively to religious activities that art was a secondary consideration for them. But once the order was fully established and the building of individual churches began, the ascendancy of religion over art was assured.

Much credit can be given to the Jesuits for their adaptability to the individuals whom they wanted to reach, and this has given rise to the belief that they also employed art only as a means to an end, that they built artistically in order to attract people. Whether or not this was their point of view can scarcely be demonstrated; certainly they intended to build *in maiorem dei gloriam.* And even if art was actually used to seduce the faithful, to intoxicate their senses with beauty and splendor, this was never a self-centered purpose, as in the first phase, but a purpose subordinated to religious, ecclesiastical-political—or at least ecclesiastical—purposes. Although the thirst for glory did not in itself disappear, piety was in the ascendancy to such a degree that the thirst for glory retreated into the background. Finally, the Jesuits represented an institution, and personal glory no longer had the same meaning for this collective patron as it had earlier for an individual.

2. SUBORDINATION OF ARTISTIC TO RELIGIOUS INTERESTS

The displacement of Humanistic ideals by the churchliness of the Counter Reformation is directly reflected in church building by the predominance of liturgical interests over purely artistic ones. The main altar in the Gesù in Rome does not stand beneath the dome, but in the choir (Fig. 23). There are other altars at the ends of the transepts and in the chapels, but they are against the wall. The position of the *baldacchino* in the center of St. Peter's in the Vatican during the seventeenth century was an exception; the altar had already been placed there. The removal of the altar from the center of the space made the longitudinal church more common than the centralized church and changed the essential character of the centralized church (when it was still used) into something specifically ecclesiastical because of the emphasis upon its periphery.

The Mass now regains its full significance. The altar becomes the spiritual center, and its favorable position becomes the point of departure for the design. Clergy and laity also receive different emphasis. The choir surpasses the transepts in size because it is reserved for the clergy. Nave and crossing are reserved for the laity. The side chapels are connected by doors so that the priest celebrating Mass has his own entrance to the separate adjacent altars. The space resolves itself into the great central hall, where the people congregate, and the surrounding peripheral passage, which contains the altars. The relationship between clergy and people becomes the essential element. Despite the intimate relationship between the two, their separation is made very apparent. They are no longer the coordinately united multitude of God's guests. And the socially privileged laymen themselves regain their special positions in the galleries, and above all in the *coretti* and loges in the choir—positions that are in the immediate vicinity of the clergy and the altar. The privileged are the prince and his retinue, or even the students from the adjacent college, who are not supposed to mix with the crowd. Galleries are common in Jesuit and other monastic churches. The priests living on the adjoining upper floors of the monastery can find their quiet place of silent devotion without being seen or disturbed, and the aged and infirm can still attend Mass without climbing stairs. The Jesuits frequently had large numbers of people at confession, and their galleries also served as confessionals.

The architecture of this period thus reflects the increased significance of the liturgy, the subordination of the laity to the clergy, and the exclusiveness of the court.

It is still not clear whether the galleries were originally reserved entirely or only partially for the clergy and persons of rank. Nor has it been resolved whether the spatial form of the Roman Gesù originated in Italy or in Spain, whether the prototype of the royal church derived from the Jesuit schema or was a collateral manifestation. We recognize for certain, however, the gradual subordination of the laity to the clergy. God dwells in *these* churches as in those of the first phase, but His throne room has also become an audience hall for the multitude. A busy army of priests mediates for this audience, and so the laity, and even God, thrive in dependence upon this priesthood. Priest and layman do not stand together before God. The priest stands between God and the laity.

The clergy is no longer secluded as it was in the Middle Ages. A Jesuit is not supposed to make amends for the sins of the world by an excess of piety. He is not an agent or substitute for the laity and does not relieve it of the task of religion. He is supposed to jolt the conscience of the laity unceasingly, to arouse in every Christian the desire for closer participation in religious life. A clergy such as this does not shut itself up in a monks' choir with its own altar or remain behind a rood screen in front of which is a special altar for the laity. This is the distinction between the architecture of this phase and that of the Middle Ages.[8]

The second phase of post-medieval architecture does not go back to the Gothic for its building program. The two are related because both accentuate the liturgy, and in this they are clearly separated from the first phase, but the second phase differs from the Gothic in the essential question of the building program. The *ascendancy* of the clergy is common to the Middle Ages and the Counter Reformation, but the latter brought the clergy into closer contact with the laity. This is expressed architecturally by the handling of the confessional. I know of no confessionals of artistic merit that date from the first phase.[9] The second phase not only made the confessional equal in importance to the choir stall by means of its decoration but also provided for it, as for the choir stall, a fixed position in the space. It was no longer a dismountable piece of furniture that could be set up anywhere. It was now a fixed goal within the interior network of circulation. The confessionals in the Jesuit church, S. Fedele, in Milan might be early examples. I do not know their exact date, but the ornament corresponds exactly to the style of carving about 1570. They are placed on the *b*-axes of the space; this makes them so clearly part of the architecture that we can assume that they were considered from the beginning as part of the building program. In the Gesù in Rome (Fig. 23) the confessionals remain where they were later installed: in front of the paired pilasters of the nave, and in front of the pilasters in the crossing.

While the increased importance of confession had its effect upon Jesuit churches, the increased importance of preaching could not make itself felt. There were pulpits in the first phase too, and these were not altered when the number of sermons increased. But the hall-like character of Jesuit churches can be, as it often has been, connected with the practical demands of a good preaching space.

The church of the second phase is a space for Mass, confessions, and sermons. Here too these purposes are co-ordinated, but their importance demands the continual presence of priests and congregation in the space. Mass can be said without the presence of the laity, but the clear prescriptions of confession, Communion, and the sermon emphasize the interrelationship between God and the world that gives the space its two-sided character. Dialogue replaces monologue. The merciful God, who can be understood through prayer and a Christian way of life, replaces the self-contained Platonic ideal. His relationship with humanity is unhindered. The church has the purpose of being the molded theater in which this interrelationship between God and man unfolds. This purpose is not fulfilled by the veneration of a Perfect Supreme Being. It is founded upon the idea that this Being demands the observance of certain behavior in exchange for redemption from sin. In this sense the central purpose is the grace that radiates from God, and in this sense also I may call the purpose of the church centrifugal—using this term, of course, not in its mechanical sense as tangential force but merely to indicate an action radiating from a spiritual center and demanding a response in the behavior of its recipients. Because it demands this response, it is dependent upon these subordinates.

3. PROTESTANTISM

The change in intention in ecclesiastical matters is thus recognizable in one concrete change in the spatial form. At the same time, religious considerations had a still greater influence upon Protestant architecture. Here too it was not the development of theology, with all its dogmas and theses, that had an influence upon ecclesiastical architecture but certain practical demands of the liturgy. There was only *one* altar. The central position of the sermon in the service meant that altar and pulpit were moved close together so that both could be seen at the same time. This produced the altar-pulpit, or the altar with a pulpit located above and behind it. The significance of music in the services made the organ one of the most important pieces of equipment. It was often located above and behind the altar-pulpit.

The service lasted for a long time, chiefly because of the length of the sermon;[10] this led to the installation of pews for the congregation, which had further architectural consequences. The freedom of movement possible in Catholic churches was impossible here. A person had to arrive at the right time and remain throughout the entire service, in order not to disturb the rest of the congregation. The passages between pews had to be left open because the people who stood concealed the view of the altar from those who were seated. Hence the demand arose for as many *seats* as possible. Since sitting consumes much more space than standing and the passages were unused during the sermon, fewer people could assemble in a Protestant church than in a Catholic one of the same size, and galleries were a practical necessity in these churches. Galleries have a different meaning from those in Jesuit churches. In neither Protestant nor Catholic churches are they structurally necessary.

The size of the Protestant church was finally determined by the normal range of hearing. The sermon produced a space of fixed maximum dimensions, and in it was placed the largest possible number of seats from which the preacher and the altar could be seen equally well. From the beginning these utilitarian considerations restricted the monumentality of Protestant ecclesiastical architecture, even if they did not make it impossible. A really creative architect could still give an air of solemnity to a space crowded with pews. The inhibition lay deeper—in the attitude of Protestantism toward art.

The Calvinists and Zwinglians entirely renounced painting, sculpture, and ornament and destroyed the old furnishings of Catholic churches in order to make them usable for their own rite. The Lutherans were less radical. But I need not go into these degrees of difference, because a total lack of imagery in the divine service is common to all branches of the Reformation: it never appeals to the eye.

The religious relationship between an individual and his God is direct. It is not really dependent upon a priest, since the Protestant has the Bible in his hands and can interpret it for himself. Certainly, the union of the congregation demands skilled speakers specially trained for divine service, but here the preacher is again coordinated with the laity. He is commissioned by the congregation to preach God's Word; he belongs to the congregation; he is its voice. Everything revolves round the "Word." In Catholicism the Word is equated with ritualistic gesture, and becomes visible. In the Protestant church the service might have been made for the blind. Just as we close our eyes in order to concentrate when listening to music, so, in the Protestant service, all distractions are removed from sight to induce greater spiritual attention. God's Word resounds from the pulpit, but it does not follow that God is in the pulpit. He has no special dwelling place; He lives in the hearts of the people. The *heart* is called the temple of God. It is evident that this makes the church a neutral place of assembly, a Sunday meeting hall that has an empty, yawning effect the rest of the week. The solemn consecration of the Catholic church lasts forever. God fills the church whether or not devotions are being offered. All its splendor and richness are there for His exaltation. God does not belong to the priest, nor is He the common property of the faithful. But the Protestant honors God by his belief and his Christian conduct. Art is not required; it has no purpose; it can only disturb, or even lead astray.

Religious belief is inherited, however, whereas artistic sensibility is born anew with each artistic individual, without regard to his faith. Thus it happens that the Protestant generations at the end of the sixteenth and beginning of the seventeenth century were filled with men who were not satisfied with the severe restrictions against imagery, who sought their right to create for the eye as well as the ear in the service of the spiritual. A flood of sculptural fantasy now flows into the ornamentation of tombs and epitaphs, pulpits, organs, altars, gallery railings, and scrollwork. It is in the Protestant churches that this world of pure imagination finds its highest expression. In general the spatial form adheres to the sober demands of the building program, which is taken literally. The richly decorative furnishings are not connected with the space.

Evangelical churches, which are developed artistically as a whole, as for example the Marienkirche in Wolfenbüttel, 1604, resemble Catholic churches. They are the glory of Protestant architecture but are not characteristic of it.

The Protestant service cannot be said to be wholly without appeal to the senses, because music is given a very important role. But it appeals to only one of the senses, as sight is excluded. This realization deepens our understanding of the Catholic church. Full appeal to the senses is still compatible with centrifugal purpose. Sensuousness is the essence of the Catholic liturgy, which is always a visible *and* audible procedure; it was also part of the liturgy in the first phase. The artistic mood of the religious ceremony is determined by whether its focal point lies in the spiritual or in the sensuous. In the Catholic church the visible symbols of salvation are crucial to the rite. It is at all times artistically oriented, whereas the intention of Protestantism is unartistic.

One cannot object that art was banished simply because of Protestant antipathy toward Catholicism, that there was a desire to remove everything that recalled Catholicism from the church interiors. The lack of art in Protestantism cannot be explained on these negative grounds alone. This antipathy certainly had some effect, but it goes back to the same roots as the lack of art itself. A purely spiritual religion was required, and when optical elements are in fact apparent in the cult, they are either unimportant or are simply remnants of the Catholic liturgy.

4. CATHOLIC SECULAR ARCHITECTURE

The essential innovation of the second phase in secular architecture is the lopsided emphasis upon the state rooms. It is true that the Palazzo Farnese in Rome has a main hall for ceremonial occasions, distinguished from all the other rooms by its great expanse and two-story height, but it is shifted to one corner of the building and has windows in one long and one short side. The effect of the hall's unusual position and height on the interior of the building, on the coordination of the remaining rooms, is not as great as we would expect. Nor does the main staircase leading up to it prepare us for an overwhelming space, because it is not placed in the center of the building. The size and height of this hall are not made apparent on the façade (Fig. 76).

There is a large hall in the center of the Palazzo del Senatore on the Capitoline Hill in Rome. A state hall clearly marked by its central location, it is the result of Giacomo della Porta's alteration, 1573, of Michelangelo's original design. As far as I can see, priority here belongs to Giuliano da San Gallo, who designed a hall more impressive in size, form, and layout than all the other rooms in the Villa Medici at Poggio a Caiano for Lorenzo the Magnificent, as early as 1480.[11]

The great hall appears from time to time in later designs, but it remained a rarity until Palladio took it up again with great regularity. Palladio's state rooms recall the vestibule-like halls marked with a loggia, common in Venice, and we can see something originally Venetian in their emphasis upon the ceremonial side of life. But about the middle of the sixteenth century a large, centrally placed hall was designed for the Palazzo Isolani at Minerbio in Emilia. Since it was designed by Vignola, it can have no Venetian source.

Palladio's great halls were entered through vestibules, and presented themselves to the guest as the center of attraction (Palazzo Chiericati and the Villa Rotonda, both in Vicenza). They were the models for later Italian dwellings, and similar rooms were soon found in Germany (Schloss Heiligenberg near Lake Constance, 1569, and Schloss Weikersheim, 1595). Only the Château Madrid in France, now destroyed, had a similar hall. France remained conservative. Much was destroyed in the Revolution, however, and what remains has not yet been adequately studied. The chief seventeenth-century examples are in the Wallenstein Palace in Prague and in the nearly contemporary Palazzo Barberini in Rome. Despite national differences in style, these are fundamentally based upon the same intention.

Coordination of the stories on palace façades was now passé. The piano nobile received the main emphasis, and the mezzanine was left unarticulated. Ground and upper stories were never treated in the same way.

The colossal order and the continuous staircases create unity in the buildings of the second phase. But the visitor is restricted to a certain fraction of this whole, and the rest of the building is closed to him.[12] It discloses only a part of its existence. The master of the house seems to have set the scene for himself. He is seen no longer in the entire complexity of his existence but only in an imposing, ceremonial mood. He calculates from the beginning on a host of admirers. He restricts them to a certain area and closes them out of the everyday life that unfolds behind the scenes. The service rooms are so arranged that they form subordinate wings unworthy of notice, and their role is simply to concentrate interest upon the state rooms. Because the owner does not reveal himself completely, he is seen by his fellows from one definite aspect; thus the intention is the same in secular architecture as in ecclesiastical architecture. The central purpose is not self-contained; it is not considered self-sufficient but could be described as aggressive or dramatic. I say here too that the purpose is centrifugal.

5. PROTESTANT SECULAR ARCHITECTURE

The social class that supports this building program is aristocratic and monarchic. Protestantism on the other hand produced in general a greater equality among men. Its highest social stratum was composed of theologians, teachers, magistrates, and merchants, and it did not commission any art that greatly exceeded the grasp of the average citizen. No matter how conceited they were, no matter how much vain self-praise they left behind in books and tomb inscriptions, they were nevertheless, as far as their buildings were concerned, on a level with their fellow citizens. Usefulness in public affairs replaced the Humanistic ideal of universality.

In Calvin's ideal republic, religiosity so thoroughly permeates all aspects of life that the contrast disappears between work and devotion, between banal act and lofty spirit. Calvin actually governed this republic, but refers to himself merely as town pastor. There is hardly any difference between church and school. This leveling of society and of life, this diminishing of contrast, also has an effect upon architecture. The secular building becomes utilitarian. What appeared crass to a Huguenot was modest to a Lutheran, but even Lutheran homes only rarely attain monumentality. Only the buildings that represent the citizens as a whole—the town halls—preserve a monumental outline and often surpass that of the new churches. The town hall nearly always has a more imposing effect in a Protestant community (in Amsterdam, for example) than in a Catholic one, because it has no competition from churches and houses. But artistic taste took refuge in ornament here just as in ecclesiastical buildings. Ornament is without purpose and is therefore independent of religious and social restraints; it became the asylum for artistic creativity in Protestant countries.

The elimination of purpose from artistic reckoning is, therefore, common to Protestant ecclesiastical and secular architecture, with very few exceptions. The four elements no longer play an equal part as the basis of artistic creation. In spatial form we could find the same sudden shift to division in Protestant as in Catholic churches and secular buildings. The corporeal forms of both become channels of force in the second phase. But light and purpose begin to play a much smaller role, or none at all. The treatment of illumination depends solely upon utilitarian needs;[13] color does not play a positive role.[14] There is no effort to achieve a perspective from one or many viewpoints. Consequently an architecture is produced that can be described as a partial art; as a result each of the elements slowly goes its own separate way. In this respect Protestant architecture is related to that of the nineteenth century.

6. PURPOSES CONCEIVED CENTRIFUGALLY

I can now summarize. Whereas in Protestantism purpose is artistically silenced, it undergoes a change in the Catholic world from an earlier centripetal to a later centrifugal intention in both ecclesiastical and secular architecture.

Third Phase (Eighteenth Century)

1. SECULAR ARCHITECTURE

I shall begin with an investigation of purpose in the secular architecture of the third phase.

France, which remained conservative in the seventeenth century, became the leader in the eighteenth. The furnishing of Louis XIV's bedroom in the center of the Château of Versailles, 1701, meant that the building program now contained an emphasis upon private life to a degree that had not been present earlier. The total subordination of the court, which now became a hierarchy of servants, produced the waiting room and the antechamber for the bodyguard (which had previously stood in the corridor). Private rooms formed a coherent unit with the state rooms. The life of the monarch as a whole became a ceremony, or at least the architecture was intended to impose this view upon the visitor. A great number of rooms was necessary in order to lodge all the servants, the higher members of the royal household, and the guests. The size and number of spaces for domestic use grew accordingly. Versailles demonstrates the increasing needs of one man. It grew only in stages. The great expansion occurred as early as 1670–1688; the chapel was added 1699–1710. (The theater was not added until the reign of Louis XV.) The building program now combined the entire household, administration, private life, and representative festivities into a single ceremonial existence centered exclusively round the monarch. It was this program rather than the spatial form of Versailles that became the model for the palaces of the eighteenth century. Examples of the perfected spatial form are the palaces at Würzburg and Bruchsal (Figs. 91–92).

The rise and spread of absolutism was the historical precondition of the third phase. The patron, whether he was a worldly or spiritual prince, was not the complete man he had been in the first phase. He was expected to have the capacity for pleasure and diversion, to hunt, play, and love. It was not his duty to *be* a great man, but he was certainly required to appear as one. He had a role to play, a role created by Louis XIV, which lasted through the eighteenth century, with changing actors, some good, some bad. The gravity of life was hidden behind the scenes. The great actor may have seemed absolute in his power, but he remained dependent upon his admiring audience, for however much court life was secluded from the people at large, it was nevertheless intended to be a continuous ceremonial performance for the entire nation. Those magnificent wrought-iron garden gates through which the crowds gazed as into a closed paradise can be considered the symbol of this. The *salons* themselves and the adjoining state rooms were designated according to their individual purposes. The main hall, used for solemn receptions, as throne room as well as ballroom, needed no furniture. A special game room, porcelain room, print cabinet, and Chinese room served the dilettantes. The long gallery, with its view of the garden, served as the dining room; the table was installed there for meals and removed afterwards. There had to be a cool grotto in the garden. A *galerie des glaces* required that the guests observe their own gracious movements and know that they themselves were being observed from all

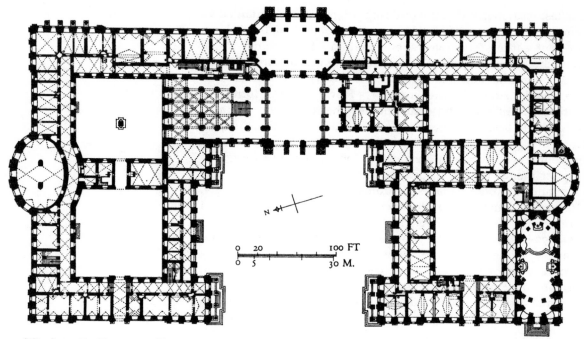

91. Würzburg, Residenz, 1719. Plan.

92. Bruchsal, Schloss, 1720.
Exterior.

sides. Affected behavior created this singularly appropriate room. The Spiegelkabinett in Würzburg (Fig. 88) is a classic in the realization of this purpose, just as it fulfilled the demand for a multitude of images and the destruction of the solid form of the enclosing body. Anyone who cannot feel at home in this room will understand that he was not made for what I call a centrifugal intention.

Only a few aspects of the highly diverse culture of the eighteenth century were translated in the building program. Neither the progress in the natural and historical sciences nor the spread of Rationalism showed any influence: only the social ideal had its effect. Man's object in life was to be observed. The mirror was indispensable; it was the most distinctive feature of the period. The essential purpose was to be mirrored, to be seen. In this respect, the third phase was merely the extreme climax of the second.

2. THE CATHOLIC CHURCH

I cannot recognize anywhere in ecclesiastical architecture a strengthening of liturgical demands within the building program. In monastic churches of this period the monks usually sat in the choir, not in the galleries. The choir was divided from the space for the congregation, but this was also true in the second phase, except for the Jesuit churches. The earlier opaque rood screen was now replaced by the splendid wrought-iron screen, resembling a garden gate (Fig. 89).[15] This ensured a similar view of life's privileged ones, who demanded that their privilege be noticed and either admired or envied. We must admit that liturgical interests are once more secondary to purely artistic ones, and yet, here, there can be no thought of the same intention as that of the first phase.

The Catholic church was still, as before, God's dwelling place. In the first phase it was erected for a God who was immutably the ideal of perfection, a Complete Being who tolerated with indifference the worship at His feet. Thus the perfection of the visible elements was more important to the rite than their appropriateness. There was not a return to this attitude in the third phase. God remained the Compassionate, Supreme Redeemer he had been in the seventeenth century, but as King of Kings he now lived like a prince. His house was a great hall. In monasteries the living quarters and work rooms in a certain sense became a closed world of toil and service, a foil for the representative gaiety of the church. The bubbling spirit characteristic of a prince found its lasting visible form, most noticeably, in the opulence and freedom of ornament. Since this ornament was spread in all its un-diluted worldliness over the space that houses the Most Holy Sacrament, we realize that God was now thought of as an imitator of Louis XIV. The sovereign built Versailles; God was not to have anything less. The faithful have never really taken exception to the boudoir aspect, the exuberance, and the sensuousness of these churches. They were all considered princely in character. The extreme climax of centrifugal thinking was thus indirectly applied to the ecclesiastical building. We receive the impression in these churches that this Compassionate Supreme Being wants to be appreciated as a cavalier, that it is most important to Him that we place His wealth, His gay, playful, and buoyant existence in the right light. This secularization of God is immediately recognizable in the sculpted and painted representations of the Trinity. The saints, who look like dancing masters, and the coquettish angels (Fig. 48) are further manifestations of this.

3. THE PROTESTANT CHURCH

Protestant architecture of the third phase created very few artistically outstanding churches. The Frauenkirche in Dresden and the Michaelskirche in Hamburg (Figs. 55–56) are certainly the most significant. The majority of churches are utilitarian buildings in which cost had a very inhibiting effect. Here too the intrusion of contemporary ornament meant a touch of worldliness and—it can even be said—of Catholic sentiment. Isolated court loges appear in the churches of Protestant princes, although they do not really correspond to the spirit of the Reformation. Pietism did not encourage church building. It strengthened personal devoutness and family worship and permitted religious devotions on weekdays. Thus interest in the church service declined.

In the history of Protestant church architecture it is not possible on the whole to distinguish a third phase in the development of purpose. The other elements went through a process of development, but purpose either stood fast or withdrew as an element of artistic creation. It existed here only in its literal meaning, just as in every utilitarian building. Since Protestantism made difficult the comprehension, the symbolization, of God, it removed the spiritual element from art. It was precisely because the Protestants made religion so entirely a realm of the spirit, depriving it of feeling, and reserving the intellect for it alone, that the whole of their architecture became ornament and thereby lost its relationship with the intellect.

Fourth Phase (Nineteenth Century)

Centrifugal intention disappeared after the French Revolution, and a utilitarian viewpoint henceforth ruled the history of purpose. What was once true of Protestant church architecture was now true of all branches of architecture. The modern state became the most important patron. New purposes arose, and with them new building types. The older purposes became autonomous and had their own development, which was expressed in their spatial forms.

The establishment of standing armies; the development of postal services and railroads, of public institutions for the sick, insane, and elderly; the growing complexity of public admin-

istration, such as in the field of justice; the spread of primary
and secondary education; the care of public collections; programs for the encouragement of music—from decade to decade
these developments produced increasingly greater specializa-
tion. The church was *one* type of building among many. It
did not set the fashion, nor did any other one kind of secular
building—not even the apartment house, which slowly
replaced the private town house.

In the nineteenth century, purpose underwent a development so richly varied that in comparison the entire preceding
period seems of little worth; but nowhere can we recognize a
decisively centripetal or centrifugal intention. Patronage
became impersonal. The owner of an apartment house inhabited the whole or part of a floor, just like his tenants. In this
and in all other buildings the occupants were transient or
were from a particular social class. They were stratified according to their financial means. (For example, the better seats at
the theater went to the people who could afford them.) Buying
power replaced personality, and at times even this could
produce an artistic building program. Personal wealth still
produced great palacelike buildings, but these disappeared in
the mass of completely impersonal buildings.

In the older church and palace there had been a permanent
inhabitant whose actual or supposed relationship to the changing visitors was a fixed and lasting one. Now buildings become
shells occasionally used by people who want to be restored
to health, to bathe, learn, read, or buy. These buildings cannot
be identified with one personality; they belong to everyone
and therefore to no one. The absent patron is not replaced by
the poetry in a theater, the science in a school, the hygiene
in a public bath; even if, as is the rule, allegorical figures bring
these general concepts to mind, these remain utilitarian
buildings.

Since a personal inhabitant is not present and cannot
be conceived of by modern man in terms of the antique muses,
all these buildings are spiritually empty until the moment
when the public itself takes up the role of permanent possessor
and autocratically permeates it with its collective demands.
This replacement of the impersonal bureaucracy by a public
with developing personality, or, rather, by the assignment of
responsibility to the public through its architects, is characteristic of the latest architecture. I need not concern myself
with this any further; I only need to point it out.

The Hofmuseen in Vienna have splendid, spacious vestibules and stairs that fill the visitor with amazement, but he
must ask himself who is so important there: it is the court,
of course. But in reality there is no one in these reception
rooms to receive him. The nineteenth century created many
similar reception halls, and they were created without thought
of any living being. It may be true that on special, rare oc-

casions a monarch receives a monarch or a city representative receives a person of note in such a hall, but these rooms are not consistent with the concept of public buildings.

If Messel's Wertheim Store in Berlin, 1896, seemed revolutionary, this was basically because the entrepreneur remained in the background and the public seemed to have the role of patron. That the public is not the patron, that buildings seem to rise without a patron—these are the common characteristics of the fourth phase. There may be examples that have a distinct intention, but the phase as a whole is uninfluenced by them.

The separation of phases in the development of purpose, therefore, is based upon polarity in the conception of personality. Perhaps the determining factor in the first phase was not the discovery of personality in general, but rather the belief that the personality was capable of autonomy and, in its way, of perfection. This assumption that independence, universality, and relative perfection were qualities within the reach of the individual had its impact upon palace architecture through separate purposes. The conception of a God who existed as an intangible, separate, and stronger force in relation to man, of a God that was nothing but the personification of the ideal of perfection, could also transform the church into an expression of absolute perfection.

In the second phase there was a sudden loss of faith in earthly perfection. Man felt humble and sinful; he had a renewed longing for redemption and an accompanying dependence upon God's grace. This change in attitude altered the spiritual direction of purpose. The individual felt completely dependent upon God and also upon his fellow men. Just as the most powerful of men depended upon the masses, so God too, because of the reciprocal relationship between Himself and the people who sought redemption, became a Being with one definite direction. The people wanted to be subordinate. They demanded *one* representative of earthly perfection; they did not expect this of everyone. Earthly perfection in a monarch was thought of as bestowed by God's grace, however, and the princes, the most important patrons of the period, were expected to *seem* perfect rather than to *be* perfect. Just as they were dependent upon ceremony and the admiration of the people, so God himself appeared in Catholic ecclesiastical architecture as dependent upon a mediating priesthood and upon a conventional, established liturgy. In Protestant ecclesiastical architecture, however, the spiritual nature of the relationship between man and God led to the creation of utilitarian buildings. God did not seem imperfect, of course, but he was no longer so completely independent, no longer an isolated ideal, as he had been in the first phase.

The contrast between a purposive intention that is centripetal and one that is centrifugal thus rests on the difference between freedom and constraint of personality.

It would be amateurish to begin with these ideas as manifestations of culture. We must begin with the concrete purposes themselves and speak of freedom and constraint in architecture only insofar as such ideas are generally characteristic of the thought of a period.

In this limited sense I can say that the first phase focused on purposes from the standpoint of a *free personality* and the second phase, from the standpoint of a *constrained personality*. The third phase gave this constraint the character of the *patron's dependence* upon the *admiring* throng; this was expressed even in ecclesiastical architecture—in Catholic ecclesiastical architecture, that is, for in the Protestant church the personality of God is radically removed from the building, and only a faint echo remains. The fourth phase is generally characterized by the *impersonality* of its architecture; hence it had no definite relationship to either of the two polarities. It remained neutral.[16]

The second phase began with the Counter Reformation and Palladio's buildings from about 1560. The third phase was in the making a hundred years later in the growing Château of Versailles; its spirit was generally prevalent after 1700. The beginning of the fourth phase coincided with the French Revolution.

5 Common and Distinguishing Characteristics of the Four Phases

1. DEFINITION OF THE FOUR PHASES

Spatial addition and spatial division, center of force and channel of force, one image and many images, freedom and constraint—these are the pairs of concepts by which I distinguish and characterize the phases of post-medieval architecture. That there are *four* pairs follows from the analysis of architecture according to four elements. Each pair of polar opposites testifies for one element only, and, since the elements represent completely different categories, each pair of concepts speaks for an entirely different aspect of a building or stylistic period.

In my discussion of the development of purpose, I said that purposive intention was the essential factor in the history of art. Intention is the content; it is expressed through purpose, which dictates form. The same distinction can be made for each of the three elements involving the senses (space, corporeality, and visibility). I have conceived of the polarity of corporeal form as one of physical forces, but underlying this formal contrast between the center and the channel of forces is an ethical one, the intention of independent and dependent personality. Similarly, the polarity of spatial form is a geometrical or formal one, but underlying addition and division is the difference between the sense of an unchangeable independence and the nervous state produced by invisible external forces. Finally, the same is true of visible form. I made a formal distinction between one image and many images; underlying that formal contrast is the contrast of content, of the intention. One image does not tempt us. It offers no surprises. It calms us. Many images disturb us. One image removes the object from us (even in interior spaces). Many images embrace us. Although the distinction between form and intention is realized in each of the elements, in the case of the three elements involving the senses the polarity is based upon the form, whereas in the case of the intellectual element, purpose, it is based upon intention. Yet even in the elements involving the senses, intention manifests itself as the function of the formal polarity; hence there exists in all four pairs of concepts a parallel structure that is ultimately based upon the contrast between independent and dependent personality.

As the four polarities follow a parallel direction, the effect of those that occur at the same time is unified. Spatial addition, center of force, one image, and the idea of freedom of personality—all point toward the same meaning. They are subordinate to a collective pole. Spatial division, channel of force, many images, and the idea of constraint of personality—all aim at the opposite meaning. They produce the opposite collective pole. The one forms an edifice that is set off from the world as finite; the other forms one that is dissolved in infinity. The first set of poles produces the conception and the feeling of the microcosm; the second, of the macrocosm. The first represents a complete, closed, self-sufficient unit; the second, a fragment that opens to the universe because it is incomplete. It should be understood that artistically this fragment is just as much a unit as the closed form with its closed spirit. If a centralized building of the first phase partially collapses because it is damaged by lightning, fire, or earthquake, it perhaps assumes a "picturesque" appearance as a ruin. It has *become* a fragment. But of course I am not talking about such accidental fragments here. I am concerned only with absolutely finished, undamaged, mechanically complete buildings, which cannot be supplemented, and which do not demand that we supply *finite* parts in order to complete them but stimulate our imaginations to complete them with infinite ones.

To be a whole and to be a part is the highest collective polarity. It is the first and only polarity that presents itself differently four times according to the analysis in the four elements. But it does not really form a fifth, distinct polarity in addition to the others.

This highest polarity of microcosm and fragment is a suitable characterization of the classical stages of the first and second phases. It denotes the contrast between Renaissance and Baroque. Naturally, this general concept *alone* would be all too diluted as a characteristic. It can have meaning only as a formula for the large number of concrete characteristics discussed in the preceding chapters, which in their turn were combined into abstract concepts in four separate polarities. This highest, pale polarity comes into its own only as the result of an inductive deliberation.

The distinction between Baroque and Rococo, however, is a *gradual* one, insofar as the forms of lower geometry used in spatial and corporeal form (which still come close to addition and one image) are replaced by appropriate forms of higher geometry. The distinction is a *psychic* one, insofar as the replacement of Baroque pessimism by the optimism of the Enlightenment causes the channel of force to shift from a tragic resistance against an immense, overwhelming power to a cheerful response to every puff of wind. The distinction is gradual and psychic at the same time, insofar as the need for exhibition that characterizes the second phase includes the whole of private life. A lasting display of splendor and affectation permeates architecture.

Neoclassicism, however, is characterized by the fact that the three elements involving the senses (space, corporeality, and visibility) make an irresolute return to the characteristics of the first phase, and the intellectual element (purpose) begins to be aesthetically eliminated, as it already had been from Protestant ecclesiastical architecture in the earlier phases.

The subsequent appearance of Romanticism and of the Renaissance Revival is not determined by a new polar tendency. The separation of all four elements only caused more partially artistic effects, and their connection with the preceding development was now essentially different from that of the previous phases.

2. SEPARATION OF THE FOUR PHASES

Before we discuss this connection, we must ask how the four phases can be separated from one another, for as yet I have characterized only the conditions of their classical years or decades. Every classical period is preceded by a period of quest in which the four separate poles are not uniformly in complete operation. The style does not exist immediately in all the elements, nor in all of them to an equal degree. This is what makes the separation of the phases from one another so difficult, even when we at length see clearly the final result to which each phase aspired.

The appearance of a symptom in the direction of the approaching classical stage in only one of the four elements cannot be considered as the birth of a new style. We demand that *several* symptoms in all *four* elements appear. It is true that it can be difficult even then to decide about any one example whether it should be considered still in the earlier or already in the later phase. (Often it will temporarily depend upon personal decision, and then perhaps be decided by scholarly agreement.) We can only be certain about the aspects of a building that are *still* Renaissance or *already* Baroque. There is no smooth transition from spatial addition to spatial division, from the radiation of force to the channel of force, but a sudden break over a zero point. It thus may be debatable whether Renaissance vestiges or Baroque symptoms are more important for a whole building. Nonetheless, the separation of phases is clearly marked, for it runs in a complicated, entangled curve through the work of art itself.

Certainly there are no sharp boundaries and decisive turning points in history! But it is hasty and superficial to conclude from this that it is impossible and inadmissible to separate the phases. There are no decisive turning points because a complete change is not finally accomplished with one stroke in all the elements. Rather, a new style partially appears in each of the elements separately. For example, symptoms of division appear while the rest of the building remains additive, or a detail loses its unique image without the whole building breaking up into many images. There are no sharp breaks because these occurrences do not prevent a later building from retaining the old style in this same detail while the new style appears in quite a different one. But it is possible to separate the phases, because we can establish a decade in which the new style begins to predominate in individual works as well as in the whole of architecture. A generation of architects that has grown up in the new style, with a new intention, begins to express itself, and from then on the style moves forward in full force toward its classical stage.

To establish this moment we must once again recall how the Baroque penetrated the individual elements of the Renaissance. The four voices sounded one after the other as in a fugue.

The corporeal form of Michelangelo's works, the Medici Chapel and the Laurentian Library, has the first voice, unless his design for the façade of S. Lorenzo in Florence is considered to be the first symptom of many images (the façade is treated as a frontispiece and is unrelated to the side), in which case optical appearance would take precedence.[1] The spatial form of the Medici Chapel (Fig. 75) is still purely additive, and the main framework of corporeal forms is still completely skeletal. Only in the tombs themselves, in the treatment of their backgrounds and in the doors and the tabernacles above them, are there pronounced symptoms of the Baroque. The vestibule of the Laurentian Library (Fig. 59) is the first case of definite spatial division because of the freestanding staircase and the height of the ceiling. The examples mentioned earlier of a splitting up of a single-nave church into a crossing or choir of three aisles have no influence on later development. They appear rather as vague preclassical forms, as precursors of a coming new stylistic direction. The Laurentian Library is Baroque in its corporeal forms but not in its optical appearance. Everything is still spread out two-dimensionally and seen frontally. Even the conception of purpose here is not markedly that of the second phase, for the library was inserted into an existing cloister, and this location dictated its spatial form.

We might be inclined to seek the first symptoms of multiple images in Venice, the home of polychromy, of polished marble incrustation (Sta. Maria de'Miracoli), and of the broken silhouette (Scuola di S. Marco). As a simple oblong hall with a transverse gallery above the entrance, Sta. Maria de'Miracoli is a spatial form that can be placed in the second phase. The form of the choir, with its elevated floor cutting into the nave, is an example of quite tentative spatial division. We shall therefore admit that there are exceptions in the first phase—they could be understood as an "undercurrent" perhaps. We could say that the separation of phases is always a question of the predominance of a majority of buildings of a similar tendency over a minority of an opposite tendency. But there is a great difference between these buildings of the first phase and those of the second, which were consciously planned to produce a multiplicity of images. The whole whimsical tendency of the fifteenth century in Lombardy and the Veneto is characterized by indifference and carelessness in design.

The buildings lack the large-scale calculation that makes the true Baroque seem so severe. The whimsical tendency of the first phase, therefore, is perhaps to be considered as an "under-current" not because it is minor but because it is capricious, lacks self-discipline, and artistically makes fewer claims. It may often be especially appealing because its charms are immediate. But the true Baroque is free of caprice. It created works of art that obey their own laws. If we speak of capriciousness in relation to the Baroque, we usually mean that it deviated from the rules compiled for the teaching of architecture, but which no architect ever followed blindly, even in the Renaissance. Once we recognize that this independent tendency within the first phase is not a forerunner of the Baroque, we shall also understand that the first symptoms of multiple images can be found only in connection with, and as a result of, certain forms of spatial division. This can hardly have occurred earlier than Sta. Barbara in Mantua (Fig. 19) and the Gesù in Rome (Fig. 23), both of which I have cited frequently. Interpenetrations alone do not produce multiple images. S. Lorenzo (Fig. 14) and Sto. Spirito in Florence, the cathedral in Faenza, and S. Salvatore in Venice (Fig. 15) are all rich in surfaces, but this does not diminish their clarity as a whole. Their forms can be correctly completed without effort. Multiple images arise only when the form eventually turns out to be something unexpected. The first example of this is the Roman Gesù (short transepts, a dome that only gradually becomes visible, the presence of galleries that can only be surmised).

Finally, purpose occurs as the last voice. Savonarola's appearance had only a short iconoclastic result. Only the Society of Jesus had a lasting effect on the people; it used art for specifically religious, ecclesiastical purposes. But once the architectural intention changed, the three formal elements *had* to be adjusted unconditionally.

I anticipated this earlier when I said that spatial addition, force radiation, and the single image are absolutely unsuited to Christianity. They contradict the concept of sinful, imperfect man and of the Merciful Redeemer.[2] When the ideas of the Counter Reformation took hold of the building program, the architects who sought a uniform effect in all four elements were compelled to reorient everything in the direction of the new purpose. The period of the Council of Trent, 1545–1563, is crucial here. I would begin the second phase of purpose with the publication of the decisions of the Council, and, since purpose draws the other elements with it, would consider this as the beginning of the second phase in general.

This final decision for the new direction comes to art from outside, from the general intellectual development, for the building program is imposed upon the architect.

It is completely understandable that the three formal elements had already—independently of the building program—turned away from the principles of the Renaissance, because a classical stage cannot long endure. It is the essential characteristic of a classical stage that it cannot be enhanced. It can only be extended, in the twofold sense of spreading over more and more territory and of being brought to bear upon more and more individual problems, in an effort to think through to the end the new principles in all their various manifestations. The classical stage so viewed is stagnant and is therefore not long bearable, especially for *those* artists who are fully conversant with its artistic principles. All problems seem to them to have been solved, and their innermost need for complete application of their creative abilities remains uncultivated. A genius with technical competence and overflowing imagination is much too confined in classical periods by the work of those who preceded him. And finally, the more one pole in each of the four elements gains exclusive control of a style, the more the period's ideal appears to be one-sided. The artist begins to feel unsatisfied. He begins to want *that* which he does not have and to work for that unattainable satisfaction by means not previously explored. So I certainly do not mean that a kind of "form fatigue" hurries on the new phase. Rather, this is the result of the feeling that all the problems of the prevailing movement have been solved, and, since the solutions are one-sided, they necessarily imply the renunciation of influences that cannot long remain renounced. That the new style itself must become one-sided at the height of its development does not inhibit the enthusiasm of the creative artist.

The formal elements are changed by internal causes, then, and this change is sealed by external causes, by the new intention. Ornament, which is without purpose, is influenced only by the internal causes. The fate of exclusively artistic matters can be observed undisturbed in ornament as if under laboratory conditions. But in the history of architecture the end of a phase is always first indicated by a change in purposive intention. At the beginning of the first phase, the introduction of a new intention in architecture was at least contemporary with the accompanying adjustment of the three formal elements. The intention may have been long present in other fields. When the first classical stage was reached, however, a partial Baroque had to arise from internal causes, but this does not mean that the full Baroque can be deduced from the development of art alone. Its appearance is linked with the total complexity of historical change, which to us seems more or less fortuitous.

A second classical stage must be seen in the mature Rococo. It is the product of a re-exerting of all the principles of the second phase and must be thought of as dependent upon the development of absolutism. Louis XIV created the new intention. The Rococo began in his last years.[3]

Isolated symptoms of Neoclassicism began to appear before the French Revolution, but the elimination of personality from architecture does not come until that time. Napoleon did not build any palaces; the Empire was already impersonal.[4]

3. CONTINUITY BETWEEN THE FOUR PHASES

The continuity between Renaissance, Baroque, Rococo, and Neoclassicism was the result of a common basis of forms. It is true that these forms underwent great changes under the influence of changing stylistic principles, but they always managed to survive, and, because of a series of intermediate stages, their origin is always apparent. The architecture from the Renaissance to Neoclassicism derives from one single source. It is admittedly touched here and there by local influences, but during this entire period no new strain was begun. Nothing in the previous architectural development had been as fertile as the introduction of the Renaissance in Florence.

To the basic stock belong the corporeal forms of ancient architecture; the spatial forms of antique central-plan buildings, insofar as they were preserved (there were more then than now); and the spatial forms of the Early Christian basilica. The sixteenth and seventeenth centuries sought new ways of using the orders, but they remained orders nonetheless. Michelangelo placed columns in the wall and in the Capitoline buildings in Rome placed small columns tight against colossal pilasters (Fig. 65),[5] but they remained columns in both cases. He invented new forms of aediculae and consoles, but they remained aediculae and consoles of antique derivation. The baluster was a newly created architectural member (attributed to Donatello); it remained in use throughout all the stylistic phases, even if it was given a triangular plan by Borromini. Even in the Rococo, when the consoles became very thin and appeared to be scattered and disheveled by the wind, the console form could *still* be discerned. And the same origin is still perfectly evident in the entablatures and gables of Rococo altars, no matter how much they were scattered incoherently in many crooked pieces.

No complete system of alien artistic forms was ever forced upon those derived from antiquity.[6] Stylistic transformation ran its uninterrupted course in uniformly closed circles. This is also true of spatial form. Ecclesiastical spatial forms were never based upon the antique temple or the Gothic church, and gradually the medieval elements were eliminated from secular architecture. Since individual purposes are created by the needs of everyday life, it is obvious that they have their undisturbed continuity. Finally, the basis is given once and for all for visible form. Even if it depends closely upon the development of glass and mirror production, upon color techniques, and on artificial illumination, the development here is never interrupted to the same extent as that of space and mass.

4. TRADITION AND ORIGINALITY

Continuity was first broken with the appearance of the Romantic movement. This and subsequent nineteenth-century modes of building are bound to the Renaissance only by tradition.

A simultaneous interaction between tradition and originality is present in all artistic activity. If we overlook the beginning of art, which does not concern us here, we shall find no artist who creates entirely from within. He grows up under the stimulus of existing works of art, lives in close communication with other artists, his teachers, and his fellow strugglers. But it is also true that every artist is capable of creating something new for himself, of adding or pouring something new into his work. Tradition and originality are conceptually opposites, but they are opposites of another kind than the polarities of stylistic history, for it is certain that we never find the one without the other. No creation is absolutely new, and anything that follows tradition exclusively is a copy and is therefore not art.

Tradition and originality are combined in different proportions in different works, in different artists, and even in different periods. The nineteenth century was not *entirely* unoriginal in architecture, but it did in great measure depend upon definite prototypes and often enough came close to mere copying. Individual creativity is encouraged when the aim of measuring the unique creation of foreign work is to accomplish something better than before, that is, to fulfill what was left unfulfilled by the previous performance. But creativity is inhibited if the aim is to create something just as good. As soon as the prototype becomes unsurpassable the force of individual creativity is thwarted.

The Renaissance broke with the living tradition of the Gothic and took for its models ancient and Early Christian architecture, but artistic originality was so strong that something new was produced. Every important architect measured the remains of ancient architecture, attempted to understand its system, and trained himself by reconstructing its ruins. Every building was a free reconstruction of ancient architecture, or a correction of the Early Christian basilica based upon the antique. Ancient architecture was considered something unattainably great and beautiful. It was an unsurpassable prototype, but a harmless one because the architect did not have it lying complete before him. The existing ruins were highly stimulating for his creative imagination. He suspected that an absolute ideal lay behind them, but he could not put his hands on it. He had first to create.

As the exact science of archaeology developed, so the stimulating force radiated by antiquity diminished. Obscure Vitruvius, who did not quite agree with the buildings, stirred up an ambition to theorize *too*. Theory, pattern books, and academies, beginning with the Vitruvian academy, accompanied the further development into the Baroque. Even if the great masters moved independently of the distilled rules of antiquity, there was still high respect for the idea, slowly developing along definite if not correct lines, of an unsurpassable antique architecture.

Michelangelo enumerated San Gallo's faults.[7] The specifically scientific conception of *correctness* stands behind such disputes and critiques, even though it has no meaning in art. Borromini designed the balustrades of the *coretti* in his Oratory of St. Philip Neri in Rome with triangular balusters, which are alternately wider at top and bottom. He justified this, not by saying that it seemed expressive or beautiful *to him,* but by referring to nature, the master teacher, which shapes even men and trees thicker above than below. The fact that the balusters are triangular could not be defended in this way, of course. He defended his alternating triangular balusters by saying that such an arrangement would permit people in the *coretti* to look down through the openings in the balustrade, without permitting those below to look up through them.[8] Even Michelangelo and Borromini acted as if they could defend the correctness of their works by logical reasoning, and other less gifted architects promoted "correctness" in their buildings. A closed chain of academic endeavor accompanied the truly original artistic development and finally (after J. J. Winckelmann[9]) combined with archaeology. From this was born art history in its modern form, that is, the approach that values the study of medieval and modern art as highly as previous ages had valued the study of antiquity.

This scientific or, to be more precise, art historical attitude toward the works and styles of the past is not characteristic of the nineteenth century alone. What became clear then had existed from the beginning in Brunelleschi's method. He had studied ruins as an archaeologist. Art history has had a scientific impact upon post-medieval architecture and has determined its relationship to tradition. As early as the Rococo, the use of prototypes was increased. Until then only the antique had been recognized, but in the eighteenth century a world of form was produced that was closer to Far Eastern art— then becoming known in the West—than to ancient art. The idea of reviving antiquity broadened into the idea of repeating any accomplished style of the past, but it was the misfortune of the generations of architects that followed that the styles that now inspired creativity were preserved not in mutilated ruins but in complete buildings.

The substitution of art historical knowledge for free imagination in the nineteenth century, the complete systemization of architectural instruction, revealed the previous, most highly creative phases as basically permeated by a scientific attitude. It is said that architecture is not an imitative art, but painting and sculpture are not supposed to be imitative either. Realism is based solely upon the study of anatomy, life drawing, painting from nature, and perspective construction, and it therefore aims at the scientific reproduction of nature. It is analogous to a so-called imitative architecture, that is, to an architecture based upon models studied historically.

In the Renaissance, perspective, nature study, and later, anatomical studies (Leonardo, Michelangelo) gave a specific character to the whole world of form without strangling the period's creative strength. Similarly, the common characteristic of the whole of post-medieval architecture is that it was created with one eye always focused upon an unsurpassable prototype, and no matter how far creative ability ventured from this prototype (altering it out of all recognition in the Rococo), historicism was constantly looking over its shoulder, and finally banished art from art.

The search for new style meant the end of this segment of post-medieval architecture. The splitting up into separate paths of the development of the individual elements caused this search to founder. Style as a whole was not taken in hand all at once. New corporeal forms were attempted without any recognition of how little they had to do with the spatial form they enclosed. Special spatial forms were developed for modern purposes, but no definite intention lay behind them. The scientific attitude made natural artistic feeling impossible.

The history of architecture was separated from artistic development and became a historical discipline. It was no longer pursued in order to find new prototypes and to recommend certain styles. It now had its own importance as part of humanistic scholarship; it led to the understanding of all styles in their limitations and development and, in addition, showed the impossibility of a Renaissance in the literal sense. Easily accessible forms, so thoroughly known and in immeasurable richness, could now be used in architecture, and yet the architect could still surrender himself to the complete freedom of creating according to his own inner voice.

Germany at least has made a beginning, and for this very reason the epoch of post-medieval architecture lies closed behind us. We can clearly recognize its common characteristics. It was one tree planted by the scientific, that is, historical spirit (the scholar Brunelleschi), brought to flower by free creative energy (the artist Brunelleschi), but predestined by its scientific beginning to dry up the free creative energy that nourished it.

Today we look back over the phases of post-medieval architecture and their inevitable end as a revelation of human history, and we stand expectantly at the beginning of a new development. Despite the revelations of the past, we cannot know what lies in the future. But we do know that we have made a new start and that it is once more a pleasure to be alive.

Notes

Preface

1. [First published, 1888; English translation, 1964.]
2. [An earlier series of writings by August Schmarsow was summed up in his *Grundbegriffe der Kunstwissenschaft*, Leipzig and Berlin, Teubner, 1905.]
3. The pairs of concepts are linear vs. painterly, plane vs. recession, closed vs. open, multiplicity vs. unity, and absolute clarity vs. relative clarity. [These are best known to English readers from Wölfflin's later *Principles of Art History (Kunstgeschichtliche Grundbegriffe; das Problem der Stilentwicklung in der neueren Kunst)*, first published in German, 1915; first English translation, 1932.]
4. [Frankl refers to the following works: Jakob Burckhardt, *Geschichte der Renaissance in Italien*, first published 1867; 7th ed., Esslingen, Neff, 1924; Alois Riegl, *Die Spätrömische Kunst-Industrie*, Vienna, Österreichische Staatsdruckerei, 1901 (Italian translation available); Heinrich von Geymüller, *Die Baukunst der Renaissance in Frankreich*, Stuttgart, 1898–1901; *idem*, *Friedrich II von Hohenstaufen und die Anfänge der Architektur der Renaissance in Italien*, Munich, Bruckmann, 1908; *idem*, *Die ursprünglichen Entwürfe für St. Peter*, Vienna and Paris, Lehmann, 1875; *idem* (with Carl Stegmann), *Die Architektur der Renaissance in Toscana*, 11 vols., Munich, Bruckmann, 1885–1908; Cornelius Gurlitt, *Geschichte des Barockstiles in Italien*, Stuttgart, Neff, 1887; *idem*, *Geschichte des Barockstiles und des Rococo in Deutschland*, Stuttgart, Ebner & Seubert, 1889; *idem*, *Geschichte des Barockstiles, des Rococo und des Klassicismus in Belgien, Holland, Frankreich, England*, Stuttgart, Ebner & Seubert, 1888.

    For a very brief account of the climate of architectural ideas within which this work must be placed, see Paul Zucker, "The Paradox of Architectural Theories at the Beginning of the 'Modern Movement,'" *Journal of the Society of Architectural Historians*, X, Oct. 1951, pp. 8–14.]

Introduction

1. [What follows is excerpted, and in part summarized, from the original Introduction, in which Frankl discusses the methodology of art history. This adds nothing to the main thesis of the present volume. His thoughts on the subject were later expressed at great length in his monumental *Das System der Kunstwissenschaft*, Brünn and Leipzig, Rohrer, 1938.]
2. [Frankl eventually published studies of the Middle Ages in which he followed the method developed here. See his *Die frühmittelalterliche und romanische Baukunst*, Wildpark-Potsdam, 1926, and his *Gothic Architecture*, Baltimore, Penguin Books, 1962.]
3. [For Frankl's later reflections upon the present work see *The Gothic: Literary Sources and Interpretations Through Eight Centuries*, Princeton, N.J., Princeton University Press, 1960, p. 776. Frankl had published a small work on Renaissance architecture prior to the present study: *Die Renaissance-Architektur in Italien*, Leipzig, Teubner, 1912. For a complete bibliography of his works see the *Wallraf-Richartz Jahrbuch*, XXIV, 1962, pp. 7–14.]

Chapter 1

1. Leonardo da Vinci, *The Literary Works of Leonardo da Vinci*, comp. and ed. J. P. Richter, London, 1883, II, pp. 25–104. [This is a study of Leonardo's architectural sketches by H. von Geymüller. Leonardo's drawing based on Sta. Maria degli Angeli is on Pl. xciv, 3. (In the second edition of 1939, pp. 19–82. The plates are numbered identically in both editions.)]
2. The dome was never built, and the vaults above the ancillary spaces were not built according to the original design.
3. The corner spaces of the Steccata have no effect upon the interior. They are connected with it only by doors.
4. Leonardo, *op. cit.*, Pl. xc, 5 [This actually has *fourteen* sides.]
5. *Ibid.*, Pl. xciii.
6. *Ibid.*, Pl. xcii, 1.
7. The inner cross arms of the ancillary centers are subordinate to the main center, but they appear to be grouped with the ancillary centers.
8. Leonardo, *op. cit.*, Pl. lxxxvi, 2.
9. *Ibid.*, Pl. lxxxv, 7.
10. Cf. the octagon with eight ancillary octagons, with and without diagonal niches (*ibid.*, Pl. lxxxviii); the octagon with eight circular ancillary centers (Pl. lxxxix); and the ancillary spaces with niches (Pls. xc and lxxxiv).
11. *Ibid.*, Pl. lxxxiv, 3.
12. It is possible that this sketch represents a plan analogous to the Steccata at Parma, that is, that the centralized spaces on the diagonals were meant to be closed sacristies without effect upon the core space. This variant is shown more clearly in a drawing by Antonio da San Gallo the Younger for S. Marco in Florence, reproduced in C. Stegmann and H. von Geymüller, *Die Architektur der Renaissance in Toscana*, Munich, Bruckmann, 1885–1908, VII, San Gallo, Fig. 1. Another Leonardo sketch, shown in plan in Leonardo, *op. cit.*, p. 47 [p. 35 of 1939 ed.], Fig. 2, and in perspective in Pl. lxxxix, shows his intention even more clearly. Another example is the church in Pl. xc, 3–4. It has short cross arms with sloping roofs and four corner chapels, which were drawn as octagons in plan but became circular corner towers in the perspective.
13. Cf. the rich combination, Leonardo, *op. cit.*, Pl. lxxxvii, 2, [This does not exactly correspond to Frankl's description.]
14. It can be said that together they form a trinomial rhythm (arch-vault-arch), but as a rule I count only the rhythm of the spaces without regard to the intervening masses.
15. The true ambulatory derived from this design is found in Ammanati's church for his Ideal City: Stegmann and Geymüller, *op. cit.*, XI, Gesamtüberblick, p. 15, Fig. 39.
16. J. Burckhardt, *Geschichte der Renaissance in Italien*, 3d ed.; Esslingen, Neff, 1891, p. 126. See H. von Geymüller's reconstruction in his *Die ursprünglichen Entwürfe für St. Peter*, Vienna and Paris, Lehmann, 1875, II, Pl. 13–14. (I now notice that even Geymüller did not see galleries in the definitive design.)
17. [A drawing (Uffizi 2) now usually attributed to Peruzzi.]
18. There is a second, rapid sketch by Bramante [more likely by Francesco da San Gallo] in which this condition is fulfilled by an essential change in the principal cross arms. They have three

bays. The palaces and colonnades, which create a square enclosing the central church, are also shown [Uffizi 104r; Geymüller, *Die ursprünglichen Entwürfe,* II, Pl. 18, Fig. 1].

19. Light through the small top openings could only be expected at certain times of the day.

20. The small rectangular windows in the vaults were clearly an afterthought. They could not save the project.

21. They show up well in the portion of the drawing reproduced in Geymüller, *Die ursprünglichen Entwürfe,* I, Fig. 19.

22. *Ibid.,* Pl. 6, Fig. 2. [Frankl later realized that this sketch was not related to Bramante's original plan in Uffizi 1 (Addenda on p. 187 of original edition).]

23. Bramante intended to accent the most important of these boundaries by marking them with columns similar to those outlining the niches in the Pantheon in Rome.

24. Cf. Burckhardt, *op. cit.,* § 48: "The first and most significant characteristic of the Renaissance is its aversion to the cross vault."

25. Perhaps the Chiesa della Madonna in Mongiovino, 1524, also belongs here. I have not seen it.

26. Leonardo, *op. cit.,* p. 42 [p. 30 of 1939 ed., which took no notice of Frankl's criticism, nor of a study that revised both Geymüller's and Frankl's conclusions, in particular finding both additive and divisive (see pp. 57–60) spatial compositions among Leonardo's drawings for churches: Ludwig H. Heydenreich, *Die Sakralbau-Studien Leonardo da Vinci's,* dissertation, Hamburg, 1929].

27. Only the drawing in Leonardo, *op. cit.,* Pl. lxxx, 5, bears out Geymüller's interpretation, but here the dome is so unclear that perhaps this drawing is only partially finished or poorly preserved. [According to Heydenreich, *op. cit.,* this drawing is better preserved than Frankl assumed from the reproduction.]

28. The vaults in many of these buildings are unusual: the dome above the Old Sacristy is composed of twelve arched severies; above the main choir of Sta. Maria delle Grazie in Milan is a shallow vault divided into eight severies corresponding to the eight arches that rise above the rectangular plan (the triangular corners are each closed by two severies); the vault of the Cappella di S. Giuseppe from Sta. Maria della Pace (now in the Brera, Room XVI) in Milan is identical. Leonardo recorded the same kind of vault (Leonardo, *op. cit.,* Pl. ciii) and also invented more complicated versions of it. The main dome of Sta. Maria delle Grazie in Milan has thirty-two ribs so placed that piers instead of windows occur on the diagonals of the drum as well as above the centers of the four main arches.

29. Plans of these buildings can be found in Heinrich Strack, *Central- und Kuppelkirchen der Renaissance in Italien,* Berlin, Wasmuth, 1882.

30. Geymüller, *Die ursprünglichen Entwürfe,* II, Pl. 20, Fig. 6, and Pls. 22–23.

31. The alteration was probably intended to make the church brighter.

32. The small lunettes in the Cappella Turini in Pescia Cathedral are dated about 1545 in Stegmann and Geymüller, *op. cit.,* VII, Giuliano di Baccio d'Agnolo, p. 2, Fig. 1 and Pl. 1.

33. The date, 1570, is chiseled into the westernmost pier of the left aisle.

34. See my "Sustris und die Münchner Michaelskirche," *Münchner Jahrbuch für bildenden Kunst*, X, 1916–1918, pp. 1–63, esp. pp. 19f. and Fig. 10.
35. [The gallery above the entrance has been rebuilt in a different form since World War II.]
36. Stegmann and Geymüller, *op. cit.*, VI, Vitoni, Fig. 1.
37. [The present interior of the church in the Foundling Hospital in Florence stems from an eighteenth-century rebuilding. There are now plans to restore it.]
38. Douai has been part of France since the Peace of Utrecht in 1713.
39. S. Giovanni Battista in Pistoia, allegedly erected 1495–1513, has short transepts.
40. This church was not finished.
41. [Sebastiano Serlio, *Il terzo libro* (*d'architettura*), Venice, 1540, *Tutte l'opere d'architettura . . . di Sebastiano Serlio*, 3rd ed.; Venice, 1619 (reprint: Ridgewood, N.J., Gregg Press, 1964), folio 65 recto.]
42. The Jesuit church in Caen is related to St. Paul-St. Louis in Paris but has cross vaults above all the spaces except the apse and the crossing. The latter is covered by a pendentive dome.
43. Rhythm often occurs in this, strictly speaking, unspatial sense. The Michaelskirche in Munich is an example.
44. The nave articulation *b a a a b* in the Theatine church in Munich is unusual. Normally the entrance bay *b* has no effect upon the rhythm.
45. Anticipated by Sta. Maria delle Carceri in Prato, 1485, where, however, it has more the effect of a crown of balusters for the entablature because of the shallowness of the relief.
46. Evidently a centralized church with ambulatory appears only on paper, as in the *Hypnerotomachia Poliphili*, Venice, 1499 (reproduced in Burckhardt, *op. cit.*, p. 45), and in Leonardo's sketches after S. Lorenzo in Milan (Leonardo, *op. cit.*, p. 50 [p. 38 of the 1939 ed.]).
47. The Salute was copied at Gostyń in Poland, 1668.
48. *Coretti* without balconies are now found in S. Eligio degli Orefici in Rome, but it is obvious that they were not part of the original design.
49. Seventeenth-century elliptical domes: S. Carlo in Naples, 1602; the Bernardas Church in Alcalá de Henares, 1617; S. Giovanni in Piacenza; S. Carlo alle Quattro Fontane in Rome, 1638; the Servite church in Vienna, 1651 (with a kind of cove ceiling above a cove with lunettes); S. Andrea al Quirinale in Rome, 1658; the Église du Collège des Quatre Nations in Paris, 1660; Sta. Maria in Monte Santo in Rome, 1662; Sv. František in Prague, 1679; the Kajetanerkirche in Salzburg, 1685; Sta. Maria della Vita in Bologna, 1686. Some eighteenth-century examples (I am too lazy to list more than half): St. Peter's in Vienna, 1702; S. Domenico in Modena, 1708; the Karlskirche in Vienna, 1716; the Salesianerinnenkirche in Vienna, 1717; the parish church in Makova, Czechoslovakia, 1719; the Electoral Chapel in the cathedral of Wrocław (Breslau), 1722; the abbey church in Legnickie Pole (Wahlstatt), 1727; the church in Sepekov, Czechoslovakia, 1730; the Church of the Magdalen in Karlovy Vary (Karlsbad), 1732; Sta. Maria dell' Orazione e Morte in Rome, 1732; the churches at Schönbrunn and Die Wies, 1736; Trinità degli Spagnuoli in Rome, 1741; the

chapel in Saragossa Cathedral, 1753; the Sagrario in Jaén, 1764; and S. Juan de Dios in Murcia, 1786.

50. This domed choir behind a spatial group was echoed in Scamozzi's design for Salzburg Cathedral.

51. It is of no importance here that the site narrowed toward the choir.

52. Sta. Susanna in Rome, 1595, also has the effect of a hall despite the presence of a chapel at each side.

53. The monks' choir, the glass wall separating it from the main choir, and the main altar—all date from the eighteenth century.

54. The lanterns in the vaults above the apses are placed *eccentrically.* [This statement is hard to understand. The lanterns are in the centers of the vaults and on center with the apses. Here Frankl himself seems to demonstrate his point: that we are easily fooled by these vaults.]

55. The intermediate spaces *a* are again subdivided into the rhythm *x y z,* so that the rhythm is actually *b x y z b/b x y z b,* and so on.

56. Arches span from point to point of the star *within* the lower surface of the dome. They form a base line of small apsidal vaults "covered" by open interstices.

57. Altered 1654.

58. There is a design from the first phase that anticipates such a blending of spaces: the pre-1536 drawing for a centralized church by Peruzzi (Uffizi 581). It also shows an early use of the ellipse.

59. I have already discussed the vaults in this church (§ 15) for it seemed easier to include them with their parallels in Catholic churches.

60. The church and convent of Maria Treu were begun in 1698; a new church was begun in 1751. It is possible, but not probable, that the present plan goes back to the first church.

61. We can probably assume that curved arches were intended for the church in Prague as well. It was designed by Christoph Dientzenhofer, whose brother, Johann, designed the church at Banz.

62. This is not quite precise, because the choir ellipse is smaller than the central one, but it is accurate enough for our purposes.

63. Another example is the Chiesa dell'Aracoeli in Vicenza [begun in 1675].

64. There are a few Pantheonlike churches in the seventeenth and eighteenth centuries too: S. Bernardo alle Terme in Rome, dedicated 1600, rises above the foundations of a corner rotunda of the ancient Baths of Diocletian. The Église de l'Assomption in Paris, 1670, is a circle without niches. A true reproduction of the Pantheon is S. Simone in Venice, 1718.

65. There are earlier examples of this in the Canigiani and Ricasoli Palaces in Florence: Stegmann and Geymüller, *op. cit.,* II, Michelozzo, p. 26 and Pl. 19. A later example is in the Palazzo Arcivescovile also in Florence, 1582.

66. The Scala dei Giganti in the Palazzo Ducale in Venice, of about 1490, is an exception. The stairway that connected the terraces of the Cortile del Belvedere in the Vatican, of about 1510, was unavoidable because of the site, and so does not contradict the rule.

67. The stairway of the Palazzo dei Cavalieri in Pisa dates from the

1560's. It is an imitation of the Capitoline stairway but lacks the central depression.

68. The great staircase in the interior was installed by Percier and Fontaine in 1817.

69. The layout is certainly of this date, although the staircase was renovated in 1759.

70. The staircase in the Hôtel Dieu in Caen is an example of a complicated curvilinear form. The first flight climbs in the center of the space to a landing from which short flights rise at right angles to the next level. From there two more flights, parallel to the first but rising in the opposite direction, climb to a higher pair of landings. Finally, two terminal flights lead back to a point above the starting point. Since the entire staircase is cantilevered, it cuts through space in a twisting curve. The steps themselves are curved and are continually alternating in width, so that the railings, which begin at each side and join at the top landing, form continuous curves slicing through space.

71. Designed 1711.

72. Cf. the staircases at Ebrach, 1716; Schönthal, 1737; and Oberzell near Würzburg.

73. Cf. the contemporary layout in the Palais Trautson in Vienna (without peripheral passage); the staircases in Schleissheim, as early as 1719; and the later staircases in the Royal Palace in Madrid, 1740; in Caserta near Naples, 1752.

74. The original stairway is illustrated in Jacques Androuet du Cerceau, *Les plus excellents Bastiments de France,* Paris, 1579, II, Pl. 12. It was a development of the garden stairway of the Villa d'Este at Tivoli.

75. Paired three-dimensional arches also appear in secular architecture, as for example in the ground floor *Gartensaal* at Pommersfelden.

Chapter 2

1. Consoles supporting an entablature occur in S. Lorenzo in Florence: in the Old Sacristy (Fig. 12), in the nave (Fig. 14), and on the exterior of the church. Individual consoles also appear later, as in the Medici Chapel (Fig. 75) and on the Mercato Nuovo in Florence.

2. The window axes of only the upper two floors coincide on the Palazzo Medici in Florence. The ground floor follows its own arrangement. The Palazzo Pitti, also in Florence, was a step forward in this regard.

3. I do not need to mention here the important differences in the handling of spandrels, window profiles, and proportions.

4. The same rhythmical alternation was also briefly considered for the windows of the Palazzo Strozzi in Florence. A model of this is preserved.

5. There are coffers that spread out radially from the center of the circular covering above the exterior pulpit of the cathedral in Prato (renovated in the seventeenth century).

6. C. Stegmann and H. von Geymüller, *Die Architektur der Renaissance in Toscana,* Munich, Bruckmann, 1885–1908, VII, Raphael, Fig. 11 and Pl. 6.

7. Perhaps this occurred earlier, in the Cortile del Belvedere in the

Vatican: see H. Wölfflin, *Renaissance and Baroque*, London, Collins, 1964; Ithaca, N.Y., Cornell University Press, 1966, p. 53.

8. [The Villa Lante is an appropriate example only if Frankl meant the columns flanking the entrance portal, which overlap the pilaster articulation of the wall.]

9. Spiral columns first became common in the seventeenth century, especially in altars, after the *baldacchino* of St. Peter's in the Vatican, 1633.

10. Other early examples are [the drawing of the façade of Sta. Maria presso S. Satiro in Milan attributed to Bramante, 1479; the Villa Madama in Rome, 1516;] the Palazzo del Te in Mantua, 1525; and the Residenz in Landshut, 1537.

11. For this see Wölfflin's detailed observations in *Renaissance and Baroque, passim.*

12. Some of the houses in the Place Dauphine in Paris, 1607, are similar.

13. Double frames of the first phase are quite different. They never collide with each other.

14. Rubens's part in this development should be studied.

15. Cf. also the painted herms in Raphael's *Stanze* in the Vatican, and in the corner room of the Palazzo Pandolfini in Florence. The latter is illustrated in Stegmann and Geymüller, *op. cit.*, VII, Raphael, Fig. 10.

16. I can mention only in passing the corresponding events in the history of painting.

17. Cf. also the Fontana dell'Acqua Felice in Rome, 1585, for example.

18. Berlin. Staatliche Kunstbibliothek, *Katalog der Ornamentstichsammlung des Kunstgewerbemuseums*, comp. P. Jessen, Leipzig, Seemann, 1894, No. 146.

19. The old Exchange in Amsterdam no longer exists.

Chapter 3

1. A theory that has recently been questioned.

2. An assumption repeated again and again in C. Stegmann and H. von Geymüller, *Die Architektur der Renaissance in Toscana*, Munich, Bruckmann, 1885–1908, *passim*, although traces of color are found only rarely.

3. Lunettes were important for the painter because, despite his scaffolding, he could obtain the illumination necessary for painting only through them.

4. It is true that the darkness of the colors in the paintings themselves adds to this effect.

5. This diagonal orientation is enhanced by supplementary openings in chapel walls and vaults that offer additional oblique vistas. The Jesuit church of St. Paul in Bordeaux, 1676, and Notre Dame in the same city have large circular openings above the doors connecting the chapels. In the church at Waldsassen and in the Kollegienkirche in Salzburg there are openings in the vaults above the side chapels.

6. A. E. Brinckmann (*Platz und Monument*, Berlin, Wasmuth, 1908) quotes the following from the *Mercure de France*, July, 1748, p. 151: "C'est qu'un bel Edifice se multiple pour l'ornement d'une Ville autant de fois que vous donnez de points différents pour le voir, au lieu que celui qui n'est vû que d'un seul point,

ne fait jamais qu'un Edifice." [A beautiful building is multiplied in its embellishment of a city as many times as you provide different points from which to view it, whereas a building that can be seen from only one point is never anything but a building.] The effects of single and multiple images upon city planning can be deduced from reading Brinckmann's book.

7. See Chapter 4 for the practical purpose of these screens.

Chapter 4

1. Ornament can be isolated and studied for itself, but whether it is part of architecture or of furniture, it undergoes the same metamorphoses.

2. Cf. the semicircular barrier behind the altar in Raphael's "Mass of Bolsena." It is very likely that these principles led Alberti to consider the profusion of altars a misuse (*De re aedificatoria*, VII, 13). He declares himself in favor of one single altar and wants it placed *in front of* the choir.

3. Ludwig von Pastor (*Geschichte der Päpste*, Freiburg im Breisgau, Herder, 1901, I³, pp. 15ff.) makes a distinction between a "false hedonistic and a true Christian Renaissance," but that is an untenable distortion. What he considers false and hedonistic is the Renaissance proper, and what he calls the true Christian Renaissance is in *present* usage designated by the word "reform" alone, in its twofold sense of Reformation and Counter Reformation. The isolated appearances of deeply religious natures (Savonarola, for example) are without effect in the period of the "hedonistic Renaissance," to continue Pastor's terminology. Only in the second half of the sixteenth century is there a general reaction that produces the absolute predominance of Christianity and the subordination of art to religious interests.

4. [For an interpretation of the meaning of the centralized church contrary to that given here, see Rudolf Wittkower, *Architectural Principles in the Age of Humanism*, 3d ed. revised; London, Tiranti, 1962.]

5. [Baldassare Castiglione, *Il Cortigiano*, begun about 1510, first published 1528. A convenient translation is that by Charles S. Singleton, *The Book of the Courtier*, New York, Doubleday, 1959.]

6. J. Burckhardt, *Geschichte der Renaissance in Italien*, Esslingen, Neff, 1924, p. 13.

7. Charles Dejob, *De l'influence du Concile de Trent sur la Littérature et les Beaux arts chez les peuples catholiques*, Paris, Thorin, 1884, p. 264: "Notons toutefois que le clergé italien qui s'explique si nettement sur les devoirs de la peinture et de la sculpture, ne règle rien sur l'architecture religieuse." He then adds remarks that I cannot refrain from quoting:

Le fait vaut qu'on s'y arrête; car, quoique l'architecte qui élève une église ne puisse commettre les fautes contre la morale, les erreurs de doctrine ou d'histoire où tomberont peut-être le peintre et le sculpteur qui la décoreront, le choix du style des proportions de l'édifice doit satisfaire le sentiment religieux aussi bien que le goût; c'est même plutôt la disposition générale de l'église qui accroît ou trouble la ferveur du fidèle que les statues et les tableaux, accessoires précieux, mais qu'au premier abord il aperçoit à peine. Comment donc de pieux prélats dont les uns ont visité la France, l'Espagne, l'Allemagne, dont les autres ont du moins prié tour à tour à Saint-Ambroise de Milan, à Saint-Apollinaire de Ravenne, à Saint-Marc de Venise, au Dome de Florence, qui suivent avec tant d'intérêt les travaux de Michel-Ange et de ses continuateurs à Saint-Pierre du Vatican, semblent-ils ignorer que la piété n'est pas également à l'aire dans tous les temples? Dans les discussions sur la reconstruction de San Petronio à Bologne on n'articule que des arguments d'esthétique et non de sentiment religieux. Le dominicain Ignazio Danti, un de plus habiles mathématiciens de son temps, commentait un traité de Vignole; Daniele Barbaro, coadjuteur du patriarche d'Aquilée, traduisait et commentait Vitruve (1556); il composait sur la perspective un traité qui s'ouvre et se ferme par une prière religieuse; mais ni l'un ni l'autre ne s'élèvent au dessus des règles techniques d'un art qui a pourtant l'honneur d'ériger la maison de Dieu.

Such is the prolix rhetoric of the French. Burckhardt observed simply that the Counter Reformation had little to say about church building.

8. Only the mendicant orders were against the separation of clergy and laity on principle. They were certainly democratic; they had no galleries.

9. The lattice between the confessor and the confessant is supposed to have been introduced only after the Synod of Seville, 1512 (Georg Heckner, *Praktisches Handbuch der kirchlichen Baukunst*, Freiburg im Breisgau, Herder, 1886, p. 129). The present form of the confessional follows the regulations laid down by the Council of Trent.

10. The congregation endured these lengthy sermons out of piety, even when they were not very interesting. Many churches appointed someone to keep the people awake by poking sleepers with a long staff.

11. See San Gallo's design for a villa with octagonal central hall (C. Stegmann and H. von Geymüller, *Die Architektur der Renaissance in Toscana*, Munich, Bruckmann, 1885–1908, V, San Gallo, Fig. 15) and the first design for Poggio a Caiano (*Ibid.*, Fig. 16).

12. A. Palladio, *I quattro libri dell'architettura*, Venice, 1570, 2, II [I quote from the Isaac Ware translation, London, 1738, p. 38]:

for as in the human body there are some noble and beautiful parts, and some rather ignoble and disagreeable, and yet we see that those stand in very great need of these, and without them they cou'd not subsist; so in fabricks, there ought to be some parts considerable and honoured, and some less elegant; without which the other cou'd not remain free, and so consequently wou'd lose part of their dignity and beauty. But as our Blessed Creator has ordered these our members in such a manner, that the most beautiful are in places most exposed to view, and the less comely more hidden; so in building also, we ought to put the principal and considerable parts, in places the most seen, and the less beautiful, in places as much hidden from the eye as possible; that in them may be lodged all the foulness of the house, and all those things that may give any obstruction, and in any measure render the more beautiful parts disagreeable.

13. In a church we must be able to *see* well, not just hear well. (I am not talking about artistic seeing, of course.) The church ought to be bright enough to enable the congregation to read the hymn-book without effort. We can recall here too the frequently quoted words of Leonhard Sturm, that the darkness (caused by stained

glass, for instance) aroused "servile awe rather than devotion, and encouraged the performance of fallacious miracles." This observation dates from the eighteenth century, but it would certainly have been accepted in the seventeenth.

14. It seems to have been mostly monochromatic.

15. There are examples in St. Gall, Einsiedeln, Zwiefalten, and Amorbach.

16. Protestantism tried throughout the nineteenth century to infuse art into its churches. The latest Protestant churches seem to achieve an artistic form despite all inhibitions and without displaying a Catholic attitude. But that exceeds the limits of my theme.

Chapter 5

1. The priority of one or the other of the elements means little to me. Many sins have been committed in the search for early symptoms of the Baroque. S. Andrea in Mantua is a pure Renaissance building. Raphael's architecture, even as it appears in the backgrounds of his paintings, deviates so little from the Renaissance norm that there is little reason to consider it. The colossal order used by Bramante on the façade of St. Peter's in the Vatican is not identical in meaning to that of the Capitoline buildings in Rome, or to those of Palladio's palaces. St. Peter's was to have been of one story, but the consistent development of the articulation round the entire building forced the inclusion of the existing Benediction loggia in the front in a colossal order. It is the result of following a true Renaissance principle. [Frankl is disagreeing with some of the statements in Wölfflin's *Renaissance und Barock*, (English translation, London, Collins, 1964. See, for example, p. 115, S. Andrea; p. 43, St. Peter's).]

2. Not everyone agrees with this. H. von Geymüller (*Friedrich II von Hohenstaufen und die Anfänge der Architektur der Renaissance in Italien*, Munich, Bruckmann, 1908, p. 27) says that "between the Renaissance, using the word in its broadest meaning . . . and Christianity, there exist intimate relationships such as no other style in history has ever shown, or ever will be able to show." [See also note 4 to Chapter 4.]

3. Purpose was chronologically primary here too. It had the first voice.

4. It is true that Napoleon thought for a while of building himself a palace.

5. One of Giuliano da San Gallo's designs for the façade of S. Lorenzo in Florence can be considered Michelangelo's source. See C. Stegmann and H. von Geymüller, *Die Architektur der Renaissance in Toscana*, Munich, Bruckmann, 1885–1908, V, San Gallo, Fig. 19 (Uffizi 2048). Compare Bramante's design for the façade of St. Peter's.

6. During the eighteenth century, forms based upon Far Eastern sources do occur, but only as a minor current, which has little effect upon the mainstream of development.

7. [A reference to Michelangelo's sharp criticism of Antonio da San Gallo's project for St. Peter's (Figs. 8–10); see James S. Ackerman, *The Architecture of Michelangelo*, London, Zwemmer, 1961, II, pp. 88f.]

8. *Opus Architectonicum Equitis Francisci Borromini* . . . , Rome, 1725, p. 10.
9. [Johann Joachim Winckelmann, classical archaeologist and first of the great art historians, whose influential *Geschichte der Kunst des Altertums* was published in 1764.]

Index <small>(Numbers in italics refer to illustrations)</small>